ALSO BY

ARTHUR M. SCHLESINGER

Prelude to Independence:
The Newspaper War on Britain, 1764–1776
(1958)

The American as Reformer
(1950)

Paths to the Present
(1949)

Learning How to Behave
A Historical Study of American Etiquette Books
(1946)

The Rise of the City
(1933)

New Viewpoints in American History
(1922)

The Colonial Merchants and the American Revolution
(1918)

MR. SCHLESINGER WAS CO-EDITOR OF
A History of American Life (13 volumes)

The Birth of the Nation

A PORTRAIT OF THE AMERICAN PEOPLE

ON THE EVE OF INDEPENDENCE

THE
BIRTH
OF THE
NATION

A PORTRAIT OF THE AMERICAN PEOPLE

ON THE EVE OF INDEPENDENCE

by Arthur M. Schlesinger

WITH AN INTRODUCTION BY

Arthur M. Schlesinger, Jr.

Alfred A. Knopf : New York

1969

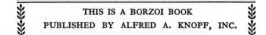

THIS IS A BORZOI BOOK
PUBLISHED BY ALFRED A. KNOPF, INC.

Published October 22, 1968
Second Printing, February 1969

Copyright © 1968 by Arthur M. Schlesinger, Jr.,
and Thomas B. Schlesinger

Library of Congress Catalog Card Number:
68–23942

Manufactured in the United States of America

Introduction

WHEN MY FATHER died on October 30, 1965, he left behind the manuscript of this book. He had written the first draft and had revised the first half-dozen chapters. (Chapter IX, in a slightly different form, was read before a meeting of the Massachusetts Historical Society and was published in its *Proceedings,* Vol. LXXIV, 1962; it is used here with the permission of the Society.) My mother, brother, and I have finished the work of revision. We have made very few changes in his text and only those suggested by his own notes or in conformity with his own practice.

The Birth of the Nation, though complete in itself, was designed as the first in a multivolume History of the American People. This series would have represented the distillation of my father's lifelong determination to bring the ordinary life of the people, their habits, beliefs, fears, and hopes, into the center of the historical enterprise. This determination grew out of the circumstances of his own life. His father had been born in Germany, his mother in Austria, and he had grown up in a small Ohio town which contained large contingents of Germans, Irish, and Negroes. Consequently, he was puzzled as a boy that his schoolbooks portrayed England as the one and only mother country. He later wrote, "I remember discussing this with my father, a great admirer of Carl Schurz, who replied somewhat wryly that apparently the only Germans worth mentioning were the Hessians who had fought on the wrong side in the War for Independence."

The boy was also puzzled that his schoolbooks left out those engrossing glimpses of the way the American people had lived in the past—how they worked, played, ventured, suffered—which he found in the books in his father's house and in the public library. "Though my thoughts were immature and unformulated, I could not help feeling there was something wanting in a history that skipped so much that seemed to me so important."

When he went to Ohio State University in 1906, he discovered the same emphasis: United States history was strictly Anglo-Saxon, and its concern was politics, war, and diplomacy, with a passing bow to religion in the age of colonization. In the meantime, the shift from the placid country town of Xenia, described with such charm in the first chapter of his memoir *In Retrospect: The History of a Historian,* to the bustling state capital of Columbus introduced him to a different aspect of American life and gave him his first sense of the city as a dynamic force in American development. When he went on to Columbia University in 1910 for graduate study, the exposure to the nation's largest and liveliest city deepened his conviction that the urban factor had been overlooked by the American historian.

A group of unusual teachers at Columbia—James Harvey Robinson with his summons to a New History, James T. Shotwell, and, above all, Charles A. Beard—reinforced my father's conception of history as "the product of a complexity of forces, governmental and personal, . . . social, economic, geographical and religious" (I quote from the preface to his *Colonial Merchants and the American Revolution*). At the same time the Progressive movement in politics was calling attention to the role of mass needs and aspirations in public affairs. In 1912 he cast his first vote for Woodrow Wilson.

It was still hard to inject unorthodox approaches into the academic curriculum, as my father discovered when he joined the Ohio State history faculty in 1912. Finally in the summer session of 1919 he was permitted to offer a course entitled "Some Revisions of American History." That autumn, at the age of thirty-one, he went to the University of Iowa as head of the history department. Here he could do as he wished. He gave "Some Revisions" again under a new title, "New Viewpoints in American History," and in 1922 introduced a new course entitled "Social and Cultural History of the United States"—the first of its sort in any college or university. The publication that year of *New Viewpoints in American History* sought to show the bearing on American history of such neglected matters as immigration, women, the labor movement, humanitarian reform, and ideas.

When my father went on to Harvard in 1924, his course on social and cultural history became the famous History 55, later History 163. In preparing his lectures, he had had to turn to writings outside the accepted historical canon—histories of religion, education, journalism, medicine, the fine arts, and the like. These works, even when competent in their own terms, tended to discuss their subjects in a vacuum, as though the developments were unrelated to the general conditions of American society. My father therefore conceived the idea of a cooperative history in ten or a dozen volumes which would portray "the formation and growth of civilization in the United States" in successive periods, treating the interests and activities of the people "not separately and independently of one another but as an integral and integrated part" of American life. This led to the *History of American Life* series, which he co-edited with Dixon Ryan Fox. As he later wrote, "Fox and I in planning this work aimed to free American history from its traditional servitude to party struggles, war and diplomacy and to show that it properly included all the varied interests of the people."

The victory of this conception has been so complete in the years since that it is hard to recall the day when social and cultural history was banned from the academic curriculum. Courses in intellectual history, urban history, the history of science, the history of immigration are today standard in American colleges; even political history is now generally conceived as an expression of social, economic, and intellectual forces. In the thirties we began to admit the immigrant into American history, and in the sixties we are at last beginning to admit the Negro (my father for many years was a member of the board of editors of the *Journal of Negro History*). A new generation of historians, many of them my father's students, have explored the problems and developed the themes set forth in *New Viewpoints* and in the *History of American Life*. My father himself gathered together a fresh collection of "new viewpoints" in his later book of essays *Paths to the Present*. American historians today operate instinctively within the social and cultural framework, drawing on the insights and methods of the social sciences and throwing new light on the qualities and dilemmas of American civilization.

My father came himself increasingly to feel the need for a new synthesis in American social history; and this became his main undertaking after his retirement from Harvard in 1954. Alas, with many public and scholarly commitments in these years,

The Birth of the Nation was all he had time to do. His family wishes to thank Madeleine Gleason for her generous and indispensable help in copying and checking the manuscript. My father would have been particularly pleased that his old and cherished friend Alfred A. Knopf should be publishing this book; and we are most grateful to Jane Garrett for the care and concern with which she has seen the manuscript through the press.

ARTHUR M. SCHLESINGER, JR.

May 1968

Contents

The Birth of the Nation

A PORTRAIT OF THE AMERICAN PEOPLE
ON THE EVE OF INDEPENDENCE

CHAPTER I

The Physical and Human Setting

THE AMERICANS WHO PLEDGED their lives, fortunes, and sacred honor to the cause of freedom from Britain in 1776 had already successfully negotiated nearly a century and three quarters of history. This was no less a span than from the Declaration of Independence to the close of the Second World War and in its own way held as great significance. For, though the colonists had retained their basic English character, removal to the new continent had developed traits and purposes for which little or no demand had existed in the Old World.

In the land they had left, vast estates abounded, villages were overcrowded, cities dirty and desperate, and opportunities for ordinary people few. Energy and talent lay fallow in a world of village Hampdens and mute inglorious Miltons. In the land to which they came, a limitless wilderness challenged to the utmost latent qualities of initiative, daring, and skill. In the meantime, new vigor was injected into the bloodstream of the original English settlers by transfusions from other European countries. In consequence, the handful of Englishmen who founded Jamestown and Plymouth had grown to two million whites of diverse nationalities and cultures.

The Atlantic was the first isolating force. Three thousand miles of water, rendering the colonies of rarely more than marginal concern to the government in London, threw the colonists on their own resources. Neglect bred a prickly self-reliance which, as time went on, royal officials on the spot viewed with growing apprehension. Yet the ocean, despite the hazards and hardships of the tiny sailing vessels, was a bridge as well as a barrier. Had the migrants been obliged to make the long journey by land, far fewer would have undertaken it. The sea passages enabled the Americans to maintain fairly close touch with the homeland through correspondence, books and newspapers, and return visits of the well-to-do. In addition, the ocean afforded the Northern colonists a profitable livelihood in fishing and commerce, and a profusion of natural harbors facilitated travel and trade from one province to another. The rivers draining into the Atlantic expedited the movement of settlers into the interior.

The land itself had even greater influence. The rich virgin soil, well watered and easy of access, inevitably made agriculture the dominant occupation, and the variations of temperature from north to south encouraged a marked degree of crop specialization. With dense woods everywhere at hand, the farmer had to clear his patch of ground before planting it. But in all other respects the "forest primeval" constituted a priceless asset. It supplied not only firewood for the household but also lumber for houses, furniture, and wagons, timber for building ships, and pitch and tar for calking them. The forest likewise provided food: berries, nuts, maple sugar, honey, and wild game. And, to add to the bounty, numerous animals—from beavers, raccoons, and other small creatures to deer and bears—contributed to the family clothing, besides furnishing a commodity for export. The quest for pelts, whether by trapping or by trade with the Indians, became a lucrative business. Had a treeless expanse instead of a massive forest fringed the ocean, the spread of settlers inland would have been greatly retarded.

Whether on land or on sea, the teeming opportunities fed the spirit of adventure and stimulated fortitude and resourcefulness. In a different fashion the Appalachians also wielded an important influence. That almost unbroken mountain wall, extending from New Hampshire to Georgia a few hundred miles or less from the coastline, discouraged the colonials from scattering thinly through the vast interior of the continent, as did the French in Canada, where no similar barrier existed. This led the Americans to develop a relatively stable and compact type of society.

The colonists had to face not only untamed nature but also untamed humans. Two civilizations here confronted each other—one dynamic and acquisitive, the other static and unprogressive. The Indians, whose ancestors had crossed the Bering Strait upward of three hundred centuries before, still lacked beasts of burden and wheeled vehicles; they still used bows and arrows and tomahawks in hunting and warfare, deprived of the advantage of firearms until they gradually acquired them from the white man. Most crippling of all, their only way of accumulating and transmitting knowledge from generation to generation was by word of mouth. "The invention of writing and of a convenient system of records on paper," as the Egyptologist James H. Breasted has remarked, "has had a greater influence in uplifting the human race than any other intellectual achievement in the career of man." It was not surprising, then, that the aborigines lingered in the stone age and dwelt typically in squalid hovels or wigwams constructed of poles, bark, and hides.

Nevertheless, the red man had adapted himself successfully to a wilderness existence, and this was something the whites had now to learn if they too were to survive. They took over the Indian's swift bark canoe for threading the streams, copied his technique of blazing trails through the tangled forest, borrowed his methods of trapping and dressing skins and of clearing plots for tillage. But for this acquired lore the settlers would have found their task infinitely more formidable.

In like fashion they made Indian corn, or maize, their basic food crop. Nothing could better have suited their requirements. It was easy to grow and could be eaten in many savory ways; and its stalks provided excellent forage for cattle. Other native edibles, widely appropriated, were sweet potatoes, squash, pumpkins, peanuts, and several kinds of beans. Still another product, tobacco, served a triple purpose. Whether used for smoking, chewing, or snuff, it gratified both men and women, besides furnishing a paying article of export. As the colonists drew farther away from the sea, they discovered a preservative for meat in the salt licks long patronized by the Indians. Since no white outpost could be

certain of enduring until it had an ample food supply, the red men
in these various respects thus contributed to the loss of their own
land.

In other ways as well the settler added to the misfortune
of the Indian. By his discovery that corn could be converted into
firewater (a translated Algonquin word), he inadvertently debauched his benefactors, seldom failing to do so deliberately
whenever it was to his advantage. His intrusion further exposed
them to deadly diseases unknown to the Indians but long rife in
Europe—smallpox, influenza, and others—to which they had no
immunity. The ravages again and again inflicted widespread fatalities, sometimes exterminating whole tribes.

Nor did the men of English stock mate with native women as
did the French and Spanish in their New World dominions. The
marriage of the Virginian John Rolfe and the so-called princess
Pocahontas in 1619 was a famed exception. Whether this proceeded from the greater availability of white partners or from
stronger racial prejudice (not evident, though, in illicit relations
with Negro women), the result was the same. Squaw men, as
those who intermarried were disparagingly known, never numbered more than an insignificant few and were found almost
entirely on the fringes of settlements where white women were
scarce.

Of all the misfortunes of the red man the greatest came from
armed clashes with the intruders. From the very earliest days the
warfare for living space went on intermittently, now in one place,
now in another. The Indians, though making their women conduct a simple form of agriculture, relied for subsistence mainly on
game; and for this they required extensive hunting grounds used
on a communal basis. The whites, for their part, intent on home-
steading and wedded to the institution of private property, would
not be denied tracts utilized so uneconomically. The policy of the
colonial authorities was to secure transfers of ownership by treaty,
but, even when the tribesmen assented, impatient settlers typically
overran the bounds. The fierce hostilities that resulted drove both
sides to massacre, torture, and other barbarities, with the better-
armed aggressors sooner or later gaining their ends.

Yet the colonists, compounding their other debts to the aborigine, derived a vital benefit even from warfare. In Indian fashion they now also scoured the woods, moving swiftly in small bands unimpeded with heavy baggage, sleeping in the open, living off the land, and stealing through the underbrush to spring surprise attacks. This training in guerrilla tactics stood them in good stead during the long years of border strife with France and her Indian allies from 1689 onward and would serve them again when they faced the British regulars at Lexington and Concord.

The last great Indian revolt in colonial America, named for the Ottawa chieftain Pontiac, took place in 1763–4 in the wake of France's expulsion from North America. Disliking their new overlords, a group of tribes formerly under French rule united to attack British forts north of the Ohio River and frontier settlements of Pennsylvania and Virginia. The suppression of the uprising enabled the Americans thereafter to give undivided attention to the critical troubles then commencing with the London government.

The English settlers, while thus combating a wild new continent and its wild inhabitants, were meanwhile coming to terms with white settlers of other stocks—to such an extent that they began proudly to see themselves as the most cosmopolitan people on the face of the globe. Thomas Paine, trumpeting his call for Independence in *Common Sense* when the moment approached, maintained that "Europe, and not England, is the parent country of America." This mingling of bloods, which Paine hardly overstated, was due partly to the conquest in the mid-seventeenth century of colonies founded by the Netherlands and Sweden, but more to mounting numbers of non-English folk who, migrating later, voluntarily shifted their allegiance. In either case these strangers had basic affinities to the Anglo-American stock and had little difficulty in merging with it. All were of European and mainly Protestant blood, belonged to the industrious middle or lower-middle classes, and sought a permanent home and brighter prospects for themselves and their children. Since few failed in this expectation, relatives and friends eagerly joined them. "In Europe," observed the French-born New Yorker Hector St. John de Crèvecœur in *Letters from an American Farmer*, "they were so many useless plants, wanting vegetative mould, and refreshing showers; . . . but now, by the power of transplantation, like all other plants they have taken root and flourished!"

The Dutch, for example, in and about New York participated in commerce, shopkeeping, and other employments alongside the English, and such names as Van Cortlandt and Schuyler attest to their continued importance in provincial politics. The Protestant French Huguenots entered no less fully into the mainstream of colonial affairs. They had fled their homeland to escape persecution when Louis XIV in 1685 withdrew the toleration that had been theirs for nearly a century under the Edict of Nantes. Numbering upward of fifteen thousand as compared with the nearly ten thousand Dutch of New Netherland, they concentrated in the principal seaports. Families like Faneuil, Revere, and Bowdoin in Boston, De Lancey and Jay in New York, and Laurens and Manigault in Charleston evidence their prominence in economic and public life.

Additions of much greater size followed in the eighteenth century from Germany and Ireland. The Germans, uprooted by repeated ravaging of the Rhine Valley at the hands of the French as well as by the political and religious repression of their own rulers, congregated largely in the Pennsylvania back country. Sleek cattle, stout work horses, teeming harvests, and huge barns earned them the name of the best farmers in America. But, living in rural isolation and intent on safeguarding their peculiar evangelical tenets, for the most part they resisted assimilation. These miscalled Pennsylvania Dutch have retained traces of their identity till our own day. From this New World center some spilled over into Maryland, Virginia, and North Carolina. A separate stream from the homeland, by-passing Pennsylvania, flowed also into upper New York and to points as far south as Georgia. When the break came with England, the German element in all aggregated around 200,000, or a tenth of the white colonists.

The other big influx was Irish only in a geographical sense. It consisted of Lowland Scottish Protestants who had originally settled in the province of Ulster in north Ireland more than a century before and had there preserved their customary way of life. They scattered through all the colonies and everywhere carried with them their stern Presbyterianism, along with anger against the British government and absentee landlords because of oppressive practices back home. Notwithstanding this bitterness the unbounded opportunities now at hand caused them to blend quickly with their Anglo-American neighbors. Unexcelled as frontiersmen and Indian fighters, they engaged also in urban business. By 1776 the Scotch-Irish numbered more than 150,000, fewer than the Germans but wielding far greater influence because of their permeation of all aspects of American life. In the final years the Scotch-Irish notables in the public service included Henry Knox of Boston, a Revolutionary general, and two signers of the Declaration of Independence: Matthew Thornton of New Hampshire and Thomas McKean of Delaware.

These two breeds, though, did not account for all the immigration. From Continental Europe outside Germany came Jews of Spanish, Portuguese, and Dutch origin, Finns and Swiss; and from the British Isles other than Ulster and England arrived native Scots, Celtic Irish, and Welshmen. But these accessions by comparison constituted hardly more than a trickle.

In a country perennially needing manpower the prevailing attitude was one of welcome. The Puritans of early New England, guarding their faith against dissenting outsiders, were but a temporary exception. The arrivals, moreover, save for the German sectarians, posed no critical problems of assimilation. Every colony at first adopted its own rules of naturalization, but as these varied from place to place, Parliament in 1740 enacted a uniform standard. Thenceforth, foreign-born Protestants and Jews after residing seven years in any province could acquire full civil rights everywhere by pledging allegiance to the Crown. The purpose as stated in the preamble was to further the economic growth of America by making migration more attractive and thus indirectly benefit the home country as well. The press, for its part, warmly greeted the newcomers. As the *Massachusetts Gazette and Boston Post-Boy* declared in its July 26–August 2, 1773, issue, "The Bosom of America is, as it always has been, an Assylum for the Oppressed of all Nations," and besides, the writer went on, the colonies profited in return from the added hands "in every useful Branch."

True, not everyone displayed equal cordiality. The outstanding example is Benjamin Franklin, who later came to know foreign peoples as no other American of his time. When deeply involved in Pennsylvania politics in the 1750's, he berated his German fellow citizens for clannishness and stupidity and for "intermeddling" brashly in elections. He darkly predicted that they "will shortly be so numerous as to Germanize us instead of our Anglifying them." Yet he printed books and financed newspapers in the German language, and other evidence as well makes clear that his strictures represented a passing and uncharacteristic mood.

Though most migrants were motivated by rebellion against conditions in their homelands, they were not congenital malcontents. In their adopted country the Old World discriminations—governmental, economic, and religious—were either slight or nonexistent. They became to an unparalleled degree masters of their own fate, with freedom to correct wrongs by lawful means should the need arise. Hence the outlanders shared with their English compatriots a fervor for preserving the rights and privileges which Britain for so many years had granted the colonists.

Naturally, then, when Britain altered her course following the French and Indian War, they for the most part supported the colonial protests and acts of disobedience and, when these efforts did not avail, helped to cut the umbilical cord. The German evangelicals were the principal holdouts on grounds of religious pacifism. Of the fifty-six signers of the Declaration of Independence eighteen were of non-English extraction, eight themselves immigrants. An inscription on a tombstone in the Shenandoah Valley of Virginia suggests the feeling of the Scotch-Irish element toward England: "Here lie the remains of JOHN LEWIS, who slew the Irish lord, settled Augusta County, Located the town of Staunton, And furnished five sons to fight the battles of the AMERICAN REVOLUTION."

Despite the unusual admixture of peoples the English remained the predominant strain in both numbers and influence. They had dwelt much longer in America with the corresponding advantage of more years of natural increase as well as of immigration. In 1776 they accounted for probably three out of every five whites. New England had the greatest regional concentration because few of the other nationalities could bear the freezing winters and stony soil. Yet even in Pennsylvania, where outlanders made up the majority, colonial life bore an indclible Anglo-Saxon stamp. It could hardly have been otherwise. Not only were all governmental institutions derived from England, but in the babel of tongues English provided the readiest means of intercommunication. It was the language of the law, the legislatures and the courts, and of virtually all the newspapers. And not least in evidencing the English stock's continued pre-eminence were such names as Adams, Otis, Franklin, Dickinson, Jefferson, and Washington during the dispute with the mother country.

Notwithstanding the advance of population, much of thc country was still but sparsely tenanted as Independence approached. The coastal area, reaching back unevenly into the Appalachian foothills, contained the largest number of people, and there the dynamic energies of American life found full play. But even in this region the virgin forest only now and then yielded to farm and plantation, and sizable towns remained few. Farther inland, lonely frontier clearings signaled the end of settlement. The Northern provinces surpassed the South in white inhabitants roughly by 1,247,000 to 727,000, though, if Negro slaves were added in, the overall figures were much the same. The peace of 1763 added to the original colonial limits the territory between the mountains and the Mississippi River formerly held by the French, but settlers, restrained in part by a royal proclamation, had as yet done little to move into the expanse. Nonetheless, the occupied areas by 1776 amounted to something like 200,000 square miles or more than twice the whole of Great Britain.

The settlers enjoyed the greatest degree of self-government known anywhere on earth—even more than the English people at home. From the very beginning every colony elected its lower legislative branch, and Connecticut and Rhode Island chose their upper houses and governors as well. In all other cases the Crown or, as in Pennsylvania, Delaware, and Maryland, the Proprietor with the Crown's consent appointed the chief magistrate and the executive council, with the latter body, save in Pennsylvania, doubling as the upper legislative house. Pennsylvania thus in effect had a unicameral system. A slighter variation from the usual arrangement existed in Massachusetts, where after 1691 the lower house, subject to the royal governor's approval, named the companion chamber.

In practice even these curbs on the popular will were little felt, since the elected representatives could in most provinces challenge them through the power of the purse—the right to refuse salaries. Few chief executives hesitated to violate instructions from London when confronted with this dilemma. As a contemporary observed, "The governor has two masters; one who gives him his commission, and one who gives him his pay." True, the possibility always remained of a veto by the Crown, but the legislators could get around that by limiting a statute's duration to the twelve months or so required to get the word back from England and then re-enacting its provisions in another form. Certain decisions of the provincial courts could be appealed; but the procedure was expensive and complex, sometimes dragging out for years, and consequently was little used. Hence in judicial as well as in legislative matters colonists pretty much determined their own course.

In exercising their autonomy, however, the lawmakers by and large met the best standards of the age. The functions of government were held to a minimum, and the burden of financial support except in moments of public danger was light. Governor Jonathan Belcher of New Jersey stated in 1749 that " 'tis 17 years since any Tax was raised on the people"; and Governor Robert Hunter Morris of Pennsylvania reported in 1755, doubtless with still greater satisfaction, that we "are not only out of Debt, but have . . . Fifteen Thousand in Bank." Accustomed to sole say in voting funds and always with an eye to limiting the amounts, the Americans defiantly cried "No taxation without representation" when Parliament, departing from precedent, enacted imperial levies after the French and Indian War.

But the legislators were less successful in handling the problem of representation in their own popular branches. Here they faced the knotty task of adjusting membership and policy to the problems of the ever-growing population of the interior. No province escaped the difficulty entirely. The older and newer sections were in chronic disagreement over such questions as defense, taxation, Indian policy, and law enforcement, with the tidewater denying or only grudgingly granting the back country desired relief. In North Carolina the friction reached the point of mob violence in 1769 and an armed clash in 1771 before the Regulators, as the back-country rebels were called, secured any redress. The issues involved were not unlike those underlying the colonial-imperial argument in the final climactic years, although in that instance the Americans, of course, had no representation at all in the British legislature.

As for government below the provincial level, no single pattern prevailed. The New England colonies relied on meetings of the qualified inhabitants of the town (that is, township). These determined the major policies and designated persons to oversee matters between sessions. Elsewhere the system ranged from municipal boards, elective or sometimes self-perpetuating (with the governor perhaps naming the mayor), to county-wide commissioners and courts in the South. Though appointed by the governor or the legislature, they functioned in fact as they willed. But, whatever the particular forms, every community effectively ran its own affairs. The principle of the consent of the governed thus extended from top to bottom of the society.

While not every adult could vote, most of the colonies granted the suffrage to all white males who owned real or personal property of a prescribed value. The theory, carried over from England, was that only men with a tangible stake in society should qualify. In addition, five colonies—Rhode Island, New York, Maryland, Virginia, and South Carolina—limited the electorate to Christians or simply to Protestants. Maryland, for all its Catholic origins, took the latter action in 1718, by which time the Proprietor himself was a Protestant. In spite of the property and religious restrictions, the settlers had far greater access to the franchise than if they had remained at home. Not only were the economic requirements easier to meet where land was abundant, but often the rules were only laxly enforced. The religious tests likewise had slight limiting effect due to the small number of Catholics and Jews in the population.

Although the secret ballot was not unknown, the voter ordinarily registered his wishes orally at the polls. Closely contested elections created storms of leaflets and newspaper arguments, evidencing the lively political consciousness of the electorate. The editor of the *New-York Gazette* in his issue of February 24, 1752, personally deplored the scurrility of some of the articles he had run, but adamantly affirmed that "all Englishmen have a right to speak their Sentiments." Freedom of the press stood in danger of legal reprisals only when the persons attacked already held office, but even in such cases printers time and again maintained their ground.

By contrast with England, the outright buying of votes was rare. Short of this, however, candidates felt at liberty to dangle the bait of free refreshments at the polls to attract supporters. The custom commanded general acceptance probably because of the welcome break it afforded in the routine of life. Nonetheless, a writer in the New York *Independent Reflector,* July 5, 1753, expressed dismay that so many persons should barter their franchise for "Beer and Brandy," "a Pound of Beef," or "a Treat" and "a Frolick." Politicians in Newport and Providence also followed this amiable practice, and although the Hartford *Connecticut Courant,* March 5, 1770, asserted that it was unknown in that colony, evidence to the contrary appeared at times in its own pages.

Nor was the usage confined to the North. In Virginia at least, election day teemed with food and drink at the expense of candidates, who usually dispensed the hospitality in person. Although a statute of 1705 sought to end the practice, it had only sporadic effect, doubtless because of the feeling that voters deserved recompense when so many traveled so far to exercise the suffrage. George Washington in four of his successful tries for the legislature spent around £140 for refreshments. In 1758 alone his election bill included 76 gallons of rum punch, 46 of beer, 21 of wine and 3½ of brandy. Thomas Jefferson also observed the fashion. Young James Madison, on the other hand, rejecting what he considered a "corrupting influence," suffered defeat when he ran in 1777. Whatever the possible abuses, however, the custom had the beneficial effect of attracting greater popular participation in politics.

Along with liberal political institutions the colonists also inherited the historic safeguards conferred by the English common law. This body of unwritten legal principles, evolved by judicial interpretation through the years, aimed to protect the individual against arbitrary acts, whether by government or by his fellows. It embraced such basic guarantees as the right of trial by a jury chosen from the vicinity, the writ of *habeas corpus* to prevent undue detention of a suspect before trial, and the even-handed administration of justice. Trial by jury was in colonial minds "that firmest Barrier of English Liberty." Hence its denial helped light the fuse leading to Independence when Parliament, following the French and Indian War, gave the power of enforcing the new trade and revenue legislation to the Crown-appointed juryless vice-admiralty courts. As John Adams put the matter, "Juries are taken by Lot or by Suffrage from the Mass of the People, and no Man can be condemned of Life, or Limb, or Property or Reputation, without the Concurrence of the Voice of the People." Understandably, from London's point of view, that voice was not to be trusted when the fate of unpopular imperial measures was at stake.

The early colonists, lacking trained lawyers and chary of self-appointed practitioners, had tended to apply common-sense ideas of right and wrong in deciding cases or, in the Puritan commonwealths, to invoke the Word of God. As the country aged, however, the rise of a professional bench and bar and a well-to-do class brought to the colonies many of the legal protections existing in the homeland. The principal American deviations from the English common law were in form rather than in substance: the elimination of archaic technicalities and the consequent simplification and speeding up of court proceedings. In some respects—notably freedom of speech and the press, the descent of real estate, and the status of married women—the rules fell short of modern standards and displeased the colonists themselves. But the system as a whole buttressed personal and property rights to an extent unknown outside the bounds of the British Empire.

The inhabitants also possessed substantial freedom in their economic life, something no other colonizing power permitted its overseas subjects. Parliament, it is true, curtailed their direct trade with foreign countries and required them to send essential raw materials to England and to refrain from competitive manufacturing, but other aspects of the economy were largely unrestricted. The colonists by and large found it more advantageous to devote their energies to agriculture, shipbuilding, and the fisheries—occupations which in some part benefited from bounties or other parliamentary favors. But they did not hesitate to flout the more onerous regulations. The restraints on commerce, for example, proved difficult to enforce and easy to evade at so great a distance from England. In fact, smuggling, even to the extent of wartime traffic with the enemy, laid the basis of many a provincial fortune. Thus when Britain, after the French and Indian War, embarked upon a strict supervision of colonial trade, the people responded with a sense of outrage.

These rights and liberties—political, legal, and economic—all hung in the balance, however, as long as France contended with Britain for supremacy in North America. At bottom the prolonged struggle constituted a rivalry not only between national states but also between antithetical theories of society. The one stood for absolute monarchy, religious intolerance, a tight monopoly of commerce, and arbitrary colonial rule. The other nurtured, or at least condoned, liberal governmental, economic, and religious institutions on behalf of its transatlantic subjects. The Americans indeed enjoyed advantages, civil and otherwise, denied to the masses in the home country.

Basically, then, Britain's triumph in the final confrontation fixed American civilization permanently in an Anglo-Saxon instead of a Gallic mold. This had greater consequences for the nation soon to be born than even the breaking of the political tie with the motherland. That unanticipated event came to pass only after England, having acquired world-wide territories from France, revised its traditional colonial policy and undertook to abridge the freedoms which the Americans had long since come to esteem as their very birthright.

CHAPTER II

The
Role of the Family

Aₗₜₕₒᵤ𝗴ₕ COLONIAL LIFE was woven of many strands—
English, Scotch-Irish, Dutch, French, German, and so on—all the
new groups, whatever their ethnic differences, shared the common
belief that the family was, in Franklin's phrase, the "sacred cement
of all societies." As Cotton Mather put it in 1693, *"Families* are
the *Nurseries* of all Societies; and the First Combinations of mankind. *Well-ordered Families* naturally produced a *Good Order* in
other Societies." Not only was the family thus decreed by custom
and by religion as the basis for sound community life, but also, in
the New World, the traditions of family solidarity were made the
more urgent by economic need.

The promotion of the family was therefore a high colonial
priority. In the early years, when men greatly outnumbered
women, some colonies offered special land grants to husbands
migrating with wives. As the Virginia House of Burgesses toler-
antly declared in 1619, "It is not knowen whether man or woman
be the most necessary." The plight of bachelors already on the
ground was difficult. To lessen it the Virginia Company in London responded to the legislative utterance by dispatching some
140 maidens over a period of three years. Fortunately single men
both there and elsewhere discovered an additional source of
supply from outside in the host of girls who paid their transportation to America by becoming indentured servants for a time.
According to the Marylander George Alsop in 1666, "They are

no sooner on shoar, but they are courted into a Copulative Matrimony, which some of them (for aught I know) had they not come to such a Market with their Virginity, they might have kept it by them untill it had been mouldy." In this fashion the novelist Defoe's eighteen-year-old niece, crossed in love in England, ran off to America and soon wedded the son of her employer.

On the confirmed and resistant bachelor fell society's unqualified disapproval. He was regarded as a shirker of his bounden duty ("the odd Half of a Pair of Scissars," said Franklin) and a deterrent to social progress. Some early New England communities sought to tempt these misfits by the offer of free building lots upon marriage. Another device was to express community disapproval by circumscribing their way of living. Connecticut authorities forbade a single man to dwell alone and assigned him quarters wherever and with whomever they determined. In general the bachelor was under special surveillance of the constable, the watchman, and the tithingman. Outside New England the unattached male was no more popular, although, except for taxes on bachelorhood in Maryland and Pennsylvania at various times, he faced no legal disabilities.

Such measures were repealed or lapsed into disuse as the years went on, but the social purpose underlying them remained fully as strong. This doubtless accounts for the complaisant attitude of a deeply religious people toward the practice known as bundling or tarrying. A custom brought from the Old World, it permitted a suitor and his sweetheart when night fell in winter to conduct their wooing in bed, provided (nominally) they did not take off all their clothes or engage in sexual relations and that her parents consented. The arrangement afforded the lovers a degree of privacy otherwise hard to find in the cramped quarters of the ordinary house, and it also saved firewood and candles. Although this engaging practice was confined largely to the poorer classes, John Adams, writing in 1761, also saw it as a good way for young folks really to know each other before marrying; and while he noted the need for "certain Guards and Restraints," he declared on balance, "I cannot wholly disapprove of Bundling."

As Adams recognized, the procedure was not so uniformly chaste as it was supposed to be. In cases of transgression, however, the erring couple could in New England usually secure absolution by open confession before the church congregation after becoming man and wife, although, of course, matrimony did not always result. Of two hundred people admitted to the church at Groton, Massachusetts, between 1761 and 1775, sixty-six or nearly one in three confessed to premarital fornication. Nevertheless, the practice was by then already beginning to show signs of decline. One blow came from the behavior of young veterans of the French and Indian War who, having learned immoral habits in the army, helped strip bundling of its innocence. Another followed fifteen years later when the French, then lending aid in the War for Independence, completely misunderstood the usage. As the Marquis de Barbé-Marbois testified, "The first French officers who were permitted it conducted themselves with so little reserve that the old people begged the mothers not to permit them this form of courtship with their daughters." As houses became larger and better heated, moreover, the original excuse for bundling waned. Nonetheless, the custom, though fading elsewhere, lingered on among the Pennsylvania Germans and some other secluded rural groups into the nineteenth century.

Sexual promiscuity for its own sake was, however, comparatively infrequent. Crèvecœur attributed the "general decency" to the fact that "almost everybody is married, for they get wives very young and the pleasure of returning to their families overrules every other desire." Still, in the first colonial days, when single women were still relatively few, the authorities set harsh penalties for "carnall wickedness," and such laws remained on the statute books. To judge from court records, infractions occurred largely among indentured servants. This was hardly their fault, since they could wed only with their master's consent, which was usually refused lest pregnancy hamper the work of the expectant mother and childbearing increase the expenses of the household. Penalties for violation were ordinarily a sound whipping and a fine for both misdoers and, in the case of the woman at least, sometimes an extension of the period of service.

In the higher ranks of society, few if any offenders were ever haled into court. Puritanism did not notably deter the upper classes: possibly the scandals of the English nobility, so fully ventilated in the colonial press, even excited them to emulation. At any rate John Hancock, the wealthy Boston merchant and future signer of the Declaration of Independence, maintained a mistress for a time before at the relatively advanced age of thirty-nine he wedded Dorothy Quincy in 1775. Robert Hunter Morris, who served as chief justice of New Jersey and later (1754–6) as governor of Pennsylvania, never married but fathered at least three natural children, one of whom, Robert Morris, became chief justice of the state of New Jersey in 1777. The president of Harvard, the Reverend Samuel Locke, a family man, lost his job in 1773 for having gotten his housekeeper with child. And Benjamin Franklin, the Boston-born printer in Philadelphia, had at the age of twenty-four a son probably by some woman other than his wife within six months of his marriage. Instances involving well-known names, though, were decidedly the exception, not the rule.

Prostitution existed to some degree in the seaports, where sailors on shore leave provided a reliable patronage to supplement what might be expected from errant townsmen. The scant contemporary reference to venereal diseases suggests that during most of the colonial period they presented no problem. Not until the 1760's did advertisements of alleged cures notably increase in the press, probably a response to adventures with "camp women" by soldiers returned from the French and Indian War.

On the frontier, where marriageable women were scarce, sex relations were reportedly of the loosest; but in older rural districts conditions might also be lax. Thus an unwed mother in Brookfield, Massachusetts, after having been fined by the county court twice earlier for bastardy, was flogged in 1740 and again in 1745 for repetitions of the offense. This incident may have come to the attention of Franklin, always in touch with Massachusetts affairs, for less than a year and a half later he wrote his anonymous skit "The Speech of Polly Baker." The fictional Polly, prosecuted in Connecticut for the fifth time on a like charge, spiritedly replied that she had merely obeyed "the first and great Command of Nature, and of Nature's God, Encrease and Multiply" and thereby had helped "add to the Number of the King's Subjects, in a new Country that really wants People." Not only was she triumphantly acquitted, but one of the judges married her. A public basically confident of its moral health could relish this salty bit of badinage.

At all levels of society the suitor was, as in the Old World, expected to clear with the girl's parents before paying his addresses. But young Americans, even then, had a tendency to ignore precedent, so that Virginia, Massachusetts, and Connecticut early set penalties of fine and imprisonment for those disregarding the custom. Sometimes fathers left wills depriving daughters of their inheritance should they wed against their mothers' wishes. In well-to-do families the European fashion of dowries and marriage portions also played some part. Franklin himself in his widely consulted *Reflections on Courtship and Marriage* (1746) advised a frank premarital discussion of respective financial resources. In the same breath, however, he censured purely mercenary unions, exclaiming, "How many play the Harlot for a good Settlement, under the legal Title of Wife! How many the Villain, to repair a broken Fortune, or to gain one!"

Whatever their station, women in the colonies had a far better opportunity for matrimony than their sisters abroad. As late as 1776 bachelors outnumbered spinsters probably by two to three or more, and earlier the ratio had been greater. Thanks to the resulting demand, girls customarily acquired husbands when very young; to have none at the age of twenty-five made them "antient maids." Sarah Rutledge, the mother of the South Carolina patriot John Rutledge, married, for example, at fourteen; Ursula, daughter of the prominent Virginia planter William Byrd I, at sixteen. The theologian Jonathan Edwards and John Marshall, the future Chief Justice, led their brides to the altar when they were seventeen. Thomas Jefferson's mother became a wife at nineteen, and Abigail Adams was that age when she wedded her John.

Franklin figured there were twice as many marriages proportionately as in Europe and that they produced twice as many children. As Gottlieb Mittelberger wrote about Philadelphia in the 1750's, "Whenever one meets a woman, she is either pregnant, or carries a child in her arms, or leads one by the hand." The urgent need for help in the home, on the farm, or in the shop made large families an economic asset. Ten or twelve youngsters were common, twenty-five or thirty not unknown. Both James Otis, the

Massachusetts patriot, and Timothy Dwight, later president of Yale, had a dozen brothers and sisters; Henry Laurens, the South Carolina revolutionary, was one of fourteen; John Marshall, one of fifteen; Professor John Winthrop, the Harvard scientist, one of sixteen; Franklin, one of seventeen; and Paul Revere, himself the third of twelve, sired sixteen. Families this large, however, were often the product of two, three, or more wives. The frequency of death in childbirth (puerperal fever was as yet undiagnosed) is a mute reminder of the cost of adding to the population. In other respects, too, the family expanded, for, besides the immediate members, the typical household included needy relatives, servants, and slaves.

Unhappily, a high death rate accompanied the high birth rate. Many mothers risked their lives to bring forth infants only for the grave. Bad diet, ignorance of hygiene, lack of medical care, and freezing homes all took their toll. Nor did the more fortunate youngsters always outlast their parents. A mortuary poem to Mrs. Sarah Thayer of Massachusetts recorded that

> She'd fourteen children with her
> At the table of the Lord.

Of the Reverend Cotton Mather's sixteen, but one survived him; of Judge Samuel Sewall's fourteen, but three; of Thomas Jefferson's six, but one.

Nonetheless, Franklin estimated that the population doubled every twenty or twenty-five years, although he did not add that this was partly due to newcomers from abroad. Politically, the confidence engendered by the rapidly mounting numbers did much to hearten the colonists in their quarrel with the mother country. As one patriot boasted in 1772, America would certainly have as many people as England in twenty years and twice as many in fifty. It was in this spirit that Franklin dryly observed six months after the outbreak of war at Lexington and Concord that, although the British had slain 150 Americans, meanwhile 60,000 more had come into the world. Neither he nor his fellows had any doubt that, as Bishop Berkeley had written nearly fifty years before, "Westward the course of empire takes its way."

Thanks to the population explosion, youngsters of fifteen

years and under made up about half the population as the Revolution approached. And for them life was implacably real and earnest. Their first and last duty was to walk in the ways of their elders, supplying obedience without question or delay. Daughters had to prepare themselves soon to take on marital cares; sons to shoulder the imminent responsibilities of man's estate; and both must be ready at an instant to face their Maker, who, it was dinned into their ears, would consign the unworthy to eternal torment. Legally, boys reached their majority at sixteen when they became taxpayers and members of the militia, by which time some of the girls were already wives and mothers. Society had little patience with what later Americans were to regard as the natural impulses of childhood and had no conception at all of the positive values of leisure and play for maturing the youthful personality. Rather, frolicsome behavior was considered evidence of congenital laziness, if not of original sin, to be corrected in chronic cases with the rod.

Under these conditions children were sometimes marvels of precocity. Charles Cotesworth Pinckney of Revolutionary fame learned to read at the age of two; Martha Laurens, the daughter of Henry Laurens and third wife of Dr. David Ramsay, read at three; and Timothy Dwight, who reputedly mastered the alphabet in a single lesson, was deep in the Bible at the same tender age. Pious literature was staple diet for the young. Edition after edition was called for of *A Token for Children, Being An Exact Account of the Conversion, Holy and Exemplary Lives and Joyful Deaths of Several Young Children* by the English clergyman James Janeway, to which Cotton Mather, not to be outdone, appended *A Token, for the Children of New-England or Some Examples of Children in Whom the Fear of God was Remarkably Budding Before They Dyed.* Best known of all was *The New-England Primer,* which from the 1680's on took the colonies by storm and continued to be republished well after Independence. Franklin's printing firm in Philadelphia alone disposed of over 37,000 copies in the years from 1749 to 1766. Its tone is suggested by the lines:

> At Night lie down, prepared to have
> Thy sleep thy Death, thy bed thy grave.

More secular in character, though hardly in purport, was *The School of Good Manners*. This best-selling juvenile, ascribed to the Boston pedagogue Eleazar Moody and based on an English manual, enjoined: "Among superiors speak not till thou art spoken to"; "Go not singing, whistling or hallooing along the street"; "Be not hasty to run out of the meeting-house when the worship is ended," and like virtuous admonitions. George Washington, at the age of fifteen culling "Rules of Civility and Decent Behaviour" from another English work, addressed such precepts to himself as "Contradict not at every turn what others Say"; "Spit not in the Fire"; and, above all, "Labour to keep alive in your Breast that Little Spark of Celestial fire Called Conscience."

Boys as a matter of course helped in the field, barn, woodshed, and shop, while girls relieved their overworked mothers as best they could by cooking and sewing, tending the younger children, spinning flax, combing wool, and lending a hand at the loom. In colonial days manual training, except where slaves were numerous, was a product of everyday routine, not as in later times a part of the school curriculum. The practice accustomed parents to the idea of child labor and caused them to accept it under very different conditions when factories began to spring up in the generation after Independence.

As the eighteenth century advanced, the stress on didactic literary fare, though not on physical toil, somewhat diminished, especially among city parents. Franklin as a youth read Plutarch's *Lives*, Addison's essays, and Burton's *Historical Collections*, as well as *Pilgrim's Progress* and Cotton Mather's *Essays to Do Good*. The *Boston Gazette*, January 20, 1772, advertised such treats "for all good Boys and Girls" as *Robin Good-Fellow, a Fairy Tale; Puzzling Cap, a Collection of Riddles;* and expurgated abridgments of *Tom Jones, Pamela,* and *Clarissa*. Another indication of the lifting clouds was *The Pretty Little Pocket Book,* describing in rhyme how to play games like marbles, leapfrog, blindman's buff, and hop, skip, and jump, though appending in each case the moral lesson to be learned. *Mother Goose,* while also available, did not become a child classic until the next century, perhaps because its jingles defied similar lofty explication.

Notwithstanding such apparent concessions, the older generation as late as Independence still displayed its basic assumption that children were miniature adults by continuing to dress the young like little grownups. Twelve-year-old sons of the well-to-do on occasion wore wigs, and their sisters enormous hair arrangements. For his stepdaughter, aged four, George Washington ordered from London an assortment of stays, stiffened coats, gloves, and masks. The vital distinction between youth and age as yet remained unrecognized. Cheerless though this kind of childhood may seem to moderns, it helped form the minds and characters of the men who led the revolt against Britain and framed the United States Constitution; perhaps in casting off the familial ties to England they were sublimating unconscious resentments against their own parents.

Both custom and law decreed that wedlock, once entered into, should be permanent. To this end most couples doubtless heeded Poor Richard's precept: "Keep your eyes open before marriage, half shut afterwards"; in any case life was so full as to allow little time for grievances, real or imaginary. Apart from rare instances in Pennsylvania, divorces were granted only in New England, and there the permissive authority generally resided in a legislative body which exercised it sparingly. To be sure, disgruntled couples now and then separated by mutual consent, and not seldom the lady, taking matters into her own hands, ran away. Indeed, advertisements in the press for truant wives were almost as numerous as those for fugitive slaves. Typical was the following in the *South-Carolina Gazette,* May 25, 1765: "Whereas my wife Mary Oxendine, hath eloped from me, this to forewarn all persons from Harbouring or entertaining her, day or night, or crediting her in my name, as I am determined not to pay any debts by her contracted."

Adultery met with harsh treatment, risking a death sentence originally through most of New England. In practice, however, humanity inclined the courts to commute the extreme penalty to lesser ones like flogging, requiring the offenders to wear a scarlet letter "A" or branding that heinous symbol on their foreheads. Bigamy created a special problem. Newcomers to America, having sometimes fled uncongenial spouses at home, felt little com-

punction about trying again where they were unknown. It was the
practice in Massachusetts to fine or whip such culprits and return
them to their places of origin by "the first opportunity of shipping." On the other hand, if one party to a marriage disappeared,
the other was commonly permitted to resume wedlock after an
interval varying from one to five years. In these cases society felt
an obligation both to the injured mate and to the community at
large to restore the normal condition of life.

To safeguard the stability of marriage the common law
granted the husband almost total authority over the person and
property of his wife—a subjection sanctioned by religion as the
logical consequence of Mother Eve's misconduct. The married
female lost title even to her clothing and other intimate possessions and forfeited control over the money and land she brought
to the marriage. Nor could she sue or be sued in a court except in
her husband's name. If she worked for outsiders, he had the same
right to her earnings as to those of his minor children, and he
could chastise her in the same degree as he did them, that is, short
of permanent disablement. Moreover, he was the children's sole
guardian and could dispose of them as he wished at death. He was
further entitled to any court damages for injuries to his wife and
in return was liable for many of her unlawful actions. As Blackstone summed it up, "The very being or legal existence of the
woman is suspended during the marriage, or at least is incorporated and consolidated into that of her husband."

Although the single woman and the widow escaped such
disabilities, this had little effect on the sex as a whole, for social
pressure hastened the former into matrimony and soon returned
the latter to that state. George Washington's sister-in-law waited
longer than many widows in taking another husband after five
months, and he himself led Martha Custis to the altar within seven
months of her spouse's death. Jefferson and James Madison were
other well-known figures to marry widows.

It is clear, however, that few husbands acted the despot to the
extent the law allowed. Whether from affection or as the price of
domestic peace, they seem generally to have followed the Reverend Benjamin Wadsworth's advice in *The Well-Ordered Family*
(Boston, 1712) to make their dominion "as easie and gentle as
possible; and strive more to be lov'd than fear'd, though neither is

to be excluded." The wife for her part undoubtedly agreed with what the poet Anne Bradstreet had written in the mid-seventeenth century:

> Let Greeks be Greeks, and women what they are
> Men have precedency and still excell,
> It is but vain unjustly to wage warre;
> Men can do best, and women know it well. . . .

Moreover, the distaff side also knew well, as a correspondent in the *North-Carolina Gazette,* July 14, 1775, needlessly counseled:

> Make him *believe* he holds the Sov'reign Sway,
> And she may *rule,* by seeming to *obey.*

Even apart from the exercise of feminine wiles, married women to a degree improved their standing in the eyes of the law as the conditions of life in a new country thrust on them responsibilities unknown in England. In certain colonies they acquired somewhat greater freedom as to property, legacies, the making of contracts, and the right to litigate. Thus New Hampshire in 1714 enabled a widow to obtain a third of her husband's estate when he had not adequately provided for her; Pennsylvania in 1718 empowered a female engaged in business during her husband's absence to sue and be sued in court; and Connecticut in 1723 provided that if a wife inherited realty it could be alienated only with her consent.

But even in such provinces the married woman in most respects still bore the relation of a subject to a ruler. It was this demeaning position before the law that prompted the sprightly Abigail Adams, chiding her husband John at the Continental Congress in the spring of 1776, to write that, while he and his male colleagues were grandiloquently asserting the rights of all mankind, "you insist upon retaining an absolute power over wives." Mentioning this outburst in a letter to her good friend Mercy Otis Warren, she explained, "I have only been making trial of the disinterestedness of his Virtue," adding ruefully that "when weighed in the balance" she had "found it wanting." The time had not yet arrived, however, when women would take organized action on behalf of their sex to correct the situation.

Although the home was the only sphere in which the married

woman was expected to move and have her being, it was by no means a narrow orbit, but rather one which taxed to the full her initiative and executive ability. Physical isolation and the chronic shortage of cash required that the typical household provide the essentials of living for itself, and this largely rested on her shoulders as the wife and mother. The family raised its own poultry and vegetables, prepared its own butter and cheese, made its own soap out of grease left over from cooking and butchering, supplied its own birch brooms, dipped its own candles, made and dyed its own cloth, rugs, and apparel, doctored and nursed its sick and injured. The term "spinster," expressive of one of these manifold tasks, continues in our language to this day, but with a connotation strangely altered from its original meaning. In addition, women sometimes helped with the sowing and reaping, and in the back country they had to know enough about firearms to repel wild beasts and Indians.

Every meal for the numerous household was a major undertaking, involving even for breakfast the preparation of such dishes as pork, beef, wild and tame fowl, Indian corn in its many forms, pies, and puddings. A rugged life demanded rugged fare. A heaping abundance rather than a yet-undreamed-of dietary balance was the object. For sweetening, most women used maple sugar, honey, or West Indian molasses, cane sugar being scarce and expensive. The special addiction of the colonists to pork arose from the ease of obtaining it, for hogs roamed the woods, feeding on acorns and roots, and needed no tending. Oddly enough, the white potato, though a native of Peru, was unknown to the early settlers. Carried by the Spaniards in the sixteenth century to Europe and there becoming a staple food, it did not reach the British colonies till Scotch-Irish immigrants introduced it in the 1720's, whence arose its name, the Irish potato.

These victuals the housewife laboriously made ready on turnspits before the huge wood-burning fireplace or in pots hung from a swinging crane over the blaze or in the capacious oven in the brickwork at the side. The day of the cookstove was yet to come. The very striking of a light necessitated the vigorous rubbing of a piece of flint against steel to make a spark to set afire tinder; but fortunately this chore usually fell to the men. To preserve perishable foodstuffs the womenfolk, having no knowledge of refrigeration or of canning, had to salt, pickle, smoke, and dry vegetables and meats. Once the settlers began living far from ocean brine, however, they found salt hard to get and had either to buy it or to seek out the saline springs and deposits frequented by the Indians and wild animals.

The absence of plumbing and water closets created further work for the housewife, but in three notable respects the advancing eighteenth century brought greater comfort as well as safety to the home. Thanks to the rise of the whaling industry and the availability of spermaceti oil, families in the coastal areas now had metal and glass lamps to supplement or replace the flickering candlelight. Then, in 1740, Benjamin Franklin invented the fireplace stove, still called by his name. This contrivance, standing apart from the wall and shedding its warmth in all directions, banished the icy chill from the fringes of the room. The Pennsylvania Germans and New York Dutch had long used stoves for heating, but few had been known elsewhere and furnaces nowhere. Next, to guard the house and its inmates from an ever-dreaded peril, Franklin twelve years later followed this device with his famous lightning rod. This invention, however, while quickly demonstrating its usefulness, spread but slowly among the rural folk.

Matrons in town mansions and on large Southern plantations and the wives of well-to-do tradesmen led a less strenuous existence than the vast bulk of their married sisters. Yet they too lacked what we would today deem essential conveniences and occupied themselves with endless exacting tasks. Even the plantation mistress did not enjoy a bed of ease cushioned by the labor of slaves, which tradition has depicted, but had to be incessantly on the move. She not only superintended the cooking and serving of meals for the family as well as for the constant stream of guests, but she also saw to it that the table was largely provisioned from her own garden, chicken yard, dairy, and smokehouse. The Northerner Philip Fithian, sojourning as a tutor on a Virginia plantation in the 1770's, regarded the feminine head of the establishment "a remarkable Economist" and quoted her as saying that she would find life infinitely boring if she did not give attention to the cattle and poultry. She and her kind, moreover, shouldered the principal responsibility for looking after the health of the Negroes along with that of their husbands and children, often preparing their own medicines for the purpose from prescriptions handed down from mother to daughter. Generally, however, women of this class did not need to spin and weave the family clothing, which their husbands could well afford to order from London.

In addition, some Southern women supervised the entire work of the plantation. The instance of Eliza Lucas of South Carolina is a shining example. Left in charge of three plantations as a seventeen-year-old girl in 1738 during her father's extended absence on military duty in the West Indies, she experimented so successfully with indigo as to make it a staple crop of the province. She also tried, unavailingly, to grow figs, ginger, and cotton, meanwhile mastering enough law to draw up wills for her poorer neighbors. Then, after marrying Charles Pinckney, a widower of twice her age, in 1744, she had some success with cultivating the silkworm, though doing less well with hemp and flax. Upon his death fourteen years later she took over the management of his vast estate, scattered in various parts of the colony, and conducted it at a profit. President Washington was one of the pallbearers at her funeral in 1793.

Eliza Lucas Pinckney was admittedly exceptional. Yet nearly all girls of the time underwent training in domestic responsibilities that fitted them, if occasion arose, to make a living outside the home. The number of such independent women, though never large, grew as the years went by and the spread of settlement increased opportunities. Generally they were widows who in many cases merely continued the occupations of their deceased husbands; but even if they were wives supplementing the family income or single women on their own, they did not incur community censure. In this respect they fared better than those who were to come after them in the early nineteenth century. Despite inherited Old World attitudes, society realized that, with more work to do than hands to do it, women could safely be allowed to contribute their mite without endangering masculine ascendancy.

Accordingly, women functioned as shopkeepers of all sorts,

innkeepers, ferry tenders, wharf proprietors, farm and plantation operators, schoolmistresses, seamstresses, sometimes also as wholesale merchants and shipowners. Between 1760 and 1775 no fewer than thirty-six women advertised millinery and dry goods for sale in the papers of Charleston, South Carolina, and at least thirteen in those of Williamsburg, Virginia, while five others at various times during these years edited newssheets in towns from Massachusetts to the Old Dominion. Three of the five were widows taking over their husbands' duties; the two others were, respectively, the mother and the sister of the man who had founded both journals. Interestingly enough, America's first poet was a woman: Anne Bradstreet, a Massachusetts farm wife and the mother of eight children. But, characteristically, she wrote simply for her own satisfaction, and it was without her knowledge or wish that an admiring brother-in-law published her verses in London in 1650, the only volume to appear during her lifetime. On the other hand, women made no headway in the legal profession or as medical practitioners except as they dosed their own families or hired out as midwives and practical nurses.

Nowhere, of course, did they possess the vote, nor did they even organize to seek it. The suffragette was a creature of the dim future. Nevertheless, the contest with the mother country from the Stamp Act onward drew them increasingly into the current of political controversy. Some contented themselves with naming their babies after patriot heroes; others banded together publicly to help the men force Parliament to repeal objectionable legislation through economic pressure. They formed societies for making and wearing homespun, for discountenancing foreign fineries, for forgoing the use of duties tea. In short, the Daughters of Liberty did their part with the Sons of Liberty in furthering the movement of resistance.

Beyond all this, the family became a key unit in social and political organization. Through intermarriage and interlocking kinship, families in a number of regions consolidated social and economic power in their hands, swaying elections, occupying high civic offices, and dominating major branches of business enterprise. Such, for example, were the Hancocks and Cushings in Massachusetts, the Browns and Wantons in Rhode Island, the

Livingstons and Schuylers in New York, the Willings and Whar-
tons in Pennsylvania, the Lees, Randolphs, and Carters in Virginia, the Rutledges and Pinckneys in South Carolina. Of the New
England mercantile class a recent student has written that, even in
the seventeenth century, "The bonds of marriage united almost
every merchant with every other merchant in the same immediate
vicinity." And of the judges in New York, Cadwallader Colden
complained in the next century that so many of them were inter-
connected with "distinguished Family" as to defeat the ends of
justice when cases involved their relatives. Generally speaking,
however, these family alliances, whether in North or South, set a
standard in governmental and commercial affairs that redounded
to the benefit of their communities as well as themselves.

These clans were largely localized; others extended across
provincial borders, some of the members having struck out for
greener pastures. The mobility which had first brought the colonists to America by no means spent itself with the original settlements. When Samuel Curwen of Salem journeyed to Philadelphia
in 1755, he repeatedly encountered relatives along the way; and
when Mr. and Mrs. John Bayard traveled from the Quaker City to
Boston four years later, they enjoyed the hospitality of Colonel
William Bayard in New York and Balthazar Bayard in Boston.
Benjamin Smith, prominent in political and mercantile circles in
South Carolina, was a kinsman of Mrs. John Adams. Similar and
perhaps even greater intermigration occurred among lesser folk.
The various Greens, for instance, who in the mid-eighteenth
century conducted printshops and newspapers in Boston, New
London, Hartford, New Haven, and Annapolis, had a common
ancestor in Samuel Green, an early-seventeenth-century pressman
in Cambridge, Massachusetts. Since poor communications and
provincial jealousies continually tended to divide the colonies,
these widespread families provided a bridge of greater understanding and cooperation. And when the crisis arose with the
homeland they helped bind together the collective movement of
resistance.

CHAPTER III

The Countryside

AGRICULTURE was the basic means of livelihood. Not only was an adequate and dependable food supply the first object of every settler, but also farming was the occupation most of them knew best and the one most had followed before migrating. The conditions of the agricultural life were, however, greatly different in the New World. Where the European peasant was characteristically bound to the soil, the American settler was always free, when the spirit moved him, to pull up stakes and push into the virgin hinterland. No section of the new country was too cold for husbandry, none too hot for labor in the fields. Land, besides being plentiful, was easy to acquire; and if perchance the authorities interposed obstacles, the newcomers seldom hesitated to take possession anyway. As some Scotch-Irish squatters in Pennsylvania righteously put the matter, "It was against the laws of God and nature, that so much land should be idle while so many Christians wanted it to labor on and to raise their bread."

The technical problems of agriculture were also different from those of Europe. Only the Scotch-Irish, who a century before coming to America had laboriously transformed the fens and wastes of Ulster into fields and gardens, had ever faced a comparable situation; but these migrants arrived fairly late in the colonial period, and even they had much both to learn and to unlearn. The settler, guided by Indian practice, made his initial opening in the forest by killing the trees in the most expeditious manner possible, either by girdling the bark with his ax to stop the rise of sap or by building fires at their bases to destroy the roots. Then, when the leafless boughs let the warm sunlight filter through, he made his first planting—invariably of corn, because of its quick growth— after which he felled the dead trunks, splitting up some to make into zigzag fences and burning the rest in great piles. So hard was this task that it took a month to clear so much as an acre; in New England the removal of stones from the soil—later to be used in walls—added to the burden. These well-established techniques would stand the pioneers of later times in good stead until they reached the treeless prairies. Once the farmer had met the family's immediate needs, he was ready to enlarge his acreage and take on other crops.

His tools, like those used in Europe, were few and primitive. The plow, his basic implement, differed little from the ones in Julius Caesar's time. The most popular kind possessed a crudely shaped wooden moldboard plated with sheet iron or old saw blades and tipped with an iron share to form the cutting edge. With this unwieldy contrivance he could turn a furrow in well-worked ground with the help of one or two oxen, but in tougher sod he needed four or six. The metal portions, made from bog ore and very brittle, broke easily and might abruptly end his whole day's labors. At harvest time he cut his grain with a sickle or scythe, then beat away the chaff with a flail, as in New England, or followed the Old Testament custom of treading it out with horses on a threshing floor, as was common in the Middle and Southern colonies. Since these implements, like his shovels, hoes, and forks, consisted mostly or wholly of wood, he could make them himself, with a blacksmith generally supplying any needed iron parts.

Along with the tools borrowed from the Old World he retained its ancient agricultural lore. He displayed vast respect for the signs of the zodiac and particularly for the moon's phases, which he could observe for himself. Since he knew the moon exerted a mysterious influence on the tides, it was only common sense to believe that it also affected vegetable life. Accordingly, he carefully attuned his labors to the heavenly indications. He sowed while the moon was on the wax to ensure rapid germination and cut down underbrush and weeds on its wane to prevent further growth. Religious teaching provided additional guidance. A drought or a flood he viewed as the act of an angry God whom he and his neighbors must placate with fasting and prayer, and with equal fervor they celebrated the presumed success of their efforts with community thanksgivings.

One traditional Old World practice, however, the colonists quickly discarded. With unlimited amounts of land available there was no longer the compelling need to replenish the soil by rotating crops or fertilizing it. It was simpler and cheaper to move on to new tracts after depleting the old. The American farmer, lacking the rooted attachment to ancestral acres that characterized his European brothers, therefore began a long assault on the fertility of the American soil.

True, there were individuals cognizant of current English writings on agricultural reform who, as the eighteenth century progressed, sought to introduce a more scientific spirit. Outstanding in this respect was the Reverend Jared Eliot. His *Essays on Field-Husbandry in New-England,* published serially from 1748 to 1759, urged the reclamation of idle or worn-out tracts by such means as drainage, irrigation, the use of fertilizers, and the alternation of crops. But almost in the same breath this enlightened soul went on to commend the "rules of Husbandry" in the Bible as truly "Remarkable" and, with obeisance to the undeniable lunar influence on plant life, to advise that bushes be hewn down and trees girdled "in the Old of the Moon." On his own, James Logan, secretary to William Penn, experimented with the hybridization of corn, and, among others, George Washington strove constantly to build up his soil and even practiced tree grafting; he was, besides, probably the first in America to cultivate lucerne, or alfalfa. But the mass of farmers continued content with things as they were. No one could have guessed that in the century just ahead their descendants would inaugurate an agricultural revolution affecting the entire world.

From Pennsylvania northward the people pursued mixed agriculture, the major crops being wheat, corn, rye, and other grains very much as in Europe. To the southward, thanks to the long summers and to special inducements of Parliament, they centered on staple production: tobacco in Maryland and Virginia, rice and indigo in South Carolina and Georgia, with the North Carolinians growing a little of each. These staples found a ready market overseas; although the law required that they be sent only to Britain, from there they were resold to the Continent, four fifths of the tobacco being so disposed of in the final years before Independence. This plant constituted the most valuable of all American exports. Cotton, the commodity which was in later times to dominate the Southern economy, received as yet only passing attention. Northern products had a more limited outlet, since they came into competition with those of the Old World except in times of crop failures abroad, but considerable amounts of wheat, flour, corn, and other provisions were regularly shipped to the West Indies to feed the slave workers on the sugar plantations. The trade in wheat and flour, a particular concern of Pennsylvania, helped make that province the most prosperous in the North.

The entire back country from New Hampshire to Georgia contributed in greater or less degree to the production of naval stores—tar, pitch, and turpentine—ship timber, and masts. Although these items could be exported to the homeland alone, British shipyards absorbed all that America could spare, and the London government from time to time offered bounties to stimulate output. Closely related was another forest pursuit, the traffic in furs, which likewise engaged all the colonies but, unlike lumbering, was a full-time job and prosecuted mainly by barter with the savages. The skins commanded fancy prices in Europe, and the traders—whom Governor Robert Dinwiddie of Virginia deemed "the most abandon'd Wretches in the World"—increased their profits by flagrantly cheating the aborigines, usually with the help of firewater. As the advance of settlement drove the fur-bearing animals ever deeper into the continent, the traders followed after them and came into competition in the Great Lakes region and the Mississippi Valley with the French, who were no less eager for the valuable Indian pelts. The rivalry in the fur trade, festering over the years, proved a major factor in precipitating in 1754 the war between the mother countries—two years before it broke out in Europe.

The husbandman in his normal round of duties also kept some livestock: beef cattle, dairy cows, swine, and goats to provide meat and milk; sheep for their wool (rather than for mutton); oxen and horses for field work. But with so much else to do he seldom gave the creatures proper care, often letting them run wild, so that they steadily deteriorated in quality and size from the time of the original importations. Only the Pennsylvania Germans, always a people unto themselves, studiously minded their stock, stabling the cattle and horses during the winters, and these practices belatedly caught on in New York and New England in the eighteenth century. As between horses and oxen, the farmer preferred the stronger and more docile beasts for plowing and the like; with a team of oxen he could tend fifteen acres of corn as easily as two alone. The raising of horses, however, supplied him with a useful article of export to the West Indies (to which he also sent salted pork and beef); and with the gradual improvement of roads he used them increasingly for riding and driving. Southern New England became the principal breeding ground. Indeed, the Rhode Islanders developed the first distinctive American strain, the fleet-footed saddle horse known as the Narragansett pacer, for which there was a demand in all the colonies. The Pennsylvania Germans also made a characteristic contribution, not a horse built for speed, but an admirable draft animal, the Conestoga horse, named after its place of origin in Lancaster County.

Meanwhile, the farmer in his other capacities was a woodman, carpenter, butcher, tanner, toolmaker, game hunter, and fisherman. After building his cabin from timber he had cut, he made the tables, chairs, bowls, chests, and beds. Then, to meet his continuing needs, he slaughtered meat from time to time; tanned hides for harness, shoes, and work clothes; chopped firewood; turned out nails, staves, barrels, and churns; carved ox yokes, gunstocks, and ax handles; manufactured carts; and supplemented the family larder by killing wild animals and fishing nearby waters. He even prepared his beer, wines, and other strong beverages from grain, fruit, and other materials at hand. In short, he supplied all the human demands that he either lacked the means to buy or else was too distant from a town to obtain. In time he not only learned to provide amply for his own household, but in many instances he also produced a surplus for sale to townsfolk and sometimes even for export. What had begun as a consequence of dire need turned

out for the vast majority of the colonists to be a rewarding mode
of existence. Even on the brink of Independence, despite the
gradual development of competing occupations in the towns,
nineteen out of twenty Americans were still tillers of the soil.
These were Emerson's "embattled farmers," without whom there
would have been no "shot heard round the world" and no victory
in the war for freedom.

The typical farm on the eve of Independence was, as it had
been from the beginning, tended by the farmer and his household.
Even in the South, where staple culture and the plantation system
abounded, small holdings greatly outnumbered the large estates.
In New England the tillers, following traditional English practice,
dwelt in compact settlements around the village green apart from
their fields and pastures, some of which were held in common.
Throughout the rest of America the farmers lived in more or less
isolated tracts separated by the primeval forest. Whatever the
particular circumstances, the husbandman led an exacting, independent, self-sufficient existence that sharply distinguished him
from the Old World peasant.

The century and a half of doggedly taming the wilderness
made an impress on the American people which, as it was renewed and reinforced on later frontiers, had an abiding effect on
the national character. Even colonials who were by vocation
lawyers, merchants, clergymen, artisans, and sailors often farmed
on the side, and no townsman, however he himself disliked bucolic
life, could entirely escape its pervasive influence.

By necessity the farmer made a religion of work. He might on
occasion ignore the Word of God, but the voice of nature brooked
no indifference or delay. In the Old World physical labor was a
demeaning occupation; in the New, the price of community acceptance. Even the great planters had to make a show of being
busy, as indeed they invariably were. And since the Bible itself
vaunted the virtues of toil—"Man goeth forth unto his work and
to his labour until the evening"—the colonist had the further
incentive of divine sanction. As Franklin warned prospective
settlers from abroad, "People do not inquire concerning a
Stranger, *What is he?* but, *What can he do?*" There naturally
arose the conviction that all men—at least all white men—were

created equal; they had only themselves to blame if they did not realize their birthright. The European conception of a permanently stratified society found little sustenance in such a soil.

Work, however, meant less the ability to do a few things well than to do many things well enough. Every man was a Robinson Crusoe. Not thoroughness but improvisation was the key to success. This schooling in dexterity instilled qualities that under the different conditions of the nineteenth century caused youths from the farm to produce some of the world's great inventions. At the same time, however, the colonists' wastefulness of soil and timber implanted a disregard for natural resources which persisted almost to our own generation, while the readiness to abandon old land for new inculcated a migratory disposition that still distinguishes the American people. For youth greener pastures ever continued to lie over the horizon.

The farmer's pressing concern with the practical and utilitarian made him indifferent if not hostile to the life of the mind. Intellectual activity for its own sake, though allowable perhaps for idle townsfolk, had no place in his scheme of things. The doer, not the thinker, achieved results in the world as he knew it; anything else was a form of malingering. He would have little truck even with writers who, like Jared Eliot, sought to improve his husbandry. By the same token he had no eye for the beauties of nature. Trees were to be cut down, not admired; rivers to be avoided or forded, not eulogized. These attitudes, too, were long to influence his descendants.

The farmer's success in overcoming heavy odds gave him an invincible faith in human progress. Unaware that this belief was an exciting new discovery of European intellectuals, he had learned from both observation and experience that man could improve his fortunes and that his children could do the same. Only the sanguine settled in America, and but for their congenital optimism they could not have endured the hardships, terrors, and loneliness that fell to their lot. Accordingly, these transplanted Europeans lacked that latent sense of tragedy which had immemorially haunted their Old World forebears. When Jefferson said, "I steer my bark with Hope in the head, leaving Fear astern," he was describing all his countrymen. Not even fatalism in religion

could long withstand this certainty of inevitable human betterment. It was not the least of the colonial farmer's legacies to the
American people.

The boundless self-confidence tended to make men feel that
government was a gratuitous burden. Where everyone was his
own master, it was natural to think that that government was best
which governed least, that its proper sphere was only to ensure
property rights, preserve order, and protect the community
against foreign invasion. Even against the Indians the colonists
relied primarily on their own resources, while communities remote
from centers of law enforcement or distrustful of official action
often disposed of their unruly elements by taking the law into their
own hands. Although the term "lynch law" did not originate until
the Revolutionary War when some back-country Virginia planters
under Charles Lynch inflicted extralegal penalties on British sympathizers, flogging and hanging them by their thumbs, the usage
itself dated back to early colonial days, with tarring and feathering
the favorite form of punishment. Both of these attitudes—the
dislike of strong government and the condoning of vigilante
methods—survived far into the national period.

These practices rendered stronger a tendency which the inhabitants had originally brought with them from England: the
willingness to defy overweening constituted authority. From Bacon's Rebellion of 1676 to the uprising of the thirteen colonies in
1775 they never hesitated to resist, by force if necessary, whatever
they considered insupportable oppression, believing with Jefferson
that "the tree of liberty must be refreshed from time to time with
the blood of patriots and tyrants." Having in the act of migrating
individually affirmed their independence of arbitrary rule, they
found it so much the easier to declare it collectively when they
thought the motherland had left them no alternative. This attitude,
too, outlasted colonial days, evidencing itself in such later upsurges as Shays' Rebellion in Massachusetts, the Whisky Insurrection in Pennsylvania, and the Dorr War in Rhode Island, as well
as in the desperate attempt of the Southern states to establish a
separate existence.

The pursuit of agriculture, though at the beginning a matter of
sheer self-preservation, came to seem to the colonists the most

blessed state man could attain in this world. A society of small independent farmers had been the dream of their ancestors; now they had achieved it for themselves and their posterity. Like the children of Israel they had issued from the house of bondage into a land flowing with milk and honey, and the acquisition of material well-being had in turn brought a freeing of the spirit. The tilling of the soil, in Jared Eliot's words, "opens to us a glorious scene and discovery of the Wisdom and Power of the Creator and Governor of the World." "To see plants rise from the earth and flourish by the superior skill and bounty of the laborer," wrote Washington, "fills the contemplative mind with ideas which are more easy to be conceived than expressed"; nowhere could he find "so great satisfaction as in those innocent and useful pursuits." Young John Adams as a law student found the "rattle-gabble" of the streets of Boston so distracting that "to put the mind into a stirring, thoughtful mood" he would flee to the "stillness, silence, and the uniformity of the prospect" of the family farm in nearby Braintree. Even after entering law practice he would calm his nerves between the trying of cases by driving the cattle to water, thinning the woodlot, and performing other simple chores. "Those who labour in the earth," as Jefferson summed it up, "are the chosen people of God, if ever he had a chosen people. . . . Corruption of morals in the mass of cultivators is a phenomenon of which no age nor nation has furnished an example."

CHAPTER IV

The Emergence of Towns

Y ET EVEN BEFORE the Revolution the agricultural paradise was in retreat. Washington, Adams, and Jefferson, for example, were all destined to spend more of their mature years in the cities they detested than in the rural solitudes they held so dear. Jefferson attributed this ill fortune to "the enormities of the times." But in fact towns had been a potent force in colonial life from the start and had offered unique opportunities to men of energy, talent, and vision. The colonial towns, indeed, had reenacted in the wilderness the historic role in the advancement of civilization which urban communities in the Old World had played from the days of Memphis and Thebes. As a writer in the *Maryland Gazette* in 1773 observed, cities had always been "the repositories, preservatives, and nurseries of commerce, liberty, and knowledge."

Almost the first object of the newcomers was to establish a village or town to serve as a stronghold against attack and as a base for colonizing the adjoining territory. The founders of Jamestown and Plymouth set an example which Europeans landing elsewhere along the coast invariably followed, as did later arrivals pushing into the interior. In time these settlements acquired indispensable functions, even in the predominantly agrarian economy. Not only did they consume surplus farm products, but towns on the ocean also exported native commodities to distant markets and brought back goods that would otherwise have been unobtainable—firearms, saws and axes, not to mention luxury items like costly fabrics and fine tableware for the Southern landed gentry. If the great planters usually carried on trade with Britain from their own river wharves and accordingly did not feel the same need for commercial centers, nevertheless, even the South had one major community.

In the towns, too, money accumulated for investment, and there also dwelt mobile groups of workers for employment in fisheries and in the merchant marine. The urban centers, more-over, nourished an active intellectual life in contrast with the toll exacted of mind and spirit by unending farm duties. Ports of entry for European merchandise, they were also ports of entry for European thought and taste, and the less strenuous pursuits of the citizens allowed more time for reflection and intellectual activity. The career of Benjamin Franklin, a city man from start to finish, showed the creative possibilities of the urban environment. Con-stant association with one's fellows not only sharpened the wits but also facilitated joint undertakings and kept the townsmen politically alert. It was no coincidence that in the contest with the mother country the cities headed the resistance, furnishing most of the leaders, organizing mass demonstrations and economic re-prisals, and rallying country support.

The principal cities when the war broke out were, in order of size, Philadelphia, New York, Boston, Charleston, and Newport, with such places as New Haven, Norwich, Norfolk, Baltimore, and Salem of secondary rank. Inland settlements were still smaller; Lancaster, a Pennsylvania-German market town, and Albany, a fur-trading and military post, were about the only ones with even modest urban pretensions. Until the middle of the eighteenth century Boston had possessed the largest population; but in the 1770's both Philadelphia (with forty thousand) and New York (with twenty-five thousand) had forged ahead, thanks to their rapidly growing and richer hinterlands, while Boston virtually stood still at sixteen thousand. Charleston (with twelve thousand) and Newport (with eleven thousand) also gained in numbers though remaining smaller than Boston. This sense of falling behind may very well have fired the Bostonians to take the lead in opposing Britain's new revenue and trade restrictions following the Seven Years' War, for, though the measures applied to all American ports, to the Bostonians they spelled utter ruin.

These centers presented low skylines of brick and wooden buildings, broken with occasional steeples and clumps of masts. Warehouses hugged the waterfront, handy to the busy wharves; behind, on higher ground, stood the shops and offices and markets. Neat private dwellings, some rising to three stories, were scattered through the town, with the poorer folk carrying on their trades in their homes. Charleston and Philadelphia alone were laid out on a checkerboard scheme—the earliest instances of city planning in America. Their wide streets running at right angles offered a pleasing contrast to the narrow and crooked roadways prevailing elsewhere. The Bostonians indeed, as a modern critic has jeered, seem to have followed the principle that one good turn deserves another. Charleston outshone all its rivals in costly mansions, thanks to the opulent rice and indigo planters who maintained residences there to escape the oppressive heat and noxious air of the back country.

The South Carolina metropolis, though, was the only one of the five towns with no public park. Philadelphia boasted its Commons, New York its Fields, Boston its Common, and Newport its Parade—places for the citizens to stroll and take their ease and conduct open-air meetings. It was in New York's Fields that young Alexander Hamilton in 1774 delivered the flaming speech against the Intolerable Acts that first brought him to public notice.

The taverns, of which every town large or small had at least one, usually bore fanciful names like their English counterparts—the Harp and Crown, the Blue Anchor, the Golden Swan, the Bunch of Grapes, the Indian King—displayed on crudely decorated signboards over their main doors. In these haunts men gathered to eat, drink, play cards, read the papers, and discuss the topics of the day. There, too, new legal enactments and notices of elections were posted, the schedules of stage lines could be consulted, and transients engage lodgings. For their further accommodation travelers could find similar hostelries at convenient distances along the more frequented roads. The one built in 1686 at South Sudbury, Massachusetts, long known as the Red Horse

Tavern, was to gain literary fame as the setting of Longfellow's *Tales of a Wayside Inn.* Restored in the twentieth century by Henry Ford, it serves as a reminder in an automobile age of an older way of life.

The five great ports were established metropolises by the time of Lexington and Concord. New York (originally New Amsterdam) was 150 years old, Boston 145, Newport 136, while Charleston and Philadelphia were approaching the century mark. Philadelphia surpassed every city in England but London in population and ranked with the largest cities of Scotland and Ireland. Its size combined with its central location made it the universal choice for the site of the Continental Congresses. As early as the mid-century a commentator in the London *Gentleman's Magazine* accounted it "as fine a city as any on the globe" of its size, with a "market-place equal to any in Europe"—contrary to the testy view of John Adams that "Philadelphia, with all its trade and wealth and regularity is not Boston."

Adams would not, however, have challenged the correspondent's further assertion that the Pennsylvania city was "as large and much better built than Bristol, or indeed any other city in England, London excepted." In the case of New York the writer even omitted the exception, observing that New York's municipal building was architecturally "very little inferior to Guild-Hall." He noted that even Charleston, America's fourth city, was as big as Gloucester. New York still occupied but a portion of the tip of Manhattan, with Broadway following the watershed of the island and the Fields (now City Hall Park) marking the town's northern limits. Boston also lay pretty much on an island, for the neck joining it with the mainland was so narrow and low that at high tide the ocean often washed over it. The settled area covered only the southern and southeastern side of the peninsula.

In the Northern cities and to some extent even in Charleston merchants and lawyers dominated affairs. The trading community had been influential from the start, but lawyers had only recently emerged from the suspicion and distrust with which they had been regarded in the seventeenth century. With few or no restrictions on admission, incompetents and shysters had flooded the practice, and the early colonists consequently preferred their own common-sense notions of justice. In 1650 the Massachusetts legislators resolved, "We are proud that we are free of the pernicious class"—an exemption, alas, of short duration—and in 1699 Governor Bellomont of New York apprised his London superiors that "the men who call themselves lawyers here . . . are almost all under such a scandalous character that would grieve a man to see our noble English laws so miserably mangled and profaned." Some colonies forthrightly forbade persons acting as attorneys to take fees.

But the mounting population and booming commercial enterprise of the eighteenth century gave new importance to business contracts, mercantile paper, property titles, and other esoteric matters, and the bar began to come into its own. Provincial authorities began licensing legal practitioners, and college graduates increasingly took up the career. In the absence of local law schools they either studied in the office of established attorneys or, if they were sufficiently well-to-do, resorted to the famous Inns of Court in London. James Otis, John Adams, and Thomas Jefferson, for example, followed the former course; John Dickinson, Richard Henry Lee, and Charles Cotesworth Pinckney and many others in Pennsylvania and the South, the latter. In fact, nearly a hundred and fifty young Americans attended the Inns of Court, especially the Middle and Inner Temples, between 1750 and 1775. Old prejudices remained—John Jay in 1777 inveighed against "designing, cheating, litigious pettifoggers, who, like leeches and spiders, will fatten on the spoils of the poor, the ignorant, the feeble, and the unwary"—but the calling was at last establishing itself on a professional basis. Bar associations arose in most of the Northern provinces to preserve and elevate standards, New York and Rhode Island leading off in the 1740's. Another stimulus came with the publication of Sir William Blackstone's *Commentaries* in London in the 1760's. Hitherto the student had been obliged to extract the theory of the common law from a mass of undigested material. Now he could view the system as an interrelated and rational whole. Copies were in immediate demand in the colonies, and the first American edition, printed in Philadelphia in 1771-2, had fourteen hundred advance orders.

By the time of Independence, lawyers, no longer pariahs, had become pillars of respectability in the community, attaining a place in American society they have never since relinquished. Known to and knowing all manner of men, they engaged actively in politics, usually dominating the legislatures, where, "skilled in the chicaneries of the Law"—Cadwallader Colden's acid phrase —they proved adept at frustrating royal governors. Drawing on English constitutional precedents as well as the natural-rights philosophy, they also wrote most of the abler vindications of the colonial position in the dispute with the mother country and furnished over half the signers of the Declaration of Independence, itself the work of a lawyer. Fortunately, too, they were at hand to help draft the new frames of government for the states and the nation. Of the fifty-five members of the Federal Constitutional Convention they provided thirty-one, four of whom had studied at the Inner Temple and one at Oxford under Blackstone.

The merchants provided the means of livelihood of the bulk of townsmen: the shopkeepers, artisans, mechanics, day laborers, carters, longshoremen, sailors, and the like. Directly or indirectly, commerce and shipping turned the wheels of community well-being. The rank and file did not resent their subordinate position, since they too expected someday through hard work to get to the top, just as those now there had done before them. The ideal of the self-made man was already an active force in American life. The hard times dogging the Seven Years' War brought employers and those dependent on them into close political cooperation. The banning of previously permitted wartime traffic with the West Indies plus a sharp reduction of British military expenditures in America and the Ministry's stiffened enforcement of the Acts of Trade injured both rich and poor, causing them to unite in non-importation and nonconsumption agreements against the further burdens imposed by London. When, however, the depression lifted in 1770, more substantial merchants, alarmed by the excesses of the mob, in large part defected from the coalition. But by that time the masses had developed a sense of their own power and felt able to act independently.

The formation of Committees of Merchants in the major ports during the early stages of the agitation testified to the growing solidarity of the traders. These bodies, besides engaging in eco-

nomic reprisals, addressed petitions to the home government for
the relief of themselves and their communities. The establishment
of the New York Chamber of Commerce in 1768 and of the
Charleston Chamber in 1774 provided further evidence of the
trend. The coastwise traffic brought men of different localities into
intimate touch, to their mutual profit. Sometimes members of the
same family carried on trade in several towns, such as the Amorys
in Boston, Salem, and Charleston and the Lloyds and Apthorps in
New York and Boston. Intercolonial undertakings of a more
formal character were rare, but the United Company of Spermaceti Chandlers, organized in 1761, fixed price ceilings for the
industry, at first throughout New England and then also in New
York and Philadelphia, and worked to bar competitors from the
field. The outbreak of war, however, brought this monopolistic
effort to an end before its example had spread to other areas of
business.

Colonial commerce was conditioned by the fact that the Acts
of Trade conceived of America as a market for British manufactures and a source of raw materials rather than as a country free
to develop its own potentialities. This accorded with the mercan-
tilist theory which dominated all European powers of the time.
Even goods going to America from the Continent had first to be
transshipped in a British port. Hence the colonists were in a
chronic debtor relationship to the mother country, expending
considerably more than they could get in return for their own
commodities. The unfavorable balance in 1721, for instance,
stood at £200,000 sterling, and with the years it became much
greater. To make up the deficiency the merchants developed
complementary channels of commerce. The West Indies were a
particularly useful market. In these tropical islands close at hand
the merchants exchanged agricultural and other native products
in part for hard money, in part for sugar and cotton for resale in
Britain, and in part for molasses, which in the distilled form of
rum they turned into coin by bartering it for slaves on the Guinea
Coast to sell in the West Indies. This last way, the so-called
triangular trade, evidenced most strikingly perhaps the merchants' infinite resourcefulness and far-flung exertions.

In addition, the New Englanders hit upon a treasure-trove in the fisheries. All their seaports sent fleets of small vessels to nearby waters or the Newfoundland Banks, with the crews working tirelessly to increase the catch, of which they received from a sixth to a tenth. Cod was the great staple, to such an extent that the Massachusetts House of Representatives hung a carving of the fish in its hall. Dried and salted, the best grades were exported to the Catholic countries of the Old World for their fast days, the poorest to the West Indies as food for the slaves, while the middlings were disposed of at home. The whaling industry centered largely in Nantucket and, though not well begun until about 1700, was prosecuted with such vigor that by mid-century the ungainly creatures—"spewing up water in the air like the smoke of a chimney"—had to be pursued in the remote Arctic and off South America. Edmund Burke hardly exaggerated when he said of the whalers, "No sea but what is vexed by their fisheries. No climate that is not witness to their toils." This marine occupation also brought handsome returns—in spermaceti, sperm oil, whalebone and ambergris (for use in perfumes). Over three hundred and fifty boats and four thousand men were employed in it at the outbreak of the war.

On the whole, as the steady economic development of the colonies shows, the imperial regulations bore lightly on the Americans until Britain reshaped her policy after the Seven Years' War. For one thing, people could buy the manufactures they needed to import more cheaply from the homeland than elsewhere; even after Independence they continued to prefer British wares. For another, Parliament provided bounties and other means to stimulate the production of tobacco, rice, naval stores, pig iron and certain other important raw materials. For still another, the traders and shippers managed to evade the more irksome restraints, aided as they were by the long and broken coastline as well as by the laxness and venality of the customs officials.

Smuggling was a well-recognized game played with the government and involved no more social stigma than in the British Isles, where the practice was almost fashionable at the time. Though carried on from the beginning in the colonies, it reached giant proportions after 1733, when Parliament overrode American protests to place heavy duties on molasses, sugar, and rum

brought in from the non-British West Indian islands—in face of
the fact that the output of the British islands did not equal two-
thirds of the molasses imported by Rhode Island alone and the
prices charged were higher. But not until the Seven Years' War
did the Ministry actually clamp down on illegal trading activities;
and when it then made strict enforcement a permanent peacetime
policy, resentment in America heightened the opposition to Britain's other commercial and revenue measures. "I know not why
we should blush to confess that molasses was an essential ingre-
dient in American independence," wrote John Adams in after
years.

Moreover, the measures against manufactures struck specifically at those articles which, when sold outside the colonies of
origin, would compete with British industries. Between 1699 and
1732 Parliament, with this in mind, restricted the production of
woolen cloth and of hats (made in America of beaver fur), and in
1750 it forbade the erection of new mills for making iron and steel
wares. In any event, the high cost and scarcity of skilled workers
rendered large enterprises in these fields hazardous. Men of capital found more certain returns in commerce, staple agriculture,
the fisheries, shipbuilding, and rum distilling.

Purely local crafts, untouched by British regulations, throve in
the towns and cities. Where the tiller of the soil was a Jack-of-all-
trades, his city brother strove to be the master of one, obtaining
the other articles and services he lacked from his fellows. Thus,
when town craftsmen built houses, tanned leather, or performed
other tasks usual to the farmer, they functioned mainly as specialists for hire. In addition, they were specialists in capacities unknown in the country—such as gunsmiths, clockmakers, silver-
smiths, wigmakers, coachmakers, glassmakers, sailmakers, and
shoemakers. Some, it is true, simultaneously pursued related
trades, like Boston's Paul Revere, who earned his living as engraver, silversmith, and wirer of false teeth. The diversified make-
up of the population provided both the skills and the variety of
demand required to satisfy a wide range of civilized needs.

These occupations were typically conducted in small shops
where the master craftsman, living upstairs, labored side by side
with one or two helpers to turn out goods generally ordered in

advance. The closest approach to modern manufacturing appeared in three other lines of endeavor: shipbuilding, rum distilling, and wrought-iron products. Here the number of employees was larger but not enough so to discourage personal relations with the employer. Besides, these employees worked pretty much as artisans on their own, not at all as factory hands in the later sense.

Shipbuilding flourished chiefly in the main New England ports and Philadelphia. The mother country placed no restrictions on the industry, indeed aided it by requiring all commerce to be carried in bottoms owned in the colonies or at home. Thanks to the abundance of suitable timber near the water's edge, the Americans could construct cheaper and better vessels, selling many of them in fact to the mistress of the seas. To fashion a ship by hand labor—the only way then known—might take more than a year. The master shipwright, working without an advance drawing, directed his men from day to day from a plan in his head. The undertaking also engaged the services of outside craftsmen: painters, carvers, coopers, ropemakers, and sailmakers. It was in a peculiar sense a community enterprise. When the war came some two thousand American-built boats were plowing the deep, comprising perhaps a third of Britain's entire merchant marine.

Rum making, another key New England business, not only supplied an essential lubricant of commerce but also the most popular colonial tipple. In 1763 Rhode Island possessed about thirty distilleries, "erected at vast expense." A decade later Massachusetts had sixty, with an annual output of 2,700,000 gallons. The third significant industry—iron—was based on bog-ore deposits scattered all the way from Massachusetts to Virginia. It provided crude utensils and tools for American use and a certain amount of raw and bar iron for export to the homeland. Although most of the iron concerns were small, a few were joint-stock ventures financed in part or in whole by British capital. Still other manufactures of more than local scope included candlemaking, flour milling, and the making of paper from rags.

With material progress had come better land communications, tending to reduce the colonists' original dependence on water transport for journeys of a few days or more. The early forest trails, one or two feet wide, broadened into bridle paths and then into wagonways. City folk, eager to build up trade with adjoining areas, provided the initiative. By 1732 roads had grown sufficiently numerous to justify the publication of a *Vade-Mecum for America: or a Companion for Traders and Travellers,* giving the routes and mileage between important points from the mouth of the Penobscot to the James River in Virginia, a distance of some seven hundred miles. Generally, however, people continued to make longer trips by boat to save both time and discomfort.

The roads almost without exception were dirt—hard and rutted or soft and muddy—and the traveler bounced over swampy stretches on top of logs laid sidewise. The drivers prudently carried axes with them to dispose of fallen trees. Bridges were few, and rivers were ordinarily forded or ferried, depending on depth. The ferries, privately run, often consisted of a single craft propelled by oar or sail or by means of a rope. For a quarter century Boston debated the building of a bridge over the Charles River to connect with Cambridge and Harvard College, but not till 1786 did it materialize. Another drawback for the traveler was the fact that every province had its own paper money, which, varying in value, confronted him with some of the problems of crossing international boundaries. Except for this, however, traveling on American roads compared favorably with those in England, and the wayfarer, happily, did not run the same risk of highway robbers. Indeed, progress to the colonist meant not what the future had yet to disclose but what he knew to be a heartening improvement over the past. Accordingly, he felt well served.

The first wheeled vehicles had been for carting rather than riding, but carriages of various types gradually came into use and by the eighteenth century were the rule with the well-to-do of town and country. These conveyances were known after the English fashion by such picturesque names as chaises, chariots, calashes, riding chairs, and curricles, their bodies being supported by leather straps instead of springs. When Parson Joseph Emerson of Malden, Massachusetts, acquired a "shay," it weighed on his conscience as an "inordinate Affection for the Things of the World." "Have I not been too fond & too proud of this convenience?" he asked in his diary. "Should I not be more in my study and less fond of driving?" In the end he sold it—to a fellow preacher. But, whatever compunctions clergymen might feel, fine equipages were the hallmark of the rich.

The vast bulk of the population, pursuing small-scale agriculture, had no need for anything but heavy wagons and carts; otherwise they went around on foot or on horseback. But in one respect they too made an advance. About 1750 some German artisans in the Conestoga Valley in Lancaster County, Pennsylvania, devised a special type of vehicle for long hauls. The Conestoga wagon had a bottom curved downward at the center to keep the load from shifting and was arched overhead with hickory ribs bearing homespun canvas to screen out the weather. The lumbering conveyance, possessing a maximum capacity of eight tons and drawn by six stout horses at the rate of ten to fifteen miles a day, not only enlarged the farmer's market area but was to acquire future fame as the covered wagon of the prairies and plains. This mode of transportation apparently inaugurated the American custom of driving to the right instead of to the left, as in England, for the teamster rode the left rear horse to whip the animals with his right hand and so found it easier to pass approaching vehicles on the right. As the monarch of the road his practice in the course of time governed all lesser traffic.

For passenger service overland the only means was the stage-coach. The first route, opened in 1732 across New Jersey from Burlington to Perth Amboy, merely formed a land link in the boat journey between Philadelphia and New York. Not until 1756 did a through line join the two metropolises, covering the ninety miles in fair weather in three days, a time which John Barnell's "Flying Machine" lowered to two in 1769. The weary traveler, arriving long after dark at a wayside tavern, started off again still weary at the crack of dawn. Ann Warder, making the trip in 1759, observed two overturned and abandoned coaches at the side of the road. In other colonies conditions in the last years before Independence were pretty much the same except that the stages usually ran more slowly and none went south of Maryland because of the few towns, bad roads, and wide rivers and inlets. It took five days to go from Philadelphia to Baltimore, four or more from New York to Boston, and two from Boston to Portsmouth, New Hampshire (a distance of but sixty miles). Most travelers pre-

ferred other means. The great era of the stagecoach awaited the
building of turnpikes in the next generation and the westward
expansion of settlement.

Far more important in promoting intercourse beyond provincial boundaries was the mail service. At first letters and parcels
had been carried by chance travelers or, in the case of official
dispatches, by special messengers. As the need became greater,
however, some colonial governments employed postriders within
their own borders. Then, beginning in 1692, the mother country
integrated and extended the system on an interprovincial basis.
The next great step occurred in 1753, when Benjamin Franklin
became a deputy postmaster for America, an office he held for
twenty-one years amidst a multitude of other duties. With characteristic efficiency he established shorter routes and more frequent
deliveries and, by introducing day-and-night riding, made it possible for Philadelphians and Bostonians to exchange letters in six
days instead of three weeks as before. Finally, at Franklin's
suggestion, Parliament in 1765 reduced the rates by nearly a
third, and the resulting rise in use more than offset the loss of
revenue per unit. Letters in those days were not enclosed in
envelopes with stamps affixed—that was not to be done until the
1840's—but were folded by the sender and sealed with wax, the
postage being paid at the other end. The bulk of the mail passed
back and forth between the larger centers and was doubtless more
commercial than personal in nature, but it stretched horizons for
inland communities as well. Along with the other improvements of
communication the postal service diminished the force of local
attachments and helped pave the way for a common sentiment
against Britain as the final breach developed.

CHAPTER V

The Labor Market

T HE DEMAND FOR wage earners in the colonies greatly exceeded the supply. Instead of a labor surplus, as in the Old World, the problem was just the reverse: a labor shortage. The overwhelming number of settlers took up land for themselves as soon as they were able, while the few who preferred the towns were no less eager to become their own masters. Indeed, the opportunity to achieve an independent and self-respecting livelihood had, more than anything else, inspired these settlers to tempt fortune in the distant wilds. Only the unambitious or unlucky were willing to work permanently for others in America. Under the circumstances, as the Welshman Gabriel Thomas observed of Pennsylvania in 1698, "Poor People (both Men and Women) of all kinds can here get three times the Wages for their Labour they can in England or Wales." Robert Beverley of Virginia, writing in a similar vein in 1705, called his colony "the best poor Man's Country in the World." And the British author of *American Husbandry* noted in the year of Lexington and Concord, "By day labourers, which are not common in the colonies, one shilling will do as much in England as half a crown in New England."

To weight the balance more favorably for employers most of the legislatures in the seventeenth century tried various methods of wage control; but the enactments could not repeal the unwritten law of supply and demand and were in time abandoned. Either the laborers would move elsewhere or employers in their

55

need would violate the statutory limits. Government intervention, on the other hand, worked successfully in an area where no single class was favored but all would gain. To ensure sufficient labor for laying and repairing roads, building fortifications, and the like the Northern colonies exacted a certain number of days' work each year of every male between the ages of sixteen and sixty, the rate of pay being determined by local officials. In the South the principle also prevailed, although slaveholders could generally satisfy the requirement through the loan of their Negroes.

Farmers seeking emergency help faced a different need and met it by calling on their neighbors, who cheerfully responded, knowing they could count on the favor being returned. The occasion might be the gathering of an unexpectedly large crop or the raising of the frame of a house or barn. In the same way the building of a meetinghouse was often a community effort. These events, accompanied by much jollity and the consumption of enormous quantities of food, rum, and cider, afforded a welcome break in the rural routine. They in no way involved employer-employee relations. Rather, they evidenced a spirit of cooperation among equals in a highly individualistic society.

The largest single body of men for hire, on the verge of Independence, consisted of seamen, widely scattered and totaling around 33,000. Many of these men were not wage earners in the ordinary sense because in the fishing and whaling industries, and during wartime in privateering, they participated in the profits of the ventures. Neither they nor their brethren on land deemed it necessary to organize to improve working conditions. In "the best poor Man's Country in the World" they already had things pretty much to their liking. Concerted action, when it occurred, hardly ever took the form of strikes, but rather of dues-paying associations to aid the sick and disabled and indigent widows and children of members. Typical of these were the Carpenters' Company of Philadelphia, started in 1724, the Marine Society of Boston, in existence from 1742, and the Friendly Society of Tradesmen House Carpenters of New York, formed in 1767. It was in the assembly hall of the Philadelphia organization that the patriots, bidding for working-class support, held the First Continental Congress.

Had the colonists relied solely upon a free labor force, they would never have succeeded in transforming the country into farms and fields and towns, for the number of such workers was too small and the cost too high. Hence from the outset the settlers resorted to a variety of supplementary means.

One recourse was the apprentice system adopted from England, whereby the colonists trained poor boys for skilled occupations. Legislatures set the standards to which the apprenticeship articles must conform, and the particular arrangements had to be filed with the town clerk or the county court to facilitate legal enforcement. An agreement usually had to have both the child's consent and that of his parents; and the term of service typically ran from four to seven years or until the youngster came of age. During the period of tutelage he lived under the roof of his master who, besides teaching him a specified craft, agreed to instruct him in the three R's (reading, 'riting, and reckoning) and to provide "sufficient Meat, Drink, Apparel, Lodging and washing fitting for an Apprentice," with two suits of clothing at the end of the relationship. In return the youth promised to be dutiful and diligent and shun alehouses and other harmful associations. Girls also came under the scheme but with less emphasis on vocational training. As a rule they were taught "Sewing, Knitting and any other manner of housewifery" in order to assist their mistress in household duties and, incidentally, in recognition of the fact that society expected them to be homemakers rather than breadwinners. Those bound to such occupations as the "Trade and art of a Tailor" or to millinery or leatherwork were very much the exception.

The system as a whole worked smoothly, causing relatively little trouble for the courts, since it yielded decided advantages for all parties concerned. In the absence of vocational schools, it offered youths the only available preparation for skilled occupations except as they might pursue parental trades. At the same time employers gained desperately needed assistance, while the public at large profited from the continuing addition of craftsmen to the always lagging supply. Apprentices suffered no social stigma, taking their places at once as respected members of the community. Indeed, toward the end of the colonial period, some rose high in political life, three becoming signers of the Declaration of Independence: Benjamin Franklin, bound to the printing trade, and Roger Sherman of Connecticut and George Walton of Georgia, to shoemaking and carpentry, respectively.

Two notable inventors of the next generation similarly got their start during these years. The youthful John Fitch, one of the pioneers in steam navigation, served under two different clockmakers, and Oliver Evans, America's first steam-engine builder, worked for a wheelwright. As in so many other cases, they found that the mastery of one pursuit opened the way to another. Indeed, the apprentice system, so well suited to colonial needs, continued long into the nineteenth century, until the introduction of machinery increasingly supplanted skilled workmen and instruction in the manual arts became a function of schools and colleges.

Despite its utility, however, the apprentice system contributed less to the labor market than did the importation of men, women, and children under contract. Not only did these additions far outnumber apprentices but, being mostly adults, they shouldered a full load of work from the start. They consisted predominantly of poor folk from the British Isles and the Continent who paid for their Atlantic voyage by indenturing themselves to a shipmaster, typically for four years, and often their children too until the age of twenty-one. Upon reaching port the captain auctioned off his human cargo to the highest bidders, usually at a substantial profit. A notice posted in the tavern or printed in the newspaper announced the sale, and the bargaining took place on board the vessel or at some nearby point on shore. The indentured servants by and large augmented the ranks of the unskilled and semiskilled, but they included a sprinkling of craftsmen—carpenters, watchmakers, blacksmiths, and the like—notably in the case of the Germans.

What impelled most to accept these arrangements was the assurance of an adequate living for a limited period after which they would enjoy opportunities of advancement impossible at home. A much smaller number, however, became indentured laborers as the result of fraud, abduction, or legal compulsion. These were of three general kinds. One consisted of vagrants and street waifs tricked or kidnaped into service. They were the victims of an unlawful traffic carried on in London and Bristol with the connivance of ship captains, who paid a pound or two for each unfortunate without asking questions. Another category comprised political prisoners exiled by the government from time to time for participation in the recurrent civil uprisings that plagued Britain from the Cromwellian wars of the 1640's to the Scottish rebellion of 1745. These were usually men of a much higher caliber. But the largest group embraced convicts of both sexes who had been given the option of punishment at home or temporary servitude in America. Their indentures ran from seven to fourteen years and occasionally even for life, depending on the gravity of the offense. This feature made them particularly attractive to the Virginia and Maryland tobacco planters, who found the four-year term of ordinary indentured servants too short for their requirements. Something like thirty thousand felons arrived in the colonies in this manner in the eighteenth century alone, about a quarter of them women.

From the British point of view the system of commutation not only rid the homeland of undesirables but softened a brutal criminal code, which exacted death for even such trifling offenses as stealing a shilling's worth of meat. Banishment, moreover, gave the culprits a chance to start over again under more promising conditions. To Franklin and many of his fellow Americans, however, the practice was "an insult and contempt, the cruellest, that ever one people offered another." But when Virginia, Maryland, Pennsylvania, and other provinces passed acts to limit or stop the inflow, London responded with a veto. It is clear that if the colonists had felt strongly enough they could have ended the traffic extralegally simply by boycotting it; and this they could never bring themselves to do, although during the struggle with the Ministry in the years preceding Independence they did not hesitate to proscribe goods from Britain. The need for manpower was just too acute.

Whether, as some contemporaries alleged, the dumping of

malefactors appreciably increased the amount of American crime is questionable save at certain moments and in particular places. In any event not a few of the exiles returned to Britain at the expiration of their sentences. Of the much larger number who chose to remain, most, it is probable, took advantage of the opportunity to turn over a new leaf, some changing their communities and names to do so more easily. This is a matter, however, upon which genealogical records are understandably reticent. Daniel Defoe, who spoke with some knowledge, had a Virginian say in *Moll Flanders* (published in 1722) that "many a Newgate bird became a great man, and we have had several justices of the peace, officers of the trained bands, and magistrates of the towns they live in that have been burnt in the hand." This indeed was the central theme of the book, for Moll herself was a transported felon who acquired an assured social position and landed wealth in her new surroundings.

If the usual historic estimates are accurate, over half the white migrants to America during the colonial period were indentured servants of either the voluntary or involuntary variety. A still greater number had committed themselves to the undertaking, but the ill-ventilated accommodations during the rough ten or twelve weeks' voyage, the bad food, and the ravages of disease took a heavy toll. In some instances the mortality was appalling. Out of a boatload of 400 Germans going to Pennsylvania in 1745, 350 died; out of 200 in 1752, 181; but even under more normal conditions the ordeal was severe, since nobody could ever feel certain of reaching shore again. These terrors and hardships should remind a forgetful posterity that the drama of American pioneering was enacted on the sea before it was on the land, that the immigrant ship deserves a place in the national saga as well as the covered wagon. Those who survived the experience found the greatest call for their services in Pennsylvania, Maryland, and Virginia. Relatively few located in New England, where the self-sufficiency of the people and the prevalence of small farming created little demand.

An elaborate body of legislation safeguarded the interests of both master and servant. Though differing in detail from colony to colony, the labor code had certain general features. The master could administer corporal punishment short of arbitrary and unnatural cruelty, forbid his servants to marry, appropriate their spare-time earnings, hire them out to others, and dispose of them by will. Servants who ran away faced stringent penalties, oftentimes an extension of their indentures. On the other hand, they were protected against inadequate maintenance as well as inhuman treatment and could take legal action to enforce their rights. Furthermore, as in the case of apprentices, they were guaranteed at the close of their tenure "freedom dues," perhaps an outfit of clothing, a sum of money, or a supply of food or tools.

The relatively few cases ever reaching the courts, whether on complaint of master or servant, suggest that the institution operated effectively. Although the need for labor made for considerate treatment by most masters, it led some to drive their workers unmercifully because of the short period of their bondage and often provoked workers to run away. Servants, on the other hand, might be lazy or refractory and unjustifiably abandon their contractual obligations. When servants absconded, masters would advertise for their recovery in the press. One instance, involving a notably conscientious employer, was George Washington's appeal in Purdie's *Virginia Gazette,* May 12, 1775, for the return of two fugitives: a twenty-year-old British-born joiner, "freckled" with "sandy coloured hair cut pretty short, his voice coarse and somewhat drauling," and a brickmaker of Scottish origin, "rather turned of 30 with light brown hair," who "talks pretty broad."

Whether the offer of forty dollars' reward brought results is unknown, but probably in most cases the runaways made good their escape, thanks to the ease of losing themselves in the widely scattered communities. Some, though, took off just temporarily as a sort of lark. John Powell, for example, informed the public in the *Maryland Gazette,* September 6, 1745, that his servant had come back after having "only gone into the country a cyder-drinking" and that the truant would again repair clocks and watches "in the best manner, and at reasonable rates." Whatever their motive, however, those who decamped were the exception, not the rule.

The most reprehensible aspect of the indenture system was its disruptive effect on the family. Husbands and wives might be sold to different masters, and parents were sometimes separated from their children for years, perhaps forever. Moreover, when servants desired to marry, masters were apt to withhold assent because of the loss of working time entailed by childbearing and infant care. The upshot not infrequently was clandestine cohabitation and illegitimate offspring—practices which even such harsh penalties as lengthening the period of indentureship failed to prevent.

Once servants received their freedom dues and struck out for themselves, only their ability and industry placed a limit on how far they might go. The great majority led useful but obscure lives that were marked, however, by a personal dignity and material well-being they would not have known in the Old World. They and their progeny composed the bone and sinew of colonial society. But there were also some who stood out from the mass. Daniel Dulany, for example, an indentured laborer from Ireland, attained fame in early eighteenth-century Maryland as a lawyer and legislator. In South Carolina, Thomas Ferguson, of Scottish background, acquired nine plantations and married the daughter of Christopher Gadsden, the Revolutionary patriot. Still others became intercolonial figures, notably George Taylor of Pennsylvania and Matthew Thornton of New Hampshire, both signers of the Declaration of Independence, and Charles Thomson of Pennsylvania, who for nearly fifteen years was secretary to the Continental and Confederation Congresses. All three, like Dulany, hailed from Ireland. At the opposite end of the scale, to be sure, were the improvident who, drifting mostly into the Southern back country, gave rise to the poor-white class.

The indenture system lingered in a few states, like Pennsylvania and Maryland, until the third decade of the nineteenth century, but the traffic in convicts and other involuntary servants necessarily ceased with the Revolutionary War. The London government, forced to seek a different outlet for its felons, turned to newly acquired Australia, establishing a penal colony there in place of mixing them with the law-abiding population. This policy of segregation, if adopted before 1776, would hardly have found favor with Britain's transatlantic subjects.

The importation of contract laborers and the apprenticing of colonial children, each in its own way, provided indispensable manpower. But under either system such persons took service only for a time, thus rendering employers periodically shorthanded. Accordingly the colonists early supplemented these recruits with slave labor, a permanent working force which would permit long-range planning and possess the further attraction of self-replenishment through natural breeding. The initial investment, though greater than in the case of apprentices or indentured servants, would moreover be virtually the final one, since the cost of maintenance would be immaterial.

Slavery was nothing the settlers had to think up for themselves, for man's ownership of man went back to the dawn of history. Old Testament worthies had engaged in the practice and on it had been built the glory that was Greece. More immediately important to the Americans, Christianity itself countenanced it, at least for pagans. The Spanish and the Portuguese carried the institution to the Western Hemisphere, where in fact the natives had already invented it on their own, and the English colonists in turn resorted to it in their need. Like the Spanish and Portuguese, they too drew the line at owning whites, as fellows in Christ, but they deemed other races inherently irreligious and therefore properly subject to thralldom. At their very door were the benighted red men and within easy reach, thanks to the enterprise of Dutch, British, and Yankee traders, heathen blacks from Africa. Both unfortunate peoples, it was held, should welcome deliverance from the miseries of barbarism to the blessings of Christian civilization. To so laudable a cause devout and high-minded colonists as well as employers crying for workers could give support.

The Indians, though, were bellicose and elusive, and became increasingly so as time went on. The settlers perforce contented themselves with those they could capture in war or buy from friendly tribes who had enslaved their own defeated enemies. The New Englanders initiated the practice with prisoners of the Pequot War (1637) and, when relations with the Indians quieted toward the end of the century, resorted to purchases from the Carolinas, where continuing hostilities produced a surplus for export. These two regions indeed possessed the greatest number of the captives. In New England they were used chiefly as domestics, working as a matter of course even for such notables in religious and public life as Governor John Winthrop, Roger Williams, and Increase and

Cotton Mather. In the two Southern colonies they worked out as hunters and fishermen—occupations in which they were skilled— but made miserable field hands. Throughout the period of British rule colonial law recognized the enslaved Indians as private property, to be bought and sold just as were servile blacks, although their bondage in some cases ran for a fixed period instead of for life.

A public sale of Cherokees took place in South Carolina as late as 1776, but by that time such events were the exception. For some years the number of Indian slaves, all along limited in supply, had been sharply falling. In general the red man proved a disappointing slave, since his traditions rejected systematic toil as proper only for squaws. Not surprisingly, the sons of the forest generally made sullen and intractable laborers and seized every opportunity to run away to their own people. And, far from profiting from enforced contact with the white man, they tended to acquire his vices and diseases, including a fatal addiction to alcohol.

The colonists might nevertheless have persevered with the idea of Indian slavery but for the increasing availability of Negroes, whose experience and traditions made them less resistant to servitude. The Negroes had mostly practiced tillage in Africa and acquired considerable skill in folk crafts. They accepted long hours of labor as their natural lot. More than that, many if not most had already undergone a heartless slavery to tribal chieftains in their own land, which perhaps made that of the Americans less galling. Also in the strange and distant clime they did not have the same opportunity as the Indians to escape to their own kith and kin. All these considerations made them an ideal form of labor in the eyes of the colonists.

The Negroes came as a rule from the west coast of Africa and its vast hinterland, oftentimes indirectly by way of the West Indies. Tribal chieftains made it a business to enslave wartime enemies and raid the countryside for others. Then, after collecting a sizable number, they marched them, naked and strapped together single file, to stations on the sea where they were bartered to white traders for dry goods, ironware, rum, and trinkets. Some traders, in addition, conducted their own expeditions. The victims, after being securely fettered, were forcibly placed aboard ship to be confined during the long ocean voyage in foul quarters too low to permit standing. The height varied from three feet three inches to three feet ten. The horrors of the Middle Passage, as it was called, stagger the imagination. Many died from suffocation or from epidemics; many others pined away or committed suicide. It was not unusual for vessels to lose a third or a half of their human freight. The captains were often cruel to the point of ferocity. Sometimes the prisoners in desperation rose up and murdered the officers and crew. Generally they lost their own lives in the attempt. On reaching port the hapless creatures were put up at public auction, singly or in lots, some being bid in by slave dealers who transported them about the country for later sale.

In the seventeenth century, when the first "Negers" were brought to America—at Jamestown in 1619—they occupied a position akin to that of indentured whites and served only fixed terms. But the very different circumstances of their coming, plus their black skins, woolly hair, and alien ways so distinguished them from the other inhabitants that before long, and generally without express legislative warrant, they were everywhere reduced to permanent bondage. In the words of the South Carolina Assembly in 1712, their "barbarous, wild, savage natures" rendered them unfit to enjoy "the laws, customs and practices of this province"—a view, however, that scarcely explained why their descendants reared under civilizing influences should undergo like treatment. Already the concept of the Negro as a subhuman race was infecting the Southern mind. Yet it was Puritan Massachusetts that in 1641, shortly after authorizing slavery for Indians, passed the first law approving the same condition for blacks. Connecticut and Virginia followed within twenty years, as did the nine other legislatures before the century closed. The Georgia authorities, when establishing that colony in 1735, originally forbade the institution, but the pressure proved so great that within a decade and a half they too sanctioned it.

By 1700 Negro bondsmen numbered between twenty and twenty-five thousand, about one in every ten inhabitants. Seventy-five years later, when the breach came with England, they totaled half a million, approximately one in every five. By contrast, the

proportion of slaves in the nation in 1860 was to be only a little
more than one in eight. This extraordinary increase in the eighteenth century, far outstripping that of the white colonists, was
due to prolific breeding as well as to continuing importations. The
vast majority of the race—nine tenths on the eve of Independence—lived in the South, where climatic conditions, large-scale
agriculture, and the luxurious life of the gentry combined to
produce an inexhaustible demand. Negro slaves made up almost
half of Virginia's population in 1775 and over two thirds that of
South Carolina. The slavery system, so disruptive of the future
harmony of the American people, had as yet, however, no political implications.

Throughout the South the Africans toiled as field hands, thus
releasing indentured servants to become overseers, foremen, and
cattle herders. A select few, recognized by their masters as possessing superior ability, performed duties in the great house,
tended the kitchen gardens, or worked as artisans. George Washington employed as many as five black girls at weaving in 1768. In
towns and villages Negroes might find further scope for their gifts
as slaves to white craftsmen. Between 1732 and 1776 the Charleston press noted twenty-eight occupations pursued by bondsmen,
ranging all the way from blacksmithing and brickmaking to tan-
ning, shoemaking, and cabinetwork. At times such encroachments
on the livelihood of white workers aroused fierce resentment. In
Charleston, where the rivalry was keenest, legislators joined the
disgruntled artisans in complaining that the Negro competition
took bread out of the mouths of freemen and discouraged them
from settling in the community. No effective deterrent action was
ever taken, however.

In the North, slavery failed to strike deep root, partly because
the small-farm type of husbandry created little demand and partly
because in any case the winters did not permit sufficient year-
round employment. Like the servile Indians, the Negroes worked
mainly as domestics. At no time did they total more than 29,000
in the Middle colonies or more than 16,000 in New England; and
only in Rhode Island did they compose as much as five per cent of
the population.

That moral objections did not account for the small number in

New England is indicated by the activity of Yankee traders in transporting "black ivory" from Africa to the sister colonies and the West Indies—a source of profit that formed a vital element in their far-flung network of commerce. The public-spirited Peter Faneuil, for instance, who gave Faneuil Hall to Boston, acquired an appreciable part of his wealth in this ghastly way. A Newport deacon, whenever one of his shipments arrived, offered thanks the next Sunday in church that "an over-ruling Providence" had permitted "another cargo of benighted heathen to enjoy the blessings of a Gospel disposition." Similarly, Cotton Mather greeted the gift of a black from his congregation as "a mighty Smile of Heaven," and other clergymen, like Jonathan Edwards and Ezra Stiles, were slave owners. Away from New England the renowned evangelist George Whitefield not only kept slaves but also was one of those to press the Georgia authorities to introduce the system. He too believed the institution to be divinely ordained for the good of both races. And with equally unexamined conscience the civic-minded Franklin in Philadelphia bought and sold Negroes, although after the Revolutionary War, having come to see the error of his conduct, he became president of an abolition society.

Thoroughgoing legislation policed the behavior of the Negroes, with the strictest regulations in the colonies where they were most populous. The basic purpose was to guarantee the master's property right to his slave, and to that end the law gave him almost unlimited authority. Unlike apprentices and indentured servants, Negroes had no vested right of fair treatment and hence no legal redress against ill usage. They were to most intents and purposes wholly at the owner's mercy, the theory being that enlightened self-interest would make him keep his human animals as sound of mind and limb as presumably he did his livestock. Without his permission they could not leave the premises or assemble in groups or be out of doors at night. For disobedience he could punish them at will, even in some colonies to the extent of maiming and killing. Running away commonly brought flogging, perhaps many times over. If the offenses were against the public peace and order, as in cases of homicide, arson, and insurrection, the state stepped in with such penalties as hanging, sale outside the colony, breaking the culprit on the wheel, or burning him at the stake.

The law everywhere prescribed that children of interracial parentage should have the legal status of the mother, whose identity it was always easy to establish. Widespread miscegenation demanded some sort of rule, and the particular one harked back at least to the Roman Empire. The interbreeding arose mainly from the daily association of indentured males with scantily clad Negro women, but as Janet Schaw, who toured the South in 1775, pointed out, owners also "honour their black wenches with their attention." For this the Scottish spinster could conceive of "no other motive or desire but that of adding to the number of their slaves"; and it would appear from an advertisement in Purdie and Dixon's *Virginia Gazette,* September 3, 1767, that half-castes also sold for higher prices. Be that as it may, owners suffered no loss of social standing by reason of their incontinence, and Josiah Quincy, Jr., a Massachusetts visitor, reported it far from uncommon "to see a gentleman at dinner, and his reputed offspring a slave to the master of the table."

In like fashion the rule of descent assigned to slavery the children of a mulatto by a white father, notwithstanding that in this case the youngsters were three quarters Caucasian; and it applied as well to those in whom the "taint of the inferior race" was still less, no matter how light their complexion might be. In short, the effect of crossbreeding was not to whiten the black but to blacken the white. Thus a decision originating in the seventeenth century condemned to servitude as long as that institution should last a people who were becoming increasingly white with each passing generation. By 1860, indeed, as the United States census conservatively estimated, one eighth of the colored population of the slave states belonged to this category. More than that, an attitude was implanted which in all parts of the country has ever since caused European Americans to class as a Negro anyone with a known trace of African blood in his veins, however far back it may have been acquired.

Slavery in the colonial period was less oppressive than it was to be under the radically different conditions of the nineteenth century. It partook much more of a genuinely paternalistic character. Rumors of slave conspiracies alarmed the public from time to time, but in most instances the stories appear to have had little basis, for actual outbreaks were few and local. A desperate stroke for freedom on several plantations in South Carolina in 1739 cost the lives of forty-four Negroes as well as twenty-nine whites before it was quelled. A series of disturbances in New York City two years later—in this case apparently for purposes of loot—brought reprisals from the authorities in the burning alive of thirteen blacks, the hanging of eighteen, and the sale elsewhere of seventy others. There were also lesser disorders, but the general situation could lead Governor James Glenn of South Carolina to report to the British government in 1751 that the bondsmen when "seasoned to the Country" were "reconciled to Servitude" and had "no Notion of Liberty."

In the North slaves were apt to be treated pretty much as were indentured servants, oftentimes living under the master's roof and eating at his table. Even in the South, where they occupied their own shabby quarters, they usually received individual oversight, since the average owner held only from about ten to twenty slaves and could know each one personally. On the great estates as well, the mistress as a rule looked after the sick and injured, and the master's family formed lasting bonds of mutual affection with the household retainers. When the number of blacks required the use of hired overseers, the conditions might be different and notoriously were, for example, on the rice and indigo plantations of South Carolina; but the instance of the Virginian George Washington, who in 1774 paid taxes on 135 Negroes, shows that this did not necessarily follow. Washington indeed went so far as to provide in his will for the aged and infirm Negroes who might outlive him.

Still, under the best of masters the blacks, except within narrow limits, had no incentive or opportunity for personal growth. Obedience, not self-development, constituted their prime virtue as slaves. They were, in Aristotle's phrase, "animated tools," not fellow human beings with the right to make the most of their natural abilities. The system, moreover, undermined the institution of the family, so vital for the transmission of moral values, for it might at any time cause the separation of husbands from wives and of parents from children. And, in addition, it permitted hotheaded and sadistic masters grossly to abuse their authority. Even so cultivated a Virginian as William Byrd II punished his Negroes on occasion by screwing clamps to their tongues, and his lady did not hesitate to beat and brand her personal attendants. Not surprisingly, slaves sometimes ran away, although this did not necessarily imply ill treatment. It might mean merely resentment at grinding toil or in the case of some an unquenchable spirit of freedom. At all events, the fugitives, handicapped by color, seldom succeeded long in avoiding recapture. On balance, however, the bondsmen were better fed, clothed, and sheltered, and led easier and probably healthier lives than if they had remained in Africa. In the words of the South Carolinian Henry Laurens regarding his own blacks, they were "as happy as slavery will admit of."

Unlike other newcomers to the colonies, the Negroes brought with them little beyond their brawn and indigenous skills, the latter standing them in good stead as artificers in America. A single ship might transport natives of many different tribes and regions, representing as many different languages and cultures—individuals who were not only strangers to one another but perhaps traditional enemies. To make confusion worse confounded, in the colonies they located wherever fortune took them, seldom associating with their own particular kind and hardly ever in sufficient numbers to perpetuate inherited ways. In effect they became a new people, neither African nor "American" but unavoidably identifying themselves with the land of their bondage. It was this discontinuity with the past, unrecognized by the dominant race, which so largely frustrated the efforts of the American Colonization Society in the generation before the Civil War to restore freed Negroes to their original home.

The displaced folk perforce learned English if for no other reason than to talk with each other, and in the process they forgot their own native tongues. That they spoke the acquired language with what Josiah Quincy, Jr., called a "negroish kind of accent, pronunciation and dialect" evidenced their lack of schooling; their drawl may also have been an imitation of the white man's speech. Nevertheless, toward the end of the colonial era, they produced a

minor poet in the African-born Phyllis Wheatley. This Massachusetts girl was fortunate in having a mistress who, seeing her
potentialities, educated her in the household and at a later time
emancipated her. Her lyrics did not reflect any racial characteris-
tics, being conventional and derivative like most verse of the
period, but they suggest what others of her color might have
achieved if given free play for their talents.

It is not surprising that African cultural survivals in America
were slight. The grief-stricken songs sung during the Middle
Passage may have inspired the later plantation spirituals. The
slaves perhaps also brought with them a strong sense of rhythm
developed by the beating of drums in immemorial tribal rites.
Similarly, the demonstrative religious observances in Africa may
have predisposed them toward the more evangelical varieties of
Christianity in their new home. And unquestionably they kept
alive certain folk beliefs such as faith in witchcraft and the
magical properties of amulets, as well as traditional animal tales,
some of which Joel Chandler Harris was to immortalize in the
stories and sayings of "Uncle Remus." But it was mostly as a labor
force that they influenced the life about them, contributing im-
measurably to the economic progress of the South.

Thus, by a combination of means—apprentices, indentured
servants, and Negro slaves—the colonists attained remarkable
success in manning their undertakings in both agriculture and
industry. Feeling little need in the circumstances for laborsaving
devices, they displayed none of that knack for major inventions
which was later to be so characteristically American. Some improvements were indeed made in the handicrafts and in such
matters as the grinding of corn and iron forging, but these at most
were minor and of only local concern.

This did not mean that latent creative ability was wanting,
although the announcement by one Thomas Mathes in Rind's
Virginia Gazette, February 16, 1769, that he had made "a machine
for the PERPETUAL MOVEMENT" suggests that it might be mis-
directed. It meant, rather, that the inventive spirit when aroused
turned to needs more critical than any felt in farming and manufactures. The Conestoga wagon, for example, helped meet the
problem of efficient land transportation, and the so-called Penn-

sylvania rifle, a no less important contrivance of German-Ameri-
cans in the mid-eighteenth century, met the demand for a more
accurate firearm. Long-barreled, with spiral grooves in the bore
to spin and direct the bullet, it was to contribute vitally to the
winning of the War for Independence and under the name of the
Kentucky rifle became the stand-by of Western frontiersmen, just
as the Conestoga wagon lived on as the historic covered wagon
of the prairies and plains. By the same token, Franklin's fireplace
stove and his lightning rod looked to the colonists' physical comfort and safety, not to increasing their productivity.

Indeed, only one province—South Carolina in 1691—established a regular patent system. Elsewhere patents were granted by
special enactments as though the legislators were surprised that
any should be called for. The flowering of invention in agriculture
and industry had to await a later and different time, when the
western expansion of the nation and the intense competition for
domestic and foreign markets ceaselessly spurred men in town and
country to devise mechanical means of lowering costs and raising
output.

CHAPTER VI

Otherworldliness

IN SPITE OF the strong religious impulse in colonization, only a minority of the migrants or their descendants formally belonged to a church. Even on board the famous *Mayflower* the greater part of the passengers, as William Bradford stiffly said, consisted of "untoward persons mixed amongst us." And, as time went on and the number of the American-born increased, so also did the preponderance of those outside the fold. One reason was the early relaxation of that intolerance which in the Old World had intensified the zeal and cemented the bonds of the sects. Another was the extraordinary mobility of the population, which made it difficult or impossible for church bodies to provide ministers where and as fast as they were needed. A third factor was the growing worldliness of the people, once the first generation with its high sense of mission had passed from the scene.

Although exact figures are lacking, a careful student has estimated that as the Revolution approached only about one in eight in New England belonged to a church, perhaps one in fifteen or eighteen in the Middle colonies, and not more than one in twenty in the South. It does not follow, however, that the rest were unbelievers. Some of them, in isolated regions, would have had to travel many miles to partake in public worship. Others considered they could lead upright lives without formal affiliation. Others had never undergone the emotional religious experience that was still generally demanded as a qualification for church membership. Certainly outright agnostics and atheists were too few to leave much historical trace.

73

The religion of the Americans had divers and bizarre ingredients. On the one hand it freely incorporated folk ideas of God and the universe, some deriving from the Middle Ages or even earlier. On the other, it proceeded from the official formulations of church doctrine. These two aspects, moreover, were regarded not as in conflict but as constituting an inseparable whole. The superstitious elements indeed, far from being weakened when carried to the colonies, found seeming confirmation in the settlers' puzzling experiences with the unfamiliar wilderness as well as in the somewhat similar fancies of the Indians and the Negroes. In fact the new country with its strange, wild coasts, mysterious forests, and lurking inhabitants impressed the pious European as a place especially suited to eerie happenings, a region expressly set aside by the Lord to battle with Satan for the souls of men.

The colonists without regard to education or social class took for granted the role of miracles or "special providences" in human affairs, that is, the direct interposition of the Almighty to express His pleasure or wrath. And this conviction underwent little change over the years. As the erudite clergyman Thomas Prince of Boston put it in 1749, God does not

> confine himself to act according to his common Course of Nature, but most wisely and justly *reserves the Liberty of acting otherwise* on all Occasions when he sees most fitting. . . . In this Manner he may in the most proper Seasons send both Droughts and Rains, and Sicknesses and Health, to particular *Places;* he may point his Lightnings to particular *Persons;* he may raise a Storm to disperse a *Fleet,* and give additional Powers to a Gust of Wind to overset a *Vessel,* or to the Waves to break her. . . . And so in Multitudes of other Cases.

To be sure, the import of the supernatural interventions was in some instances baffling. Thus, when a calf was born at Ipswich in 1646 with three mouths, three noses, and six eyes, Governor John Winthrop of the Massachusetts Bay Colony confessed in his journal, "What these prodigies portend the Lord only knows, which in due time He will manifest." And indeed, before the end of the year, it appeared that the strange event, attended with such supporting phenomena as an encircled noonday sun, three suns at dusk, and the coldest winter ever known, were divine indications of the impending foundering of a valuable New Haven ship. It was deemed beside the point that the vessel was "very crank-sided" with a top-heavy cargo.

Comets excited particular dread. Alexander Nowell, a Harvard tutor, affirmed in 1667 as "an universal truth" that "experience Attests, and reason Assents, that they have served for sad Prologues to Tragical Epilogues." Nathaniel Morton stated in *New Englands Memoriall* (1669) that the comet which had hovered over the land for two months during the winter of 1664–5 had forewarned a sinful people of a threatened foreign invasion, deaths by thunder and lightning, and extensive crop failures. Boston's Increase Mather, who in 1681 devoted a sermon to "Heavens Alarm to the World . . . Wherein Is Shewed, That fearful Sights and Signs in Heaven are the Presages of great Calamities at hand," developed the theme at exhaustive length two years later in a learned treatise, *Kometographia*. This work, a veritable handbook on the subject, recounted "all the Comets which have appeared from the Beginning of the World" with the "evil Events" attending them.

Similarly, earthquakes were, in the Reverend Cotton Mather's phrase, *"moving Preachers* into *worldly-minded Men."* Unheeded omens had preceded the tremors that frightened New Englanders in the late autumn of 1727: a bitterly cold spring, a hot, parching summer, a devastating September hurricane. When the first shocks came, a vast fear-struck audience assembled in Boston to listen to this younger Mather discourse on *The Terror of the Lord.* "I see none *Asleep* at this Time," he jeered. " 'Tis a Congregation of *Hearers* that I am at this Time Speaking to." Detailing the moral laxities which had occasioned the divine correction, he declared, "The smell of sulpher, which is affirmed by many to have been plain to them, adds to a Fearful expectation of a Fiery Indignation in Gods Time. . . ." Other pastors spoke in like vein; one congregation collected 150 new members in three weeks. And the Reverend Thomas Prince, to remove all doubt as to the matter, compiled his *Earthquakes, the Works of God and Tokens of His Just Displeasure,* describing "some late Terrible Ones in other Parts of the World." It was reprinted in 1755 "with additions by the author" when New England again underwent severe shocks.

The Creator, it was no less piously believed, chastised erring

mankind in many other ways as well. Thus Increase Mather
ascribed the bloody Indian uprising of 1675–6 under King Philip
to heavenly castigation for the New England settlers' ill-treatment
of the red men, just as in 1711, after a destructive conflagration in
Boston, he delivered a graphic sermon on "the Sins which provoke
the Lord to kindle Fires." Six years later, following a disastrous
snowstorm, the Provincial Council, speaking for the civil authorities, summoned the people to humble themselves before the Lord
for "the Tokens of His Displeasure," evidenced especially "in the
late excessive Snows and Tempests." And in the same strain
Thomas Prince during the prolonged summer drought of 1749
took as his Sabbath text: "And if ye will not for all this hearken
unto me, then I shall punish you seven times more for your sins"
(Lev. XXVI. 18). Curiously enough this idea of a meddlesome
deity has survived in legal documents to our own day in the phrase
"acts of God."

But the Almighty could smile as well as smite. As rewards for
piety He bestowed fair weather, good health, abundant harvests,
and, not least, success in battle. During the third war with France,
for instance, the Reverend Jonathan Edwards attributed the capture of Louisburg in 1745 to "God's so extraordinarily appearing
to baffle" the enemy, and Thomas Prince, preaching on "The
Salvations of God in 1746," included as a shining example the
sending of a tempest that "put a total end" to a French fleet
approaching Boston and "bore them away in the Night."

This same belief in special providences affected the religious
thought of the Middle and Southern colonies, although since the
clergy in those parts printed their sermons less often than in New
England the evidence is not so abundant. In Virginia, for example, according to a contemporary writer, a series of "Ominous
Presages" had foretold Bacon's Rebellion in 1676: "a large
Comet every Evening for a Week . . . Streaming like a horse
Taile Westwards"; "Flights of Pigeons in breadth a Quarter of the
Mid-Hemisphere," whose weight broke the limbs of trees; and
"Swarms of Flyes" (probably seventeen-year locusts) ascending
for a whole month "out of Spigot Holes in the Earth." A related
but more harmful belief also prevailed as in New England. This
was that the colonial population was only partly visible, the

unseen portion consisting of troubled or infernal spirits from the abode of the dead, whom the Lord for his own inscrutable reasons permitted from time to time to roam the earth.

A phantom, tormenting a family in Newbury, Massachusetts, in 1679, performed such frightening acts as lifting a bed from the floor, hurling a cat at the mother, and seasoning the victuals with ashes, until at length, as Increase Mather solemnly reported, "it pleased God to shorten the Chain of the wicked Daemon." A less imaginative ghost in Hartford, Connecticut, in 1683, contented himself with merely flinging stones and corncobs through the windows and down the chimney, and even these disturbances ceased when the occupant of the house returned some clothes he had withheld from their owner.

Far more sinister than such visitants were the witches—flesh-and-blood beings, generally women, who reputedly exercised malevolent powers by leaguing themselves with Satan or who had unknowingly been taken possession of by that archfiend. Some performed their unholy work by means of their incorporeal or spectral bodies, others by assuming the appearance of black cats; and in either case only their victims were able to see and identify them. Diabolically inspired occurrences were recorded early in most of the colonies; and in all of them, as in Great Britain, the punishment for the offense was death in conformance with the Scriptural injunction: "Thou shall not suffer a witch to live" (Exod. XXII. 18). In Europe during these same years witch panics sent untold thousands to the gallows and the stake. In England alone the fanatical Matthew Hopkins brought about the execution of sixty suspects in Essex County in 1644.

By comparison, the Americans displayed extraordinary restraint. In the entire colonial period only thirty-six persons, as far as documents disclose, were sentenced to death, and none at all in the eighteenth century. In the 1650's three luckless women on vessels bound for Virginia and Maryland were hanged for allegedly conjuring up storms. Indeed, in both colonies the commissions issued to county magistrates specifically directed them to investigate purported cases; but although a succession of accused were brought to trial, Rebecca Fowler of Calvert County, Maryland, in 1685 was the only one ever to pay with her life. Likewise in Pennsylvania the Quakers unquestioningly accepted the fact of witchcraft, although the surviving court records fail to reveal any convictions. For a lesser offense, however, that of practicing geomancy (divination by means of casting a handful of earth about), one George Roman of Chester County in 1695 suffered a fine of £5 and the loss of his books on occultism. It was left to Connecticut and Massachusetts to exhibit the greatest zeal. Commencing with Achsah Young in Windsor, Connecticut, in 1647, at least twelve women were sent to the scaffold for the crime before the wholesale death-dealing at Salem Village (now Danvers), Massachusetts, in 1692.

That dread outbreak of witches—the "Plot of the Devil against New-England," according to Cotton Mather's *Wonders of the Invisible World* (1693)—was a case of community hysteria that started innocently enough when two little girls in the pastor's household repeated to their teenage companions the terrifying accounts of Barbadian voodooism told them by their half-Negro, half-Indian slave woman. Joining forces, the youngsters, whether from mischief, feverish imaginations, or an urge for self-dramatization, began denouncing grownups of the town—and later of nearby places—for practicing the black magic upon them. At the trials that ensued the "afflicted children," seated conspicuously in the courtroom, shrieked and jerked and fell into fits as palpable proof of the truth of their charges. So convincing were their antics and so potent the effect of mass suggestion that a number of those arrested confessed to being witches. Before the madness ran its course fourteen women and six men (one an ordained minister) were executed, with two other unfortunates dying in jail while awaiting trial.

To Chief Justice Thomas Hutchinson, reviewing the episode seventy-five years later in his *History of the Province of Massachusetts-Bay,*

> the whole was a scene of fraud and imposture, began by young girls, who at first perhaps thought of nothing more than being pitied and indulged, and continued by adult persons, who were afraid of being accused themselves. The one and the other, rather than confess their fraud, suffered the lives of so many

innocents to be taken away, through the credulity of judges and juries.

Unhappily, he added, "none of the pretended afflicted were ever brought to trial for their fraud. . . ."

Hutchinson's estimate of the episode may in modern eyes seem oversimple, but by 1767, when it was penned, his opinion as to its spurious character bespoke a widely held view, though not one that necessarily rejected the potential existence of witches. Samuel Sewall, one of the judges in the Salem proceedings, did not go so far, for instance, when in 1697 he made public his regret for the naïveté of the court in assessing the evidence, nor did the Massachusetts legislature in 1711 in voting damages to some of the victims' families. As late as 1720 three children in Littleton, near Boston, accused a woman of bedeviling them—she died before the alarmed community haled her into court. Hutchinson himself admitted that even when he wrote there were still people about who, "from the reluctance in human nature to reject errors once imbibed" or out of "respect to the memory of their immediate ancestors," justified the Salem verdicts. In fact, however, no prosecutions for the crime occurred anywhere in New England after that affair.

Elsewhere, however—in Virginia in 1698 and 1706, Pennsylvania in 1701, Maryland in 1702 and 1712, and North Carolina in 1712—trials were conducted for the offense, but these seem to have been the final ones in America and none apparently brought a conviction. The great English jurist Sir William Blackstone spoke for the vast majority of the colonists as well as of his own people when in 1769 he wrote in the fourth volume of his *Commentaries,* "To deny the possibility, nay, actual existence of witches and sorcery, is at once flatly to contradict the word of God, in various passages both of the old and new testament," but, he went on, "one cannot give credit to any particular modern instance of it." In contrast with the colonies, the last witch trial with a death sentence took place in England in 1712, in Scotland in 1722, in Germany in 1775, in Spain in 1781, in Switzerland in 1782, and in Poland in 1793.

From an institutional point of view America presented the greatest diversity of beliefs of any land on earth. The reason is not far to seek. From the beginning of the sixteenth century to the middle of the seventeenth the Old World had been rent with theological dissension, and the vast transatlantic continent offered a natural refuge for the persecuted minorities.

The largest single denomination in 1776, the Congregationalists, traced their descent from the Puritans of early Massachusetts. Before leaving the homeland they had considered themselves part of the Church of England, differing with it only in aiming to "purify" its doctrines and liturgy of the "corruptions" inherited from Roman Catholic times. Behind the shield of the Atlantic, however, they erected what was in effect an independent sect. Of their 658 meetinghouses all but seven were in New England. The Presbyterians, second in size, were later arrivals, being largely an outgrowth of the massive Scotch-Irish migration of the eighteenth century. At the end of the colonial era they possessed 543 churches, mostly in the Middle provinces and the hinterland. Meanwhile, the Baptists, founded in Rhode Island by Roger Williams, had spread in every direction, standing third among the denominations with 498 congregations on the eve of Independence.

The Church of England, or Anglican faith, the oldest in America, ranked next in strength. Introduced by the colonizers of Jamestown—a piece of wood nailed to two trees served as the earliest pulpit—and acquiring bands of followers throughout the colonies, it had its principal base in the South, where in the closing days before the Revolution more than half of its 480 churches were to be found. The Methodists, who opened their first chapel in New York only in 1767, were as yet merely an evangelistic movement within the Anglican fold dedicated to preaching the Gospel to the humble classes. The last of the major sects, the Society of Friends, or Quakers, had come into their own when William Penn founded Pennsylvania, but they had many adherents as well in North Carolina, Delaware, New Jersey, and Rhode Island, with a total of 298 meetinghouses in 1776. These five denominations accounted for four fifths of all Christian places of worship.

Of the remainder most people belonged to groups that had removed to America directly from Continental Europe, the one exception being the Catholics, centering in Maryland and largely English in make-up, who totaled 50 churches in 1776. There were the Lutherans from Germany and nearby with 151 congregations, largely in the Middle colonies and the South; the German Reformed with 125, chiefly in Pennsylvania; and surviving from New Netherland days, the Dutch Reformed in New York with 123. In addition, some small Pietistic bands of Teutonic origin—the Mennonites, Dunkers, Schwenkfelders, and others—lived to themselves in interior Pennsylvania; and, beyond the pale of Christendom, Jewish synagogues had lately come into being in Charleston, New York, Philadelphia, and Newport, with adherents mainly of Portuguese or Spanish blood.

In spite of the bewildering array of religious organizations the members, for the most part, derived their idea of God from the infallibility of the Bible. About six thousand years before, in the nearly universal view, the Lord had created Adam and Eve, the first mortals, with the world in which they and their posterity were to dwell; in punishment for disobeying His commands He had expelled them from the Garden of Eden and cursed all their descendants with original sin; but through the crucifixion and mediation of Jesus, the Son of God, they might escape everlasting damnation and attain salvation in an afterlife by becoming members of the true church. The Almighty, moreover, was an intimate personal deity, not an aloof observer. He judged the daily actions of men and sought ceaselessly to save their souls from the blandishments of Satan. The entire conception embodied dramatic elements of plot and counterplot, of anguish and ecstasy, against contrasting backgrounds of stark evil and radiant hope.

Within this large consensus there were theological differences, but these can easily be exaggerated—as, indeed, they often were in the sometimes heated controversies of the seventeenth century —and they tended to lessen as the colonies aged. A modified Calvinism provided the dominant belief of the mass of churchgoers. The great Genevan had expounded the doctrine of unconditional predestination—that is, the Lord in His inscrutable wisdom and "totally irrespective of human merit" had foreordained certain persons (the "elect") to eternal bliss, all others (the "reprobate") to eternal torment. But the Puritan divines, who were the foremost colonial Calvinists, softened this stringent dogma—and some had begun to do so even before leaving England—by suggesting that those not initially of the elect might still achieve that status through righteous conduct and God's saving grace. In any event, the original doctrine could hardly have withstood the stubborn optimism and self-reliance of the Americans. Calvinism, more or less as so defined, undergirded not only the Congregationalist creed but also that of the Presbyterians, Baptists, Anglicans, and the Dutch Reformed. Their divergences related to secondary matters.

Of the principal religious bodies the Quakers stood farthest from the Calvinist position. The Friends sought God not in the letter of the Scriptures alone but in the dictates of their hearts, relying primarily upon an "Inner Light" to guide their steps in holiness. Therefore they spurned all formal worship and a "hireling clergy," allowing every member to speak out in meeting as the spirit moved him. They refused, moreover, to swear judicial oaths (expressly forbidden by the New Testament); and, like the Pietistic sects, they further declined to bear arms (as contrary to the Sermon on the Mount) and wore plain attire to symbolize their Christian humility.

For most people, colonial religion was less concerned with doctrine or with introspection than with tangible results in character and conduct. Indeed, the most striking differences between the groups appeared in two other respects: their organizational structure and their relationship with the secular government. Aside from the highly individualistic Quakers, three types of internal organization prevailed in the principal denominations. At the one extreme stood the Congregationalists, who, as their name implied, practiced autonomy in their individual congregations. Each elected its own preacher and other officers and conducted its affairs as it saw fit. Interchurch conferences, though held from time to time, served merely in an advisory capacity. The Baptists, who had originated in America out of a doctrinal dispute with the Congregationalists, followed an identical plan.

At the opposite pole were the Anglicans, or Episcopalians, who, when establishing the Church of England after Henry VIII's break with Rome, had modeled their organization on the Roman

Church, eliminating the Pope, however, and in due course making the Archbishop of Canterbury their spiritual head. Theirs was a system of centralized authority in which the bishops decided everything of importance irrespective of either the lower clergy or the laity. The colonial members fell under the jurisdiction of the Bishop of London, who alone could ordain their ministers. Distance, however, so weakened his control that the vestries in the local parishes, notably in Virginia, acquired a dominance in ecclesiastical concerns unknown at home. The Virginians, unlike English parishioners, not only managed the church property but also usurped the function of the bishops by appointing and dismissing their parsons. Accordingly they often came close to congregational self-government.

To correct the situation, calls came from both sides of the water for an American episcopate—for one or more bishops residing on the ground. The agitation reached its height in the final colonial years, when it became entangled with patriot fears of overweening British power in matters of taxation and trade and so lent the project the sinister appearance of a move to further impose "ecclesiastical bondage." Assurances by its advocates that non-Anglicans would not be affected failed to still the popular clamor. In reality, however, the proposal lacked the support of the Ministry and in any case would probably not have succeeded. Although no other sect of the time possessed a hierarchical framework, the Methodists perpetuated this feature of the parent body when they set up their religious organization after the Revolutionary War.

Halfway between the democratic Congregational system and the aristocratic Anglican arrangement lay the Presbyterian. Unlike the Congregationalists, the Presbyterians, as in Scotland, held to a common church government under the binding authority of synods composed of lay and ministerial members. Unlike the Episcopalians, they rejected gradations of the clergy, placing them all on an equal footing. More than either, the Presbyterians in their reliance on federalism and representative institutions anticipated the political make-up of the future United States. The Dutch and German Reformed denominations also followed this plan.

Paradoxically, the two sects that varied most in internal structure—the Anglicans and the Congregationalists—were also the two most alike in their external relationship with the civil authorities. Both the Church of England and the Congregationalists, as one of their offshoots, found a church-and-state connection to be a natural one, and each denomination was so situated in certain colonies as to bring it about. Anglicanism thus became the legally established faith throughout the South (though in Maryland not till 1702) as well as in four southern counties of New York, its revenues arising, as in the case of the mother country, from taxation of all the inhabitants regardless of religious affiliation. In Massachusetts the Congregationalists at first held a comparable position, even the suffrage being confined to their members; but at Britain's insistence the provincial charter of 1691 abolished this illiberal restriction on voting, thereby opening the way for the Quakers, Episcopalians, and Baptists—the principal religious minorities—to divert their taxes to their own faiths. This came about in the second quarter of the eighteenth century. Congregationalism was also established along similar lines in neighboring Connecticut and New Hampshire. So in 1776 nine of the thirteen colonies still provided financial support for one or more preferred denominations.

In the early days the pastor, especially in New England, had been the leading member of the community. He was not only the spiritual guide, on intimate terms with the Lord, but also usually the most learned person; and on both scores he was considered an unfailing fount of wisdom on public and private matters. He was indeed the first professional man to appear in the colonies, preceding the schoolmaster, the lawyer, and the doctor, although he himself might act on the side in one or other of these capacities. When a visitor at Andover, Massachusetts, asked the Congregational minister Samuel Phillips whether he was "the parson who serves here," that worthy tartly rejoined, "I am, Sir, the parson who rules here"; and probably none of his fellow-townsmen would have challenged the assertion.

But the passage of time wrought changes in the minister's position as business and other secular interests absorbed the increasing attention of the people and even of some members of the cloth. Instead of entering the clergy able youths now found other openings for their talents. Between 1700 and the Revolutionary

War at least forty-eight preachers in New England had to sue their parishioners for unpaid salaries. The parson's voice—except in times of "revivals" of religion—became merely one among many in the hustling, bustling communities. The divines who exerted an influence on the popular mind during the quarrel with Britain were the notable exceptions.

Nor did New England and the Congregationalists exhibit the only instances of growing worldliness. In Philadelphia, the Presbyterian synod in 1720 held a pastor guilty of fornication (although it allowed him to resume his duties after a month because of his "signs of true repentance") and tried others for such derelictions as bigamy, drunkenness, and stabbing. In New York City in 1747 the Dutch Reformed consistory, coping with a different but more chronic problem, urged its ministers to preach no more than fifty minutes or an hour so as "to increase the audiences" and "remove the complaints about long sermons."

Even more spectacular issues arose in the Anglican strongholds to the south. There the requirement that American candidates had to journey three thousand miles to London for ordination had hampered the development of a strong native ministry. As a result, most of the positions went to English rectors who had frequently lacked the zeal or discipline to succeed in their homeland. As early as 1624, the Virginia legislature felt obliged to forbid churchmen to "give themselves to excesse in drinking or ryott, spending the time idelie by day or night, playing at dice, cards, or at any other unlawful game"; and it passed statutes of like import in 1669 and 1705, but without the hoped-for results.

In Maryland the situation was equally distressing. At Patapsco, for example, a woman who flogged the "Reverend N———l W———r" was let off with the fine of a single penny, "it being imagined by the court," said the *Maryland Gazette*, June 16, 1747, "that he well deserved it." Horatio Sharpe, governor of the province from 1753 to 1769, cited numerous examples of "scandalous behavior," "immoral conduct," and "prostituted life" among recreant pastors. In 1771 the Assembly enacted a law subjecting the clergy to special scrutiny. As in every age, however, the backsliding of the few doubtless excited more notice than the piety and disinterested services of the many.

In reaction to the spiritual ebb a mighty effort was put forth by

dismayed souls in the 1740's to reverse the tide. The Great
Awakening, as it was called, affected all classes, ages, regions, the
educated as well as the ignorant, those outside the churches as
well as those within. Only the Catholics stood aloof. True, most of
the Episcopal clergy decried the upsurge of emotionalism, as did
the body of Quakers, but many of their adherents succumbed. As
though preparing the ground for the event, revivals had taken
place among the Dutch Reformed in New Jersey in the 1720's,
and among the Congregationalists of inland Massachusetts and
Connecticut in the mid-thirties, but in each case a distressing lull
had followed. Something more was evidently required to dispel
lethargy and reanimate religion in all the colonies.

George Whitefield, a free-lance Anglican preacher from the
mother country, provided the needed leadership. A man of
passionate eloquence, this Oxford-trained son of a Gloucester innkeeper had demonstrated his capacity for the task by his widespread conversions among the English working class. In successive
tours of the colonies from 1739 onward he addressed huge gatherings, sometimes, like Christ's disciples, in the open air. "It was
wonderful," attested Benjamin Franklin of Whitefield's Philadelphia visit, "to see the change soon made in the manners of the
inhabitants." When the Episcopal rector in Boston, Timothy Cut-
ler, greeted the evangelist with "I am sorry to see you here,"
Whitefield unhesitatingly retorted, "So is the devil!" On every
hand local clergymen hastened to forward the cause—Congregationalists like Jonathan Edwards, Thomas Prince, and Eleazar
Wheelock in New England, Presbyterians like Samuel Blair and
the four Tennent brothers in the Middle colonies, and the Baptists
Samuel Davis, John Waller, and others in the South. With the help
of such "sons of thunder" the Awakening spread irresistibly from
town to town and swept all before it in the rural parts. It was the
first universal and spontaneous movement in the history of the
American people.

Though an outgrowth of colonial conditions, it corresponded
with, and doubtless derived impetus from, the contemporary
Wesleyan agitation in Britain as well as the Pietist stirrings in
Germany and Bohemia. There, as in America, a revulsion had
occurred against the formalism, pedantry, and frigidity that had

lessened the appeal of Prostestant worship. As Whitefield put it, "the Reason why Congregations have been dead, is because dead Men preach to them. . . . how can dead Men beget living Children?" The call was for a rebirth of personal piety, a return to the old-time religion with its uncompromising stand on original sin and the Lord's power to grant or withhold salvation.

Jonathan Edwards, for example, discoursing on "Sinners in the Hands of an Angry God" in 1741 at Enfield, Connecticut, portrayed an Almighty who held the unconverted "over the pit of hell, much as one holds a spider or some loathsome insect over the fire." To His "mere pleasure" alone, he thundered, "is to be ascribed . . . that you did not go to hell last night." The hearers, we are told, responded with "a great moaning" and "shrieks & crys." James Davenport, from a Congregational church on Long Island, and others conducted such vigorous revivals in Connecticut that the legislature in 1742 enacted a law to expel from the colony as vagrants outsiders who preached without the consent of the regular minister and a majority of the members, and it pronounced Davenport himself "disturbed in the rational Faculties of his Mind."

The scenes, mounting in turbulence as time went on, alienated many of the early friends of the Awakening. Regarding one of the meetings the Reverend Charles Chauncy of Boston wrote in *Seasonable Thoughts on the State of Religion in New-England* (1743):

> Numbers of People continued the greatest Part of the Night, in the utmost Disorder. They were *groaning, crying out, fainting, falling down, praying; exhorting, singing, laughing, congratulating* each other, which they did by *shaking Hands* and *Embraces* (the latter was commonly practised by *different Sexes*) and by the *fifth* Night, there were almost three Hundred thus affected,

while of another occasion he reported,

> there were *threescore* Persons lying, some on the Floor, some across the Seats, while others were held up and supported in great Distress.

The primordial instincts aroused in dense throngs by reiterated emotional appeals assumed command. And, as might be expected

from what we have come to know of the relation of the physical
and psychological changes during puberty to the process of conversion, boys and girls were among the most impressionable
auditors. Their actions curiously resembled the behavior of the
"afflicted children" of Salem days half a century before, with now
the Lord instead of Satan supposedly the instigator.

By 1745 the movement had largely spent its force. The souls
reclaimed in New England alone were reckoned at from 25,000 to
50,000, but such figures, even if reliable, do not reveal to what
extent the effects proved lasting. In 1760, The Reverend Ezra
Stiles of Newport, Rhode Island, looked back on the Great Awakening as a time when "Multitudes were seriously, soberly and
solemnly out of their wits," and Edwards himself confessed in
1751, "I cannot say that the greater part of supposed converts
give reason, by their conversation, to suppose that they are true
converts." Even in the case of the true converts the unceasing
emphasis on the impermanence of human existence and the terrors of hell had centered their attention on personal salvation. It
directed their concern to improving themselves rather than the
communities in which they lived.

On the other hand, by its nondenominational character the
Awakening had stressed the underlying unity of the Protestant
groups and made it easier for communicants to shift from one sect
to another. Moreover, it intensified the zeal of the very devout,
although it also created dissension over the use of emotional and
disruptive methods, notably among the Congregationalists and the
Presbyterians. To the Baptists and the Methodists, these methods
came more naturally, which put them in the way of becoming the
great popular sects of the future. In due course, too, the more
active type of piety led to the founding of the College of New
Jersey (now Princeton) by the Presbyterians and of Dartmouth
by the Congregationalists.

Finally, the Awakening gave birth to the greatest metaphysical
work ever penned in America: Jonathan Edwards's treatise *Freedom of the Will* (1754), a distillation of his lifelong reflections
regarding this crucial aspect of God's relation to man. Far from
an emotional presentation, as might be expected, it was a superbly
wrought argument to demonstrate that freedom of the will con-

sisted in man's being able to follow his inborn propensities whether good or bad, not in his ability to reverse them, which only the Omnipotent could do. Whatever comfort this afforded Edwards then took away by asserting that man could not escape divine retribution when his acts were evil, even though they were beyond his control. A belated effort to restate and refine the Calvinistic dogma of predestination, the book left an impress on American theological thought for the next hundred years. James Boswell, the biographer and friend of Samuel Johnson, confessed that his only relief from its relentless logic was to forget it, but Dr. Johnson disagreed. "All theory is against the freedom of the will," he commented, "all experience for it."

That was doubtless the reaction also of the run of Edwards's down-to-earth countrymen. As a satirical rhyme put it in a New York paper (whence it was reprinted without comment in Purdie and Dixon's *Virginia Gazette,* February 11, 1771):

> If all Things succeed, as already decreed,
>> And immutable Impulses rule us,
> To preach and to pray is but Time thrown away,
>> And our Teachers do nothing but fool us; . . .
> Then no Man can stray, but must go the right Way,
>> As the Stars that are bound in their Courses:
> But if, by Free Will, we can go, or stand still,
>> As best suits each present Occasion,
> Then fill up the Glass, and conclude him an Ass
>> Who preaches up Predestination.

The agonizing soul-searching of the 1740's had the unexpected side-effect of stimulating rationalistic approaches to religion among the intellectual classes. This attitude was a carry-over of the European Enlightenment. Arising in seventeenth-century France and England, the Enlightenment reached its height in the eighteenth. On the negative side, its adherents questioned arbitrary authority, whether secular or spiritual; on the positive, they affirmed man's capacity through his mental faculties to explore all things human and divine. Impressed by Newton's demonstration of a harmonious and self-regulating universe, they asserted the primacy of natural law over supernatural intercession, of the moral life over received dogma, of reason over mystery. In their eyes the only valid belief was deism, which envisaged God as the great engineer who had designed and fueled the machinery of the cosmos and afterward stood aside to let it run of itself. They viewed the Bible as an aid to men's understanding. Where the colonial evangelists bemoaned the decay of ancient piety, the deists considered religion of the traditional sort not a matter of then and now but rather of now and then.

Rationalistic writings soon found their way into the libraries of Harvard and Yale as well as into the homes of many cultivated Americans, while the young people who attended British universities encountered the views there. John Locke's *Essay Concerning Human Understanding* (1690) wielded the greatest influence. The treatise repudiated the accepted belief in innate ideas—those "which the soul receives in its first being"—maintaining instead that men necessarily "correspond with the general harmony of nature" and that all knowledge proceeds from sense impressions derived from the external world, that is, from reason confirmed by experience. As though echoing Locke, the Reverend John Wise of Ipswich, Massachusetts, a dauntless warrior for both ecclesiastical and political democracy, declared in his *Vindication of the Government of New-England Churches* (1717), "Those Persons only who live in Obedience to Reason, are worthy to be accounted free. . . ." Gradually others in and out of the pulpit took up the same refrain.

The mingling of British and American officers during the third war with France in the 1740's did something to spread such views, but it was the shock of the Great Awakening which brought them significantly to the fore. Charles Chauncy, for example, condemned the emotional excesses on the ground that "an enlightened Mind . . . ought always be the Guide of those who call themselves Men." So also held his Boston colleague, the Reverend Jonathan Mayhew. "God," Mayhew said, "has not only given us liberty to examine for ourselves; but expressly required us to do it." Both men vigorously combated the doctrine of Calvinistic determinism with its corollary of man's moral helplessness.

Of avowed deists America possessed few or none before the Revolution, but of people deistically inclined the number increased in the final colonial years, especially among the better educated. They never composed more than a small segment of the population, and, being unorganized, they often belonged, nominally at least, to some church. The company included such outstanding men as John Adams in Massachusetts, Stephen Hopkins in Rhode Island, Benjamin Franklin and Dr. Benjamin Rush in Pennsylvania, and Thomas Jefferson, George Washington, and James Madison in Virginia. It was, by and large, men like these who took the lead in uniting the colonists against the threatening measures of Britain. As faithful sons of the Enlightenment they condemned what they considered political unreason quite as much as they did theological unreason. As a matter of course the signers of the Declaration of Independence appealed to "the Laws of Nature and of Nature's God" and to the "Supreme Judge of the world" for the rectitude of their course. The personal God of John Calvin and Jonathan Edwards could scarcely have received a more signal disavowal.

This development expressed part of the new religious consensus that characterized the Americans of 1776. After more than a century and a half the colonists, experiencing a wide gamut of spiritual vicissitudes, had arrived at broad conclusions about the role of religion in society. A pattern of convictions and practices had emerged which in sum gave American Christianity a distinctive and abiding cast. Basic was liberty of worship or, at least, toleration of historic Protestant differences.

This had hardly been the intent of the two first colonies. The Puritans, settling in Massachusetts to safeguard their own cherished creed, rigorously suppressed divergent opinions whether coming from within or without their ranks. They were reformers who did not themselves wish to be reformed. In the 1630's they expelled Roger Williams and Anne Hutchinson from both the church and the colony for unorthodox teachings, and in the 1650's they harried Quaker missionaries, even to the extent of hanging four. As the clergyman Nathaniel Ward put it in 1647, dissentients "have free liberty to keep away from us."

Anglican Virginia during these years proved scarcely less harsh toward Quakers, inflicting fines, imprisonment, and banishment, though stopping short of death. In the 1640's the authorities even moved against Puritan settlers, causing many of them to flee to Maryland, and the colony passed a law to expel any Catholic priest who might venture to take up residence. Indeed, as late as January 1774, James Madison, hearing that "not less than five or six Baptists" were held "in close jail" in a neighboring county, could still bewail that the "hell-conceived principle of persecution rages among some." This flare-up of bigotry, however, was definitely a throwback, no longer typical either of Virginia or of the age.

The intolerant course of a few colonies which in their beginning years aped Old World practices tends to obscure the fact that most colonies from the outset expressly legalized a wide range of religious choice. Thus the charters of New York, New Jersey, the Carolinas, and Georgia ensured freedom for all Protestants, regardless of sect. So too did the second charter of Massachusetts, in 1691. Things had indeed changed in the Puritan fastness when so eminent a cleric as Cotton Mather could rejoice that the "zeal of former times" no longer incited the persecution of "erroneous and conscientious dissenters by the civil magistrate."

Lord Baltimore, the founder of Maryland, wanted, as a Catholic, to provide a sanctuary for his oppressed fellow religionists in England, but he did not thereby propose to exclude Protestants, whom he expected to settle in greater numbers and hence build the colony more quickly. The two purposes worked at odds, however. Right from the beginning the Protestants comprised the majority element, and, although the provincial lawmakers at Baltimore's behest adopted the famous Toleration Act of 1649, later legislatures withheld its benefits from Catholics, first during the period 1654–1660, and then in 1689 permanently. In 1702 the Church of England was set up as the established religion, and Catholics thereafter were permitted to hold services only in private houses.

Three colonies declared against any restrictions at all on worship. Following the precepts of Roger Williams, who had removed to Rhode Island upon being exiled from Massachusetts, the Rhode Island Assembly in 1657 pronounced "freedom of different consciences" as "the greatest hapines that man can posess in this world." Similarly William Penn later in the century welcomed to his domains of Pennsylvania and Delaware all adherents of God regardless of creed. In these commonwealths, then, every believer—Protestant, Catholic, or Jew—could, in Voltaire's phrase, "go to Heaven by the way which pleases him."

Practical considerations had from the start been working against a compulsory uniformity of belief, even in colonies with government-entrenched faiths. A sparsely populated land demanded brawn and brains for its development without regard to religion. Moreover, the multiplicity of denominations—the greatest in any country on the globe—fostered an atmosphere of mutual forbearance if for no better reason than the self-interest of each particular group; and this mood received enthusiastic support, of course, from the vast number who belonged to no church. Pressure from the London authorities, eager to promote more rapid colonization, tended in the same direction, especially after Parliament's passage of the Toleration Act of 1689. That statute, while not removing the requirement of universal financial support of the state religion, freed Protestant dissenters in the homeland to attend any services they liked.

The Great Awakening paradoxically helped by minimizing ancient sectarian distinctions. Whitefield put the matter strikingly in an imaginary dialogue with a revered Old Testament patriarch before a Philadelphia audience. "Father Abraham," he inquired, "who have you in heaven? Any Episcopalians?"

"No."
"Any Presbyterians?"
"No."
"Any Baptists?"
"No."
"Any Methodists, Seceders, or Independents?"
"No, no!"
"Why who have you there?"
"We dont know those names here. All who are here are Christians."

Of like influence were rationalistic and deistic approaches to religion. As the venerated John Locke had put it in his *Letters on Toleration* (1688), nobody was bound "by nature" to any particular creed but should as a matter of right select the one he deemed most effectual for his salvation. Toleration, however, had its limits. No more than Whitefield did Locke concede the freedom to Catholics, who themselves refused ecclesiastic liberty to others and, moreover, professed an allegiance to the Pope incompatible with that to their own country. And he further denied the boon to unbelievers in Christ.

Thus, as the situation stood in 1776, freedom of worship belonged by law solely to Protestants, except in Rhode Island, Pennsylvania, and Delaware. Although this fell far short of the absolute ideal, the great body of colonial religionists could follow their preferences without fear of official penalties. Nowhere did they have to subscribe, except through tax payments, to a dogma or ritual against their convictions. The system of tax-supported churches, while still prevailing in most of the colonies, no longer interfered with the celebration of other creeds.

Catholics, on the other hand, continued to experience various legal disabilities. In most colonies they were forbidden to conduct public services and in all of them—even Rhode Island, Pennsylvania, and Delaware—to vote or hold office. The same political proscription applied to Jews in every colony save New York and to atheists probably everywhere. Yet in this predominantly Protestant world the total number subject to statutory restraints was very small, and in any event the repressive legislation seems not to have been strictly enforced. Practical tolerance went far to offset legal intolerance in a society growing constantly more secular. Even in Maryland, with its past harshness toward Catholics, it was possible for members of that faith in 1763 to open a church in Baltimore without molestation.

But to an increasing number of Americans practical tolerance was not enough, nor was even legal tolerance. This the Virginia Revolutionary Convention forthrightly proclaimed in its Declaration of Rights in June 1776. The pertinent provision as originally drafted pledged "the fullest toleration in the exercise of religion, according to the dictates of conscience"; but James Madison, dissatisfied with the implication that government possessed the power to confer an inherent human right, had the wording altered to "all men are equally entitled to the free exercise of religion, according to the dictates of conscience." Thus Virginia, in the spirit of Roger Williams and William Penn, put the case squarely on the basis of a principle transcending man-made law and in a form applicable to Catholics and non-Christians as well as to all distinctions of Protestants. The post-Revolutionary era was to see this unqualified position adopted universally.

A related outgrowth of the century and more of religious life was the emerging conception of the church as a purely voluntary association dependent on the members for support. This was the price of survival for groups cut off from public funds, but in any case it accorded with the sturdy self-reliance that marked the colonists in all their activities. Far from dampening spiritual ardor, the opportunity of forming their own congregations was evidently a stimulus to faith. It not only accounted for the multiplicity of Protestant sects but also for the very existence of the Catholic and Jewish minorities. Even the government-allied faiths had to function on this basis outside their own colonies. With their eventual disestablishment following Independence, voluntarism was to be the only style of religious organization.

Still another bequest of the colonial period was the accent on emotional preaching. The scholastic presentation of doctrines typical of the early years had given ground under impact of the Great Awakening to melodramatic appeals, with a corresponding advantage to those groups featuring the method. At the same time the Awakening had demonstrated the great effectiveness of itinerant ministers and informal exhorting by laymen and the uneducated. All these practices would bear even greater fruit in evangelizing the settlers who were soon to pour into the region beyond the Alleghenies.

The colonial observance of the Sabbath, or Lord's Day, wielded continuing influence. An inheritance from the mother country, this custom constituted a dramatic instance of the alliance between church and state. With minor variations, every legislature prohibited on the Sabbath all trading, unnecessary work, travel except to church, hunting, fishing, and amusements, usually on pain of fine or detention in the stocks. Above all else Sunday—a word eschewed because of its pagan origin—must not be fun day. Puritan Massachusetts, Quaker Pennsylvania, and Anglican Virginia stood as one in this, although the actual enforcement suffered somewhat south of New England in regions where the population was highly diversified or an aristocratic class tended to set its own rules. Boston's Josiah Quincy, Jr., touring South Carolina in 1773, described the Sabbath there as a time "of visiting and mirth with the rich, and of licence, pastime and frolic for the negroes"; he considered that the only honest course would be for the authorities to remove the regulations or else "see them better executed." But, whether honored in the breach or the observance, the universality of the enactments afforded the hardest-working people in the world the blessed opportunity of one solid day of rest in every seven. For that brief span idleness was a duty imposed by both divine command and human law. So deeply rooted was the usage that it persisted with little change well into the next century and even today gives the Sabbath a distinctive character.

An additional consequence of the religious experience was the belief that between Sabbaths the Lord applauded the amassing of property, indeed that wealth almost constituted a visible badge of His favor. Asceticism played no role, even in the small Pietistic groups or, if so, not for long. Self-denial in material things could hardly offer a compelling spiritual goal in a land where every prospect was pleasing. The clergy lost no opportunity to decry the sins of sloth and improvidence and acclaim the Christian virtues of diligence, foresight, and thrift. Although the *Book of Proverbs* cautioned that "A good name is rather to be chosen than great riches," it took away much of the effect by enjoining, "Go to the ant, thou sluggard; consider his ways, and be wise." In Poor Richard's homely version, "God helps them that help themselves." Never were worldly ambition and otherworldliness clasped in fonder embrace.

The Puritan divines, for their part, constantly warned against the corrupting possibilities of wealth, but never against wealth itself when honestly acquired. The Reverend Joseph Morgan of New Jersey in *The Nature of Riches* (1732) went so far as to depict the avid pursuit of gain as a yoke assumed by the rich for the sake of the poor. The Anglican churchmen to the south likewise viewed benignly their parishioners' accumulation of vast estates; and even the Quakers, who at first practiced plain living as a principle, in the end found it compatible with their creed to pile up fortunes in land and trade and gratify expensive tastes. In 1769, when they formed no more than a seventh of Philadelphia's population, they furnished twelve of its seventeen wealthiest citizens. The acquisitive spirit, so sanctioned from on high, continued as an enduring American trait, sometimes with results contrary to Christian ideals. But it also supplied the ethical impulse for sharing one's means with the less fortunate, one of the noteworthy aspects of the national character.

As a final product of colonial religious life men learned that they could hold their own ideas of the ultimate good while respecting the right of others to think differently. Spiritually at least, all men were created equal. Every sect taught the worth of the individual and the brotherhood of man, though with drastic reservations as to the black race. Moreover, most of them provided practical training in cooperative efforts and ecclesiastical self-government. All these were factors which strengthened democratic tendencies at work in other spheres of the American scene and were to have a durable effect.

CHAPTER VII

Urban
Growing Pains

With the emergence of towns came urban problems—new and perplexing challenges for a people accustomed for the most part to a rural way of life. Daily association with neighbors meant unfamiliar opportunities and pleasures, but it also imposed curbs on one's former freedom of action. Townsfolk had to take into account the common good if for no other reason than to derive benefits in return.

At first, they assumed civic obligations reluctantly, ignoring them as long as they could and then seeing to it that they were performed at as little cost as possible. The presumption was that every adult male as a matter of course would be willing to contribute time and energy to the safety and well-being of the community. This simple arrangement worked well enough as long as a town was small enough to constitute a sort of enlarged family, with everybody feeling a responsibility for everyone else. But, as population increased and relations became more impersonal, the voluntary system revealed serious shortcomings and left the authorities no alternative but legal compulsion. Even so, they still sought if possible to avoid any charge to the taxpayer. Indeed, their own remuneration usually took the form of fees received from the individual served or of a share of the fines assessed. Only gradually did regular compensation become attached to municipal positions and then only to the more important offices and at scarcely more than nominal amounts. A partial justification for this frugality was that even in the major places the incumbents needed to give but a portion of their time to the duties.

All these attitudes were a legacy from Britain, where London and other cities had undergone, or were still undergoing, a similar evolution. In America the pressure of mounting urban needs naturally bore most heavily on Boston, Newport, New York, Philadelphia, and Charleston, the leading centers, and in these places the principal advances were made. Boston, the oldest of the five, set the pace until about the middle of the eighteenth century, when it gave way to Philadelphia, the youngest and about to become the largest. But even in the closing colonial years the call of civic duty and the prestige of municipal office made so little appeal that both Philadelphia and New York fined citizens who declined their more responsible positions. In the Quaker city the mayoralty itself at times went begging because men preferred to pay a penalty of £20 to £30. Everywhere certain essential public services, such as fire fighting and the construction of sidewalks and sewers, continued to depend largely or entirely on private initiative and support.

The streets at first were dirt after the manner of country roads, thick with dust in dry weather and almost impassable in wet. But in the eighteenth century, thanks to expanding populations and the greater burden of traffic, the authorities in the Northern cities began to surface the principal thoroughfares with stones or shells from the beach, levying the expense in whole or in part on the abutting property holders. An unpaved shallow trench in the middle served the purpose of drainage. In 1713, however, Boston demonstrated the superiority of gutters at the sides, although only Philadelphia and Newport followed this example before the end of the colonial period. Charleston indeed struggled along with its original dirt streets for many decades. In all the towns, moreover, the pedestrians had a difficult time, since the laying of sidewalks was left entirely to private whim and support. Boston, surprisingly backward in this regard, had no footpaths at all, the citizens trusting to rows of posts to fend off passing horses and vehicles.

To the townsfolk the increased traffic afforded gratifying evidence of growth, but their country cousins viewed the scene with astonishment if not dismay. In the words of a young Rhode Island medical student in Philadelphia in 1774, "Here the thundering of Coaches, Chariots, Chaises, Waggons, Drays and the whole Fraternity of Noise almost constantly assails our Ears." In the effort to abate what John Adams called the "rattle-gabble" in Boston the Massachusetts legislature in 1747 forbade vehicles to pass by the State House during its sessions, but in the end it had to block off the way with iron chains. The assault on the hearing, however, had less serious consequences than the hazards to life and limb. These in time caused all the populous centers to enact severe penalties for reckless riding and driving. With equal optimism they sought to keep the streets clear of rubbish and other debris by imposing on each householder the duty of removal in front of his own premises.

An adequate fuel supply, too, became a problem just as soon as the towns outgrew their original limits and the people could no longer rely on logs and fagots carted or sledded in from a neighboring forest. Prices then invariably rose, and, when the cold season proved especially long, the poor found themselves in dire straits. During the bitter winter of 1740–1, for instance, the Boston town meeting voted £700 for their relief. Coal was not unknown, but the cost restricted its use to the wealthy. This commodity came from Britain in ballast, occasionally also from Nova Scotia, Rhode Island, or Virginia, but never in sufficient quantities to replace wood.

Food, however, was plentiful everywhere, making the colonists probably the best-fed people in the world. A family, if it wished, could raise its own victuals, supplementing them with fish caught in a neighboring stream and with wild game from the woods; or it could satisfy its wants at one of the market houses owned or licensed by the town. The provisions, offered for sale by farmers on stated days each week, included a variety of meats as well as of cereals and vegetables; and as the eighteenth century advanced, official standards of weights, measures, and quality went far to protect the customers against fraud.

The disposal of sewage, on the other hand, was never adequately solved. During the first century of settlement a household, if bothering about it at all, had no choice but to bury or burn its wastes or else deposit them in reeking surface drains or in some convenient body of water, thereby starting the great American tradition of pollution. But with greater size Boston and Phila-delphia began to allow citizens at their own expense to construct underground conduits or sewers, and the sister cities presently followed. Even in 1776, however, the installations were only spotty, leaving the most effective scavenging to the good offices of roving swine and goats and, in the case of Charleston, to buzzards.

The fire hazard also increased with the years, but it had been serious from the beginning. This was because the settlers, using the material at hand, had generally constructed their buildings of timber throughout and, for purposes of mutual protection against the Indian peril, had huddled them together. One of the early preventive measures was the prohibition of wooden chimneys. As further safeguards the authorities maintained licensed chimney sweeps to clean out accumulations of soot and instituted the curfew, which, ringing at nine o'clock every evening, warned the townsfolk to bank or extinguish their hearth fires and douse all other lights until four thirty the next morning. In a sense, the entire community comprised the fire department, each house-holder being obliged to keep one or more leather buckets to help neighbors in quenching a blaze. When shouts or bells sounded the alarm, all rushed to the scene, formed a double row to the nearest source of water and passed the brimming pails up one line, re-turning the empties down the other.

Boston's initiative in acquiring a "fire engine" from England in 1679 led the other towns in the eighteenth century to follow suit, but the new system produced hardly better results. The prim-itive machine, constructed of wood or of wood and copper and lacking a hose, consisted simply of a tank on wheels with a pump at which relays of men strained to force the water out through a nozzle. Some notion of its effectiveness may be gathered from the boast of a Boston firm in 1733 that the superior brand it made was capable of throwing "a large quantity of Water twelve feet above the ground."

Time did bring about substantial improvement in the orga-nization of fire fighters. Boston, unwilling to trust any longer to a spontaneous outpouring of citizens, instituted in 1712 municipal brigades whose members, subject to call, were excused from jury service and other civic duties in lieu of pay; and other major towns presently copied this plan. Nevertheless, even in these places, the prime reliance was on volunteer companies, with Boston again taking the initiative in 1717. These self-appointed firemen enjoyed no privileges or exemptions, but they developed great *esprit de corps* and in their zeal to outdo rival companies were sometimes suspected of starting a blaze in order to be the first to extinguish it.

Typical of the conditions of membership were the regulations of the original Philadelphia company, which the transplanted Bostonian, Benjamin Franklin, organized in 1736. "Our articles of agreement," he says in his autobiography,

> oblig'd every member to keep always in good order, and fit for use, a certain number of leather buckets, with strong bags and baskets (for packing and transporting goods), which were to be brought to every fire; and we agreed to meet once a month and spend a social evening together, in discoursing and communicating such ideas as occurred to us upon the subject of fires, as might be useful in our conduct on such occasions.

As the years went on, the companies came to communicate ideas on matters of broader civic import; and when the troubles arose with Britain, many of them cooperated with patriot committees in economic reprisals against the home government. Indeed, a specially formed Anti-Stamp Fire Society in Boston in 1765 went so far as to resolve that, under "the deepest Impressions of Concern for their injured Country, and of righteous Indignation at its Oppressors," they would not save the stamp office from burning unless other buildings would be endangered thereby.

The advances in fire fighting, however, still lagged woefully behind the need, with the result that the last half-century or so before the Revolution witnessed the worst conflagrations of the whole colonial period. In no other regard did the residents fail so badly in meeting the demands of urban living. Boston thus saw over one hundred structures consumed in 1711 and nearly four hundred in 1760, with lesser disasters in between. Charleston, also a chronic sufferer, lost 334 homes and countless shops and warehouses in its greatest fire, that of 1740. The toll in each place might have been still higher but for the expanding use of lightning rods after the mid-century, particularly on public edifices. The better fortune of Philadelphia and New York throughout the colonial era was due primarily to their larger number of brick and stone buildings.

To offset the cost of fires to property owners, an insurance company was established in the second quarter of the century in Boston and another in Charleston; but neither survived more than a few years, the holocaust of 1740 bankrupting the Charleston venture. Twelve years later Franklin fathered an undertaking which not only made good then but has continued to the present time. Modeled on a London propotype, the Philadelphia Contributionship for the Insurance of Houses from Losses by Fire offered its services to all persons living within ten miles of the city. A further attempt in Boston in the 1760's also apparently succeeded. These modest enterprises, though arising too late to be of much benefit to the colonists, prepared the way for the comprehensive institutions of later years.

Unfortunately, no help in fighting fires was to be obtained from waterworks, which nowhere existed in the colonies. Springs, wells, cisterns, and rain barrels satisfied domestic wants; and along the streets of every sizable town were wells, publicly or privately owned, for general use, sometimes on payment of a fee. Philadelphia, for example, in 1771 had three or four to the block in its thickly settled sections, making 498 in all, of which about a quarter belonged to the city. Moreover, the pumps as places of common resort were used for posting official notices and proclamations. In 1774 New York in an admirable spurt of enterprise projected a municipal system based on a reservoir with hollow log pipes extending to "every Street and Lane" and "so contrived as to communicate with extinguishing Fire-Engines." But the oncoming war indefinitely delayed its completion, leaving Philadelphia to install the first important waterworks in 1801.

Policing was another problem that urban growth rendered more acute. During most of the seventeenth century every adult male had taken his turn at being a day constable or night watchman without compensation, on pain of supplying a substitute or paying a fine. The watches, carrying lanterns on their rounds, would reassure the townsfolk that they were being well guarded by calling out the hours and the state of the weather. But, as the difficulties of maintaining order increased, the principal communities found it necessary to organize paid forces with relatively fixed personnel. Something resembling a police department thus emerged. Even so, newspaper critics found occasion to complain. When some "malicious and evil minded Persons" one night in 1742 stole the door off a Boston watchhouse, a newspaper writer commented sarcastically that "the Watch-Men ought at least to take Care of their own Lodgings"; and ten years later a New Yorker disparaged the patrols of that place as being mostly "idle, drinking, vigilant Snorers, who never quell'd any nocturnal Tumult in their Lives." Nevertheless the evidence indicates that the preservation of law and order in American towns was more effective than in comparable Old World ones.

Evildoing flourishes in the dark, and one obstacle to better enforcement was the fact that until the close of the colonial period the streets were lighted only with lanterns hung from the windows of private houses. A writer in the *Massachusetts Gazette and Boston News-Letter,* February 27, 1772, perhaps knowing what had already been done elsewhere, pleaded for the "introduction of public Lamps" as tending "both to secure our persons from insult and abuse and our property from robbery and violence." The idea had some time before taken hold in Philadelphia, which in 1751 established a municipal system of whale-oil lights mounted on wooden posts, with provision for lamplighters and for the fining of persons who broke the lamps. New York followed in 1761, Charleston in 1770, and Boston in 1774; Newport alone of the major centers clung to the older method. Indeed, Philadelphia's 320 lamps in 1767 made it the best lit city in the British Empire.

Urban crime, though alarming enough to the colonists, never attained serious proportions. As long as the towns were small enough for everybody to know everybody else, community opinion acted as a deterrent; and, even when expanding populations altered this, the easy economic conditions rendered life and property safer than in Old World cities. In Pennsylvania, for instance, according to fairly complete statistics, only thirty-eight persons were convicted of murder from the first days of settlement to September 1775, or a little more than one every three years, while the corresponding figure for burglaries was less than one a year, a record all the more surprising in view of that province's great mixture of nationalities, the continuing frontier disorders, the presence of British-deported felons, and the temptations to criminality presented by the wealth centered in Philadelphia. The most frequent offenses there, as in the other colonies, were of a different order—petty thievery, drunkenness, assault and battery, and sexual irregularities.

Prostitution, as has been noted, throve in the leading ports, fostered by the undersupply of marriageable women as well as by the habits of sailors on shore leave. In an attack on the problem the Massachusetts legislature as early as 1672 prohibited under stiff penalties the erection in Boston of "a stews, whore house or brothel house," but with what result is suggested by the fact that a hundred years later, in 1771, the Boston press carried an obituary of "Man of War Nance," described as a "likely looking Woman" with "a bad Character for Chastity and Sobriety." In 1734, 1737, and again in 1771 mobs broke up particularly flagrant bagnios; and conditions in the other cities were little if any better. In 1744 a Philadelphia grand jury protested that "disorderly Houses" had so multiplied as to give one neighborhood "the shocking name of Hell Town"; and twenty years later a Charleston grand jury remonstrated against the "bawds, strumpets, drunkards, and idle persons" infesting its streets. Nor were masculine offenders against chastity always of humble station. The Massachusetts patriots, for example, discovered in 1775 the treachery of their trusted associate Dr. Benjamin Church from a letter he had indiscreetly confided to his mistress for delivery to the British army. "There is seldom an Instance of a Man guilty of betraying his Country," sententiously declared Samuel Adams, "who had not before lost the feeling of moral Obligation in his private Connections."

With the major towns geographically isolated from one another, it is strange that a greater number of lawbreakers did not simply move on to other places when conditions became too hot for them in their local communities. One who did so was "the famous and Notorious Villain," Tom Bell, son of a respectable

Boston shipwright, who embarked on his nefarious career while a student at Harvard. Expelled in 1733 for "scandalous neglect" of his studies, petty thievery, and "complicated lying," he turned to greener fields, wandering up and down the coast for the next decade or so, at times lining his purse with funds obtained by posing as a temporarily straitened member of the Winthrop, De Lancey, Fairfax, or some other eminent family, at times employing his talents as a forger, counterfeiter, or horse thief. The *New-York Post-Boy,* November 5, 1744, warned its readers that Tom was at the moment believed to be "walking about this city with a large Patch on his face and wrapt up in a Great Coat, and is supposed to be still lurking." Whenever the law caught up with him, he usually managed to break jail or to escape punishment by some "cunning Stratagem." Then, surprisingly, in 1750, at the age of thirty-seven, the versatile rascal took up schoolteaching in Patrick Henry's county of Hanover, determined, so he informed Hunter's *Virginia Gazette,* to "wipe off the Odium that his former Manner of Life had fix'd on him." When last mentioned in the press a few years later, he was plying that pedestrian occupation in Charleston, South Carolina, and soliciting subscriptions for his memoirs, which, unfortunately for a curious posterity, never seem to have materialized.

Hardly less colorful but with overtones of comedy was the Cinderella-like story of Sarah Wilson, who had begun her erring career in England by stealing some of her mistress's jewels. Deported for the offense to Maryland in 1771 as an indentured servant and soon escaping from her owner, she miraculously turned up in Charleston early in July of the next year, elegantly arrayed and feigning to be none other than Sophia Carolina Mathilda, Marchioness de Waldegrave and sister to Queen Charlotte, whose picture she displayed as a sort of passport. To what was doubtless her cynical amusement, all doors were immediately opened to her, as were also all purses when she assured her hosts of offices and other royal favors at her disposal. After living off the fat of the land for four months she then made her way northward, repeating her triumphs in Philadelphia, New York, Newport, Boston, and Portsmouth. An offer of a reward by her master in mid-1773, though widely copied in the press, failed for some reason to end the masquerade. As late as July 17, 1775, the *Newport Mercury* reported the fictitious peeress as returning from that place to New York. Therewith she vanishes from history.

The most ruthless criminals had disappeared from the scene a generation or so before the Revolution. They were the sea rovers who with crews of desperate men operated out of the leading ports during the thirty years after 1690. They capitalized on the fact that amid the chronic wars with France and Spain the distinction between privateering and piracy was often difficult to draw and that they could count on the connivance of complaisant Crown officials in the colonies as well as of members of the mercantile community. Freebooters brazenly strode the streets of Philadelphia because, it was alleged, Governor William Markham's son-in-law was one of them. In New York, Governor Benjamin Fletcher and his wife accepted gifts from them and even entertained the outlaw Thomas Tew at their table. When queried about this by his London superiors, his Excellency blandly explained that he was only trying to reform the misguided man, particularly "to reclaime him from the vile habit of swearing." Unscrupulous merchants, for their part, not only assisted in disposing of the cargoes but also sometimes helped finance the expeditions.

The forays of notorious pirates like Stede Bonnet, John Quelch, and Edward Teach ("Blackbeard") excited terror all the way from Brazil to Madagascar and the Indian Ocean, until at last the colonial authorities brought their careers to a violent end. One of the number, Captain William Kidd, though apparently only a reluctant recruit, has found a niche in American legend, and people still search hopefully for his buried treasure. This respected shipmaster sailed from New York in September 1696, with a royal commission to hunt down buccaneers; but when a whole year passed without sighting any, his crew, balked of their anticipated loot, went into marauding on their own account, with Kidd retaining command against his will, or so he subsequently claimed under oath. To add to his later difficulties, he brained an insubordinate sailor with a bucket one day in a fit of rage. Arriving at Boston in July 1699, Kidd after some delay was arrested and sent in irons to London for trial. There the judges rejected his plea that he had been coerced into filibustering and that two of the captured vessels had carried French passes and were therefore lawful wartime prizes; nor could they agree that the killing of the seaman should be considered only as manslaughter. Protesting his innocence to the end, Kidd was convicted of both piracy and murder and met death by hanging. As late as 1760—sixty years later—although freebooting had long since become a rare occurrence, two men were executed for the crime at Newport.

Urban mass violence reflected in part the lack of more wholesome outlets for animal spirits. The mob assaults on the brothels in Boston were one example; and regularly on the night of November 5 gangs from the north and south ends of the town celebrated Guy Fawkes day by engaging in anti-Catholic demonstrations. Increasingly, too, mobs in Boston and elsewhere sprang up to resist navy impressments and to attack revenue officers and informers seeking to enforce the Acts of Trade. But it was not until the Stamp Act that the outbreaks became epidemic. Even the hoodlums from Boston's north and south ends buried their differences to unite in the demonstrations; and better-class citizens often encouraged them to express the resentment of the populace toward the ministerial measures. Although the proceedings were criminal conspiracies in British eyes, no American jury ever convicted a participant.

The disorders reached crisis proportions in clashes with British garrisons at New York and Boston in 1770—magnified by the colonists as the Battle of Golden Hill and the Boston Massacre— and again in the Boston Tea Party three years later. It was this last disturbance, engineered by the patriots after the royal governor declined to send away the East India Company without payment of the obnoxious tax, which goaded Parliament into altering the democratic features of the Massachusetts charter and closing the port of Boston. But the Ministry had acted too harshly and too late. A people accustomed to taking the law into their hands now responded with armed rebellion.

The punishments prescribed for lawbreakers were for the most part excessive or bizarre by modern standards, when not both. For example, New York in 1776 provided death for sixteen acts when committed the first time—including counterfeiting, forgery, burglary, horse stealing, and arson—and for as many more upon a second conviction. Delaware demanded the extreme penalty in twenty instances, Pennsylvania in eighteen, Connecticut in fifteen. Colonial law, after the Old World fashion, sought to safeguard the community against what it ranked as major crimes by terrifying and irrevocable retribution. The codes made no allowance for the relative gravity of the transgressions, extenuating circumstances, or the possibility of reforming the convicted. Every individual was presumed to be a free moral agent who had willfully chosen to go wrong.

Even so, the number of capital offenses was far less than in England and the treatment of malefactors more lenient. For one thing, the comparative smallness and amiability of the colonial town made the problem less formidable. For another, the spectacle of felons expelled from Britain turning into useful members of society contributed to a more humane attitude. In practice, moreover, the letter of the law was often nullified by juries refusing to convict when the penalty seemed disproportionate, while other mitigations came about through the exercise of the pardoning power or the commuting of the death sentence to banishment. And, increasingly, evildoers saved their lives by pleading benefit of clergy.

This curious usage had arisen in medieval England to enable churchmen charged with major crimes—murder, arson, treason, and the like—to be tried in ecclesiastical courts, which did not administer capital punishment, instead of secular ones, which did. Over the years the practice spread in somewhat modified form to the temporal courts. It was at first made available to all persons who read Latin, then to all who read English, and finally, in 1707, to the illiterate as well. However, to prevent their claiming the privilege a second time, the culprits, in a crude anticipation of modern fingerprinting, were branded on the thumb.

The judges in all the colonies but Connecticut followed the English example, granting the exemption for all crimes except murder, treason, and piracy. In New York alone the concession was invoked no fewer than seventy-three times between 1750 and 1775. To cite a Massachusetts example, the Boston printer John Boyle laconically noted in his diary on February 25, 1773: "James Bell, Shoemaker, tryed for the Murder of his Wife on the

5th. Jany last, and found Guilty of Manslaughter; but pleading the Benefit of ye Clergy was burnt in the hand and discharged." The occasion that lives in history books took place a few years before when the two soldiers convicted of manslaughter in the Boston Massacre were let off with the lesser punishment. This deep-rooted but archaic method of tempering justice with mercy persisted until after Independence; Massachusetts gave it up in 1785, and by 1800 the other Northern states and Virginia, as well as the new federal government, followed suit. The rest of the original thirteen acted more slowly, South Carolina delaying till 1869. Great Britain itself did not cease the practice until 1827.

For lesser breaches of the law the colonial wrongdoer, also after the English fashion, underwent a variety of picturesque and degrading punishments, such as being whipped at successive street corners, or confined for long hours with his feet in the stocks or his head and hands in the pillory, or exposed on the gallows with his neck in the noose. A delinquent was lucky to escape with a mere fine. As especially fitting the misdeed, a malicious gossip or common scold—seemingly always a feminine offender—was required to stand gagged before her house or with a cleft stick on her tongue and, in aggravated instances, to endure the ordeal of the ducking stool. For graver transgressions short of capital crimes the unfortunate might suffer the lifelong stigma of having his ears cropped or cut off or of being branded on the hand or face with a letter telling the nature of his guilt. In accordance with a roughly alphabetical plan, "A" signified adultery, "B" burglary or blasphemy, "C" counterfeiting, "D" drunkenness, "F" forgery. A humane substitute in cases of adultery was to stitch the symbol onto the female offender's clothing, which was the fate of Hester in Hawthorne's *The Scarlet Letter*. For cumulative effect the penalties might be combined, as when "one Lindsay," convicted of forgery in Worcester in 1769, was sentenced to the pillory for an hour, then thirty lashes, and finally, to being seared on the hand.

Public humiliation was regarded not only as heightening the punishment but also as a means of identifying the culprits to the community at large. The townsfolk, for their part, found the sight a welcome relief from the daily routine. The whipping post, the stocks, the pillory, the ducking stool, and the gibbet all served as agencies of gruesome entertainment, with a constantly changing plot and cast of characters. Some five or six thousand persons, many from the countryside, witnessed the hanging of the two pirates in Newport in 1760, and the entire population of Charleston turned out in 1767 for the hanging of two horse thieves. To cash in on such occasions, enterprising printers struck off handbills and leaflets spiced with lurid woodcuts and the alleged dying words of the departed. Young Benjamin Franklin hawked about the streets of Boston a ballad of his own composition celebrating the downfall of the redoubtable Blackbeard—an effusion which he ruefully characterized in his old age as "wretched Stuff, in the Grubstreet Ballad Stile." The *Life and Confessions* of Herman Rosencrantz, executed in Philadelphia in 1770, ran through two editions of two thousand each in a single month.

Conspicuously absent from the round of punishments was the familiar modern method: imprisonment. The colonists held that a wrongdoer should settle his debt to society by a single quick payment, whether it be death, mutilation, or some lesser atonement. Locking up the offender meant the withdrawal of needed labor from the community, and, besides, it would create a tax burden that might be aggravated if his dependents became public charges. To be sure, "gaols" were to be found in all the colonies, but these buildings, typically of flimsy construction and unheated in winter, served almost exclusively for detaining prisoners until they were tried or the penalties inflicted. The inmates had to provide their own food or depend for their fare on kind-hearted outsiders, with the result that they sometimes perished of starvation, as did three of those in custody in Philadelphia in 1772.

The principal exception to the rule against imprisonment was the treatment of delinquent debtors, whose sentences ran until their obligations were discharged. Here all other considerations gave way to the fear of their fleeing to parts unknown and the related hope that confinement would either make them disclose any hidden resources or bring their friends to their rescue. The law ordinarily drew no line between large and small debtors or between fraudulent and honest ones, nor did it usually assure an equitable distribution of the assets among several creditors. The first to prosecute was the first to collect. Because of society's need for labor, however, the system differed from that in England by allowing the indebtedness to be commuted into a term of service to the creditor or some other master, but this option was not often resorted to. Instead, the unfortunates languished in jail without means of earning their release. An anonymous Newport pamphlet in 1754 dwelt at length on *The Ill Policy and Inhumanity of Imprisoning Insolvent Debtors,* and newspaper writers worried the theme on occasion; but it was difficult for the people of the time to envisage any rational alternative. In fact, it was not until many years after the Revolution, with the rise of wage earners as a force in political life, that imprisonment for debt was finally abandoned.

The drift of humanity to cities created a host of problems unknown or little felt in rural communities. Although the colonists made uneven progress in trying to meet these problems, they learned from experience as they went along. In their provisions for the convenience and safety of urban life, the leading American towns compared favorably with their counterparts abroad. Moreover, they laid the foundations of what would eventually be a great urban civilization.

CHAPTER VIII

Stirrings of
a Social Conscience

THE MULTIPLYING EXPRESSIONS of consideration for the unfortunate were omens of an emerging social conscience. Although the Americans lacked the tight class structure and accumulated wealth that sustained works of philanthropy in the mother country, more and more colonists as time went on gave of their substance to projects of public value. Both their own rise from humble beginnings and their devotion to Christian ideals nourished a fellow feeling for those in the community who, otherwise no different from themselves, had been hampered by conditions for which society itself must in part accept the blame. Moreover, the flow of private generosity to America from Britain, most notably in the field of education, set them an inspiring example.

From the outset individuals made modest contributions to the cause of college education: books, equipment, tracts of land, money for buildings and scholarships, even on occasion food. Then, with the emergence of a well-to-do element in the cities, the gifts grew larger and, as the Revolution approached, embraced broader social objectives. Peter Faneuil's present to Boston in 1742 of a market house with a civic auditorium above (known to posterity as "the cradle of liberty") was hailed by a contemporary as "incomparably the greatest benefaction yet known to our Western shore"; but, if so, the donor soon had rivals, for in 1747 Abraham Redwood gave Newport £500 to found a public library; and in 1751 James Logan willed to the city of Philadelphia a building and three thousand books for public use, with an endowment for maintenance. Shortly afterward, moreover, the townsfolk there raised upwards of £5,000 by popular subscription for establishing the Pennsylvania Hospital; and in 1764 John Hancock's uncle, Thomas, bequeathed £600 toward the erection in Boston of an insane asylum (never constructed, however).

Chronic poverty, or pauperism, presented a different kind of problem, although in a country of abounding economic opportunity it never approached the dimensions common in the Old World. What there was of it centered in the leading ports. In these communities disasters at sea, contagious diseases, and the wars with the French took their principal toll, and there, too, the ne'er-do-wells as well as the maimed, the halt, and the blind tended to congregate. Marine catastrophes alone accounted for over one thousand widows "in low circumstances" in Boston in 1742. Nevertheless, the Reverend Andrew Burnaby, accustomed to the terrible destitution of his native England, marveled that in traveling the twelve hundred miles from Williamsburg, Virginia, to Portsmouth, New Hampshire, in 1760 he did "not see a single object that solicited charity."

This freedom from beggars was an outcome of the system, which had grown up through the years, of placing the primary responsibility for aiding the indigent on financially able members of their families. That, to be sure, was also the English plan, but it operated more successfully in the colonies, where the needy were fewer, financial competence was more prevalent, and families were perhaps more closely knit. Young people on coming of age were required to succor impoverished parents and grandparents, as husbands, of course, had to support wives and children. The purpose underlying this legislation was to buttress the institution of the family, save the destitute from the disgrace of public dependence, and also economize the town's funds.

It was only when relief from these sources was unavailable that the local authorities took a direct hand. They might then board or lodge the infirm and the old in private homes at public expense and apprentice orphans and illegitimate children to some useful occupation until the age of twenty-one. In cases of temporary privation they might further dispense outrelief—food, fuel, and garments. And as a preventive measure many towns employed a "warning-out" system to exclude or eject newcomers without assured means of support. In addition, the major population centers in time established almshouses—Boston as early as 1662, Philadelphia in 1732, with the other large towns and even some smaller places following before the close of the colonial era. These methods of public assistance had importance for the future in recognizing the principle that, when private alternatives failed, the obligation lay on the taxpayer to help those who could not help themselves.

In still other cases benevolent individuals and groups stepped into the breach. Private legacies, for example, supplied the funds with which Boston built its almshouse in 1662; and the Virginian Matthew Godfrey in 1716 bequeathed to Norfolk County his slaves and the income from his thousand-acre estate for assistance to the poor. Charity sermons in the churches opened people's hearts and pocketbooks; and the Quakers, true to their humane principles, displayed signal interest, even to the extent of anticipating municipal action in Philadelphia by erecting an almshouse at their own cost in 1729. Mutual-aid associations of craftsmen and seamen afforded further help; the New York Marine Society is still functioning today. Most striking perhaps was the solicitude of persons of common national backgrounds for their distressed, notably the Scots, who, the first in the field, had by 1776 planted their St. Andrew's Societies all the way from Boston to Savannah. The Irish, English, and Welsh, though less active in this regard, formed kindred organizations; and even the Germans, who in general avoided the cities, established *Gesellschaften* for the purpose in Philadelphia and Charleston in the 1760's.

It was mass calamities, however, which evoked the most dramatic exhibitions of benevolence, erasing provincial and ethnic lines to unite the colonists in a single overarching effort. The Charleston fire of 1740 brought gifts for relief from as far off as Massachusetts. The Boston fire twenty years later merely repeated the story on a larger scale. In Virginia, George Washington subscribed £12, and the entire sum from private and public sources exceeded £13,000. The Boston Port Act in 1774, shutting off opportunities for employment, aroused an unexampled response.

Up and down the seaboard popular gatherings helped stimulate concern, and men went from door to door and from street to street to collect contributions. Soon great quantities of wheat, livestock, cheese, rice, and other foodstuffs poured in on the stricken town, as well as clothing, firewood, and gifts of money, which alone totaled nearly £8,000. In this case, to be sure, patriotism spurred charity, but basically the relief endeavors sprang from abiding wells of human compassion.

Of a different order was the problem presented by the victims of drink. Undoubtedly the ruggedness of colonial life promoted intemperance, but the settlers had brought the propensity with them from Britain, where, if Defoe and Fielding are to be believed, the situation was at least no better. Although the Americans did not condemn drinking as such, indeed drank themselves and saw much good in it, they deemed excessive indulgence a violation of the divine will depriving His creatures of their God-given manhood; and from direct observation they deplored it as a prolific womb of poverty, broken homes, and crime. In 1744 a Philadelphia grand jury, of which Benjamin Franklin was a member, noted as a further unfortunate consequence that profanity had "grown of late so common in our Streets."

No one, however—not even the most pious—cried out for teetotalism or prohibition. The remedy, rather, lay in moderate consumption— temperance in its yet undistorted meaning. Significantly, the notable attempt of the founders of Georgia to impose a measure of sobriety on the infant colony by banning distilled liquors hardly went any further; and even this slight divergence from custom met such opposition locally that it had to be abandoned nine years later. The colonies, moreover, welcomed the alcoholic traffic as a source of revenue, devoting the proceeds to defense needs or other worthy objects. In this fashion the Connecticut legislature in 1727 appropriated the yield of that year's rum levy to Yale College.

Drunkenness, according to the Maryland Assembly in 1639, consisted in "the notable perturbation of any organ of sence or motion." Colonial regulations to abate the evil included the licensing of taverns, fixed hours for the selling of liquor, limits on the amount that could be bought at one time, and the proscription of sales to minors, apprentices, indentured servants, Negroes, and Indians. In 1760 Virginia and Maryland felt a further need to pass specific acts to remove the temptation from clergymen. Habitual offenders might be branded with the letter "D," sentenced to the stocks, be whipped or fined, or even in extreme instances disfranchised.

But if articles in the press and blasts from the pulpit signify anything, the perturbation did not improve; on the contrary, it grew worse. The *Newport Mercury* in the 1760's, for instance, harrowed its readers with a front-page screed entitled "The Drunkard's Looking Glass: Or, a short View of their Present Shame and Future Misery"; and in Philadelphia, Dr. Benjamin Rush in 1772 embarked on his lifelong campaign against ardent spirits from a medical standpoint in a pamphlet entitled *Sermons to Gentlemen Upon Temperance and Exercise,* an exhortation urging the replacement of rum and whisky by beer. The only people, however, to take group action were the Quakers, who, beginning in the seventeenth century, urged their members to give up distilled liquors altogether. It was not until the second quarter of the nineteenth century that reformers, despairing of partial measures, declared war on intoxicants in every form.

Restrictions on the sale of alcoholic beverages to Indians and Negroes reflected no humane spirit; they were designed rather to ensure peace and good order for the sake of the whites. Even so, these regulations as they applied to the Indians were a dead letter in the backcountry, where liquor was an essential lubricant of the fur trade as well as a means of drugging the savages into parting with extensive lands. In a broader sense, the colonists had a complex attitude toward these lesser breeds, blending scorn for peoples considered to belong to a different and lower species of mankind with a Christian desire to do something to assist them. The Indians had won their ill repute by ungratefully taking up arms against the superior civilization; the Negroes, for precisely the opposite reason of meekly serving that civilization as slaves.

Behind the colonial view lay the agelong European prejudice against men with strange skins and alien creeds. Although the noble-spirited Moor in Shakespeare's play was a Christian, Desdemona's father could not refrain from reviling Othello for causing

her to seek "the sooty bosom of such a thing as thou." Uplift work
among tribesmen willing to heed it fell almost exclusively to the
churches. Whether the red men were regarded as being the children of God or of Satan—a nice point never wholly resolved—
their plight called for religious ministration. For over forty years
until his death in 1690 the Massachusetts Puritan clergyman John
Eliot went through New England preaching to the Indians in their
own tongue, even translating the Bible into the local Algonquian
speech, a prodigious if not very rewarding task, since the language
had previously been unwritten. Eliot, moreover, contrary to most
of his white brethren, considered that it was Christ's intention to
allow the aborigines to retain enough land to subsist and grow in
spiritual grace. By the eighteenth century all the faiths showed
more or less interest in this field, the Anglicans being the most
systematic through missionaries sent out by their Society for the
Propagation of the Gospel in Foreign Parts, chartered in London
in 1701. That the attempts at conversion bore meager fruit
doubtless owed much to the fact that, unlike these dedicated souls,
the colonists with whom the savages ordinarily dealt behaved in
such a manner as to make the white man's religion seem a gross
imposture.

The attempts at education yielded even poorer returns. Here
the churches acted as indirect agents. Congregational Harvard
hopefully provided for the instruction of Indian boys, as did the
Anglican College of William and Mary and, when they were
founded, the Presbyterian College of New Jersey at Princeton and
the Congregational Dartmouth; but the sprinkling of these youths
who attended—only one ever graduated from Harvard—derived
little benefit from a curriculum ill adapted to their comprehension.
Special schools of a more elementary character, such as the
Reverend Eleazar Wheelock's Indian Charity School at Lebanon,
Connecticut, founded in 1754 with funds from England, offered
more practical subjects; even so, the results were usually disappointing. Indeed, these high-minded ventures simply confirmed
the popular belief that the aborigines were beyond civilizing and
thus helped implant the view—which would not become vocal
until the nineteenth century—that the only good Indian was a
dead one.

Since nearly all Negroes were in bondage, their chances for spiritual and mental improvement depended on the masters to whom luck had assigned them. The early belief that if slaves were Christianized they would have to be freed discouraged slave-owners from undue exertions on their behalf; but even after the Maryland, Virginia, and other legislatures in the 1660's had later declared to the contrary and the law officers of the Crown in 1729 removed any remaining doubt, most masters remained indifferent if not opposed to their evangelization. They apparently did not even see in man's faith a means of instilling a humility that would make the servile people better workers. Some owners, especially in the plantation provinces, held that churchgoing would give the bondsmen less time for their work; others that it might foster notions of race equality; still others that in any event the blacks had no souls to save. Undoubtedly, a further factor was that religion among the Southern whites themselves tended to be nominal.

Although the Society for the Propagation of the Gospel in Foreign Parts spent more energy on converting Negroes than Indians, and other church groups were active to some extent, the obstacles inherent in the master–slave relationship proved too great for any considerable or lasting results. The teaching of reading and writing, usually incidental to spiritual instruction, made still less progress. By 1776, however, special schools for the race, under Anglican auspices, had been established in the North at Philadelphia, New York, and Newport, with one even at Williamsburg, Virginia; but the number of individuals affected was far too small to leaven the mass.

Even in the North and among the devoutly religious no significant body of sentiment opposed slavery as such except for the Quakers. Few colonists quarreled with the Bishop of London's view in 1727 that "the Freedom which Christianity gives, is a Freedom from the Bondage of Sin and Satan," not freedom of the body. Although at one time or other nearly every colony in the eighteenth century passed legislation to tax further additions from Africa, the motive was primarily to obtain revenue or to check the inflow long enough to ensure the peaceable absorption of those already on hand. In any case, many of these acts were negatived by the home government in the interest of British merchants engaged in the trade.

The Quakers alone officially discouraged their members from owning slaves, even going so far before the end of the colonial period as to disown recalcitrants. John Woolman, an itinerant minister of Mt. Holly, New Jersey, and Anthony Benezet, who for a time directed a Friends' school for Negroes in Philadelphia, were their outstanding spokesmen. Woolman in his *Journal,* published in 1774, warned, "These are the souls for whom Christ died, and for our conduct towards them we must answer before Him who is no respecter of persons." He would not use sugar because it was the product of West Indian slave labor. Benezet, holding like Woolman that "the Negroes are equally entituled to the common Priviledges of Mankind," departed from the usual Quaker attitude of moral suasion by proposing in a pamphlet in 1762 that they be freed by law and after a probationary period be given homesteads, perhaps in the region beyond the mountains.

The doctrine of the rights of man, advanced during the dispute with Britain, brought additional support to the cause. Thus James Otis in his pamphlet *The Rights of the British Colonies Asserted and Proved* (1764) declared, "The Colonists are by the law of nature free born, as indeed all men are, white or black," and an echoing voice in Rind's *Virginia Gazette,* March 10, 1767, affirmed that "freedom is unquestionably the birthright of all mankind, Africans as well as Europeans." But those who pursued the natural-rights line to this logical conclusion were the rare exception, and even in Otis's case it was a subject mentioned once and never later renewed.

The steps actually taken by the patriots went no further than the adoption of agreements not to buy slaves freshly brought in, which of course left the institution itself untouched; and these measures were but incidental to a much wider boycott of British importations. From 1769 onward popular gatherings in every Southern colony but Maryland took a stand against the British slave trade; and in 1774, following the Boston Port Act, Rhode Island and Connecticut, where alone the people controlled all branches of the government, enacted the ban into law. But the Rhode Island legislature, after high-mindedly declaring that those "engaged in the preservation of their own rights . . . should be willing to extend personal liberty to others," expressly authorized participation by its constituents in the slave trade outside Rhode Island. The First Continental Congress, however, meeting at Philadelphia later in the year, forbade activity in the traffic as well as the purchase of newly imported Africans and applied the terms to all the colonies, again as part of the broader economic war on Britain.

Although the interprovincial assemblage repeatedly asserted the natural-rights philosophy on behalf of the white race, the delegates, in many cases themselves slaveholders, perceived no inconsistency in morals or law in excluding one fifth of the American population. For this the reason was plain. They regarded the blacks as a species of legal property to whom the principles simply did not pertain; such folk could not conceivably be considered as belonging to the body politic. Nor, according to their lights, were the members of the Virginia Convention in May 1776 any more illogical when they affirmed in their famous Declaration of Rights that "all men are created equally free and independent" without supposing for a moment that this applied to Negroes.

Most revealing of all in this respect was the action three months later of the Second Continental Congress when deliberating on the text of the Declaration of Independence. Jefferson had inserted in the draft a long passage indicting George III for violating the "most sacred rights of life and liberty in the persons of a distant people" and "carrying them into slavery in another hemisphere, or to incur miserable death in their transportation thither." The delegates rejected it, proclaiming instead in more general language that by virtue of "the Laws of Nature and of Nature's God that all men are created equal." The very man who penned this "vehement philippic against negro slavery," as John Adams termed it, was himself the owner of some two hundred slaves. The original language was deleted, Jefferson later said, "in complaisance to South Carolina and Georgia," but, he added, the Northern members also "felt a little tender under those censures; for tho' their people have very few slaves themselves yet they had been pretty considerable carriers of them to others." An English friend of the colonists, Thomas Day, commented dryly, "If there be an object truly ridiculous in nature, it is an American patriot signing resolutions of independence with the one hand, and with the other brandishing a whip over his affrighted slaves."

As in the case of slavery, the colonial attitude toward war was thoroughly pragmatic. Valuing peace as conducive to their everyday pursuits, the Americans considered armed strife a deplorable interruption. Yet people living in the wilds had to be ready at a moment's notice to repel marauding Indians; and the colonists as a whole, as subjects of the British king, were unavoidably drawn into the mother country's European contentions. Despite the width of the ocean the battlefields of the Old World extended to the New. But, if circumstances made the Americans a warlike people, they did not make them a military one. Discarding the European system of a professional soldiery, they relied from the outset upon a haphazardly armed and clad militia— citizen troops who typically elected their own officers and underwent only occasional training. An aversion to paying taxes for a regular establishment may have been a factor, but, more deeply, the colonists were reluctant to view fighting as a normal function of society. In fact, the seaboard members of the legislatures voted funds only grudgingly for the defense of backwoods settlers, and throughout the repeated conflicts with France the lawmakers waited to provide Britain with supplies and men until convinced that their own immediate interests were in jeopardy.

Only a few church groups, however, notably the Quakers, heeded the scriptural injunction, "Thou shalt not kill." The "premeditated and determined destruction of human beings," wrote Anthony Benezet in his *Thoughts on the Nature of War* (1766), was "a sad consequence of the apostasy and fall of man; when he was abandoned to the fury of his own lusts and passions." For over half a century William Penn demonstrated the practicability of the divine way by keeping peace with the Pennsylvania Indians through a policy of fair treatment. But the doctrine of trusting alone to Heavenly protection created problems for a sect which, wielding at the same time the reins of government, had responsibility for the lives of non-Quakers as well as their own. At first the Assembly under popular pressure made appropriations for defense after hostilities had once erupted, salving their consciences by voting minimum amounts for objects left carefully undefined. Thus in 1740, following the onset of the third war with France, they designated the money "for the use of the King, for such purposes as he should direct." But as time went on the leaders came to realize that the responsibilities of power required them to forsake their principles or compromise them into a nullity. Hence in 1756, alarmed by General Braddock's defeat the year before by the French and Indians on Pennsylvania soil, and facing the final struggle with the Gallic foe, the Friends as a body withdrew from the government, tactfully leaving military preparations to more willing hands.

Henceforth the Quakers confined themselves to purging the sin from their own hearts. More worldly members like James Logan, for many years a high provincial official, justified defensive war, holding the absolute doctrine to be too far advanced as yet for mankind; and, when the War for Independence came, individual Friends found it possible to square their scruples with service in the field. The other nonresistant sects in Pennsylvania, such as the Mennonites, Dunkers, and Moravians, preserved their convictions untarnished. Possessing relatively few adherents and living to themselves, they escaped the Quakers' dilemma of having to defend the lives and property of the population in general.

Although the bulk of the Americans were not pacifist-minded, and although patriot spokesmen freely indulged in bellicose rhetoric as the crisis with England deepened, the basic disposition of the colonists is shown by the fact that even the hot-tempered crowds, unlike nationalist mobs in the new nations of the twentieth century, invariably flinched from inflicting death. As the British historian W. E. H. Lecky has observed, no people in history have been "more signally free from the thirst for blood, which in moments of great political excitement has been often shown both in England and France." The rioters contented themselves, rather, with pelting their victims with brickbats and dung, damaging their property, tar-and-feathering them, and hanging them in effigy. The six or seven fatalities attending these disturbances all came at the hands of the British.

Even so, "D. R." in Purdie and Dixon's *Virginia Gazette*, January 17, 1771, roundly rebuked writers who "signified their

Joy at the Prospect of a War." "What is War?" he demanded, but a "License of Robbery and Murder." It entails "the Fatigues, the Dangers, the Sickness, the Wounds, the Death of Thousands; the Desolation of Provinces; the Waste of the Human Species; the Mourning of Parents; the Cries and Tears of Widows and Orphans." In words that have a modern ring he charged that some people nonetheless welcome the calamity so that "Trade may be brisker, that Money may circulate, that they may add a wretched Sum to their Estates." In reality, however, the colonial leaders, far from desiring a military solution of the difficulties, hoped almost to the end to obtain redress from Britain through peaceful petitions and economic reprisals. War, when it came, was the unanticipated result of pent-up emotions which on both sides had at last burst all bounds. It will probably never be known who fired the first shot on Lexington Green, but the point is not important, for by then each party was ready for bloodshed.

The colonists in their approach to social betterment were hardheaded, never wasting time on abstract goals but seeking only to do what could be done. Sir Thomas More, his imagination fired by the discovery of America, had in 1516 published *Utopia,* a book that contributed a new word to the language by picturing a land where all property was held in common, nobody worked more than six hours a day, and everybody enjoyed abundance. But those actually living in America—in any event those of British blood—dreamed no such dreams. They were by disposition gradualists, interested in improving conditions piecemeal and step by step, whether in succoring the poor, abating intemperance, or befriending racial minorities. Apart from the Friends there was no dedicated reform group, secular or sectarian, in the colonies, and the Quakers typically confined their efforts to their own adherents. How firmly this empirical attitude was imbedded was shown on two occasions when Englishmen at home sought to impose preconceived notions of a way of life on their transplanted countrymen.

Upon the initiative of the Proprietors of the Carolinas, John Locke in 1669 drew up for prospective settlers an organic law known as the Fundamental Constitutions. This document, avowedly framed to "avoid erecting a numerous democracy," provided for a social order, feudal in character, consisting of an American hereditary nobility, a landed aristocracy, a peasantry, and a legislature so constituted as to vest the control in the great landholders. It was Locke's only specific application of the principles of government which, in their general terms, pervaded the thought of all Americans. But this cumbersome structure, conceived in the quiet of his English study, could scarcely have been less adapted to a hardy frontier folk three thousand miles away. The Fundamental Constitutions met with stubborn resistance at every turn and after thirty-three years had to be abandoned without its provisions ever being put fully into effect.

The other attempt arose out of motives of human compassion. In 1732 James Oglethorpe, a member of Parliament interested in the reform of English debtor prisons, obtained with some fellow philanthropists a royal charter for the founding of Georgia as a haven where the worthy Protestant poor of Britain and nearby countries could make a fresh start in life. Since the colony would also serve as a military buffer against the Spanish in Florida, Parliament joined with private subscribers in supplying funds for it. Those qualifying as settlers were transported without charge and given plots of land with clothing and subsistence for three months. To assist the process of rehabilitation the Trustees, as the English directors were called, forbade Negro bondage so as not to restrict opportunities for free labor and outlawed the traffic in ardent spirits. In short, the venture sought to achieve two of the principal humanitarian goals of the time—the relief of poverty and the prevention of drunkenness—as well as one that still lay in the future—the abolition of slavery. In the first dozen years the Trustees sponsored some 2,500 colonists in this fashion, while many others went forth on their own initiative.

But from the outset troubles arose, for the settlers, impatient of paternalism, demanded the rights and privileges exercised by their neighbors in other colonies. For one thing, the Trustees until very near the end denied them an elective legislature. For another, the individual landholdings, which the Trustees had limited in size to prevent the development of great estates, were so small or so infertile as to discourage enterprising owners; and although the restrictions were grudgingly modified as the years passed, the colonists continued to protest. The regulations against drink and slavery indeed created such formidable problems of enforcement that the one was revoked in 1742 and the other in 1750. Understandably, the Trustees became discouraged as matters got increasingly out of hand, and in 1752, a year before the charter was to revert to the Crown, they voluntarily surrendered their authority. Once again the scheme of master planners distant from the scene foundered on the shoals of intractable human nature.

Little or no better fortune attended projects conceived in America. These in every case emanated from non-English sections of the population, and they differed strikingly from the Carolina and Georgia enterprises in contemplating a Utopian type of life for small groups of the like-minded living in isolation. In 1736, soon after the Georgia experiment got under way, Christian Priber, a Saxon immigrant bemused with the European tradition of the "noble savage," began urging on the Cherokees of the southern Appalachians a plan for a cooperative society which should also be "a City of Refuge for all Criminals, Debtors, and Slaves, who would fly thither." In Paradise, as he modestly named the proposed community, "the law of nature should be the sole law," all property and all women be held jointly, and the children be raised under common oversight. Had the scheme ever materialized, he could hardly have assembled a more unpromising lot for the purpose; but before he proceeded further than selecting the site, the colonial authorities in 1743, alarmed by Priber's further activity in promoting a hostile confederation of Southern tribes, flung him into prison, where he died a few years later.

The communities actually realized were founded by pietistic sects, which, having suffered persecution in Europe, seized the opportunity in America to dwell apart from the world and practice primitive Christianity by all working for the good of all. The occupations they pursued were farming and handicrafts, and the degree of collective ownership varied somewhat from group to group. Toward the end of the seventeenth century some Dutch followers of Jean de Labadie undertook a settlement on this basis in Maryland, and a band of Germans led by Johann Kelpius established another near Germantown, Pennsylvania, but neither lasted two decades.

The Quaker commonwealth, however, was distinctly hospitable to altruistic enterprises, and other sects of German origin took advantage of the friendly atmosphere in the eighteenth century. In 1732, the year of the founding of Georgia, a group of Seventh-Day Baptists under Johann Conrad Beissel organized a community known as Ephrata in Lancaster County. In addition to holding all important property in common, Ephrata stressed celibacy and required both sexes so to clothe themselves as to conceal "the humiliating image revealed by sin." In the 1740's and 1750's the Moravians inaugurated flourishing societies, off the beaten path, at Bethlehem, Nazareth, and Lititz, Pennsylvania, with another in Wachovia, North Carolina. Life in these communities was simple and austere. None, though, numbered more than a few hundred members, and it was the religious rather than the economic bond that held them together. Indeed, the Moravian colonies, while otherwise maintaining their identity, succumbed to private enterprise in 1762, and Ephrata followed in 1786.

These experiments in human perfection made little or no impression on the people at large. This was not only because the projects stemmed from strangers in their midst. The average colonist was too confident of obtaining what he wanted in life by his own efforts to sacrifice self-reliance to the dubious advantages of any regimented system. Already enjoying by Old World standards a heaven on earth, he saw no reason to surrender present benefits in order to anticipate Heaven above. The undertakings nevertheless revealed an aspect of the American character that, however peripheral, foretokened similar idealistic ventures in the national period.

CHAPTER IX

The
Aristocrats

THE COLONISTS accepted the idea of a graded society as given and immutable. It was the only system they had known in Europe, and they had no thought of forgoing it in their new home. Indeed, the act of migration had given them a personal stake in perpetuating it; for in America the meek were at last inheriting the earth. Here it was man alone, not his ancestors, who counted. Even the humblest folk could hope to better their condition, and the equality of opportunity that had now become theirs meant as well the opportunity to be unequal. The indentured servant, the apprentice, the common laborer—everyone in fact but the Negro bondsman—could expect in time to stand on his own feet and move upward in the world.

Still, other factors worked against a faithful duplicating of Europe's stratified order. As David Ramsay pointed out in his *History of the American Revolution* (1789), no remnants of the feudal age existed to thwart or hinder men's advancement. The occasional noblemen who went to America deserted their accustomed "splendor and amusements" only for temporary exile, usually in order to cash in on a colonial proprietaryship or a royal governorship. Even that selfless man of God, Count Zinzendorf of Saxony, left America in 1742 after thirteen months of laboring fruitlessly to unite the various German Protestant sects in Pennsylvania. Thomas Fairfax, settling in Virginia from England in 1747 at the age of fifty-four, was unique among the permanent comers in bearing so high a rank as baron, and he lived out the remaining thirty-four years of his life for the most part unobtrusively on his frontier Shenandoah Valley estate.

Some settlers, notably in Virginia, were untitled younger sons or kinsmen of peers, while to the north many belonged to the English landed or mercantile gentry. By Old World standards, though, they were members of the upper middle class and at best could provide but the entering wedge for an aristocracy. They not only lacked noble title but suffered from the want of a royal court to act as a stimulus and model. Nor could they rest their social edifice, as did the privileged caste at home, on a hereditary class of landless peasants and destitute workingmen. The enslaved blacks alone served the purpose, but they were to be found mainly in the South, where indeed the patrician order achieved its fullest development.

In the case of a few of the early colonies the London government sought by fiat to establish artificial class distinctions, but these efforts, occurring in the middle of the seventeenth century, all came to grief. The English authorities, accustomed to titles of nobility at home, were blind to the very different conditions existing in the overseas wilderness. The settlers were scattered, strong-willed, and still scrambling for a living; the thought of a social straitjacket not only outraged their sense of self-respect but also tended to deter prospective settlers. John Locke's blueprint of a quasi-feudal order in the Carolinas represented one attempt. Another took the form of the power granted Lord Baltimore as Proprietor of Maryland to confer "whatever titles" he pleased. In the first instance, the purpose, as has been seen, was to avert "a numerous democracy"; the Maryland charter, on the other hand, put the case affirmatively, asserting that, short of such a provision, "every access to honors and dignities may seem to be precluded, and utterly barred, to men well born." Baltimore, however, for reasons undisclosed, never exercised the prerogative. Consequently, the plan of an American-based peerage, which collapsed after a brief trial in the Carolinas, did not even make a beginning in Maryland.

For the settlers to build a stratified society on their own initiative and in their own terms was, however, quite another matter. This they proceeded to do in colony after colony as rapidly as time and circumstances permitted. In the case of Massachusetts, however, they did not have to wait. Not only were the founders themselves drawn from Britain's rural and urban gentry but also, as good Puritans, they considered their superior station divinely ordained. In the words of their first governor, John Winthrop, "God Almightie in his most holy and wise providence hath soe disposed of the Condicion of mankinde, as in all times some must be rich some poore, some highe and emminent in power and dignitie; others mean and in subieceion." Accordingly, they immediately assumed the key positions in government and society, sharing the honors with the foremost clergymen. They overreached themselves, however, when they sought to legislate class differences in dress. Despite the heavy penalties for disobedience, ordinary people in this new land did not understand that they were to be perpetually ordinary. To no avail did the legislature in 1651 express "utter detestation" that men "of meane condition, education and callings should take uppon them the garbe of Gentlemen by the wearinge of Gold or Silver Lace" and the like, and that "women of the same rank" should "wear silke or tiffany hoodes or scarfes." Both there and in Connecticut, which had adopted somewhat similar regulations, the resistance to them was so stubborn that they were presently allowed to fall into disuse.

In other respects, however, the aristocracy strengthened its primacy, and as the years went on, families with fortunes newly made on land or sea won admittance to the circle. The traveler Joseph Bennett wrote in 1740 of Boston, "both the ladies and gentlemen dress and appear as gay, in common, as courtiers in England on a coronation or birthday." And the author of *American Husbandry,* surveying the New England scene thirty-five years later, reported that although social demarcations were less glaring than abroad, "gentlemen's houses appear everywhere" and on the "many considerable land estates . . . the owners live much in the style of country gentlemen in England."

In New York, while the colony was still New Netherland, the Dutch West India Company had introduced a system of patroonships—immense tracts along the Hudson that the recipients were to cultivate with tenants bound to them in a semifeudal relationship. But only a few of the grants were actually made before the British took over in 1664, and of these, only Rensselaerswyck, in what is now Albany County, was to work out well. The English governors in their turn followed the Dutch example to the extent of awarding enormous estates to favored individuals. On this basis a privileged class evolved, which divided political and social preeminence in the province with the leading merchants and lawyers of New York City.

Although the historical background in Pennsylvania was different, the story there was the same. Despite the lowly antecedents of most of the Quaker settlers and their devotion to "plain living," an aristocracy of great landholders and merchant princes arose. John Smith, an old-time Friend, looking back from the year 1764, sadly depicted the change that had come over Philadelphia. During the first twenty years, he said, as the members began to accumulate means, they commenced "in some degree conforming to the fashions of the World," and after another twenty, when "many of the Society were grown rich," vanities like "fine costly Garments" and "fashionable furniture" became usual. Indeed, the foremost families, not content with handsome urban residences, also maintained country estates as retreats from the intense heat of the Philadelphia summers.

But the Southern aristocracy attained the closest resemblance to the English landed gentry. Here, in a predominantly rural economy, men on the make enjoyed the decisive advantage of an extensive servile class as well as of broad acres. Here also, to a degree unknown in the North, the Virginia patrician William Fitzhugh spoke for his class in avowing that his children had "better be never born than illbred." Josiah Quincy, Jr., visiting South Carolina in 1773, wrote, "The inhabitants may well be divided into opulent and lordly planters, poor and spiritless whites and vile slaves." The Bostonian, however, overlooked the fact that, different from the other Southern provinces, the select circle in this one also included successful merchants, thanks to Charleston, the only important seaport south of Philadelphia. Thomas Jefferson, analyzing from more intimate acquaintance the free population of Virginia, listed at the top "the great landholders";

next, "the descendants of the younger sons and daughters of the aristocrats, who inherited the pride of their ancestors, without their wealth"; thirdly, "the pretenders, men, who, from vanity or the impulse of growing wealth, or from that enterprise which is natural to talents, sought to detach themselves from the plebeian ranks"; then, "a solid and independent yeomanry, looking askance at those above, yet not venturing to jostle them"; and, finally, the "degraded" and "unprincipled" overseers, the smallest group. His description applied equally to Maryland.

The Southern gentry, however, possessed an energy and resourcefulness uncharacteristic of its Old World prototype. To maintain its position the members had to be men of affairs—tireless and responsible directors of a system of agricultural labor alien to the homeland, which, moreover, was used for the raising of staple crops uncultivated there and grown on great and often scattered plantations. They could not, however much they wished, constitute in the same sense a leisure class.

Two concepts of land inheritance derived from English law furnished potential support for an aristocratic order. The principle of primogeniture ensured that the total family realty would descend automatically to the eldest son in default of a will. This arrangement prevailed not only throughout the South but also in New York and Rhode Island, and in the modified form of a double share for the eldest son existed in all the remaining colonies but New Jersey. Entail, the other aspect of the English system, enabled an owner to leave his estate intact to a specified heir or line of heirs. This practice had legal sanction everywhere. As a matter of fact, however, neither method was much used, for where land was so plentiful there did not exist the same need as in the mother country to guard against dissipating a patrimony. Moreover, these devices, even when employed, did not work the same hardship on the disinherited, since by their own means they could acquire independent holdings and thereby actually enlarge the economic base of the upper class.

The English-appointed governor and his entourage in the provincial capital formed the apex of the social pyramid. These personages and their womenfolk emulated the pomp and glitter of the royal court at home and furnished a pattern for the great landholders, mercantile princes, and the like who composed the native aristocracy. A beadroll of such families in the eighteenth century would include the Wentworths of New Hampshire; the Bowdoins, Quincys, Hutchinsons, Olivers, Faneuils, and Hancocks of Massachusetts; the Redwoods, Browns, and Wantons of Rhode Island; the Trumbulls and Ingersolls of Connecticut; the De Lanceys, Schuylers, Van Rensselaers, Livingstons, and Coldens of New York; the Logans, Allens, Morrises, Willings, Pembertons, and Shippens of Pennsylvania; and, in the plantation colonies, the Dulanys and Carrolls of Maryland; the Byrds, Randolphs, Carters, Masons, Pages, Fitzhughs, Harrisons, and Lees of Virginia; and the Rutledges, Pinckneys, Draytons, Laurenses, and Izards of South Carolina.

Families like these buttressed their position by matrimonial alliances both within and across provincial boundaries. To cite a few cases, the New Yorker John Franklin married Deborah Morris of Philadelphia, and her fellow townsman William Shippen married Alice Lee of the Old Dominion. The Allens of Philadelphia, the Redwoods of Newport, the New York De Lanceys, the Ervings of Boston, and the Izards of Charleston took mates in three or more colonies. So considerable was the fame of the outstanding clans that a plausible rogue like Tom Bell could wheedle money from the gullible by merely claiming to belong to one or the other of them. The rare instances of gentlefolk marrying beneath their station excited dismay within their social group. To William Byrd II, for example, it was nothing short of a "tragical Story" when a wellborn Virginia girl in 1732 played "so senceless a Prank" as to marry her uncle's overseer, "a dirty Plebian."

By custom and official usage members of the gentry enjoyed the privilege of attaching certain honorific tags to their names. As in England, they alone could qualify as "Gentlemen," and only they had the right to the designations "Esquire" and "Master," although the latter term tended in ordinary speech to be pronounced "Mister." Oddly enough, "Mistress" and "Mrs.," the corresponding forms of address for the distaff side, denoted both married and unmarried ladies until late in the colonial period. The common man, for his part, contentedly answered to "Goodman" —his day of being called "Mister" was yet to come—and his

helpmate responded to "Goodwife" or "Goody." Equal consideration for class distinctions governed the allotment of pews in
Congregational churches, where persons resisting their assign-
ments were sometimes haled into court. And at Yale until 1767
and Harvard until 1772 even the order of reciting in class and the
place of students in academic processions expressed the social
standing of their parents.

Not being to the manner born, most people aspiring to gentility had to learn from scratch how to act like their betters.
Luckily, manuals for the purpose lay at hand. The great majority
were English importations, but to meet the rising demand colonial
printers as the years went on put out their own editions. These
treatises followed originals appearing in France and Italy, where
since the age of chivalry the standards of approved behavior had
been set for all Europe. Among the writings most often listed in
American booksellers' announcements and the inventories of private libraries were Henry Peacham's *The Compleat Gentleman*
(1622), Richard Brathwaite's *The English Gentleman* (1630),
Richard Allestree's *The Whole Duty of Man* (1660), and, for
feminine study, Lord Halifax's *The Lady's New Year's Gift: or
Advice to a Daughter* (1688), the anonymous *Ladies Library*
(1714) and the unsigned *Friendly Instructor* (1745), and William Kenrick's *The Whole Duty of Woman; or, a Guide to the
Female Sex from the Age of Sixteen to Sixty* (1761). Even the
commonsensical Benjamin Franklin wrote his wife from London
in 1758 that he wanted their daughter Sally to "read over and
over again the *Whole Duty of Man* and the *Lady's Library*."

These handbooks held up integrity, courage, justice, courtesy,
and piety as the hallmark of the gentleman, with modesty, chastity, tenderness, godliness, and unquestioning submission to one's
husband as the essentials of a gentlewoman. Wifely docility not
only befitted the inherent inferiority of the sex but also attested
lasting penance for the first woman's disobedience. If her yoke-
fellow proved unfaithful, wrote Lord Halifax, she should "affect
ignorance" of it; if he were a sot, she should rejoice that the fault
merely offset her own many frailties; if he were "Cholerick and Ill-
humour'd," she should avoid any "unwary Word" and placate him
with smiles and flattery; if he was unintelligent, she should take

comfort in the thought that "a wife often made a better Figure, for her Husband's making no great one." The writers, when treating behavior in company, instructed the ladies what to wear, how to arrange a dinner, what diversions were proper, and how to converse (with the admonition: "Women seldom have Materials to furnish a long Discourse").

On the principle that as the twig is bent the tree's inclined, special guides were addressed to the young. Thus Eleazar Moody's *The School of Good Manners* prescribed a plethora of "don't's" for the children of 1715—in the home, on the street, at school, and in the company of adults. Typical examples follow. "Never speak to thy parents without some title of respect, as, *sir, madam, &c.*" "Pull off thine hat to persons of desert, quality or office; shew thy reverence to them by bowing thy body." "Spit not, cough not, nor blow thy nose at the table, if it may be avoided." Young George Washington, culling his own personal rules from another English work, appropriated such precepts as: "In writing or Speaking, give to every Person his due title According to his Degree and the Custom of the Place"; "Wear not your Cloths, foul, unript or Dusty"; and "Kill no Vermin as Fleas, lice ticks &c. in the Sight of Others." Even as a grown man Washington betrayed his continuing interest in the subject by buying in Williamsburg in 1764 an American reprint of the then century-old *Whole Duty of Man*.

The gentry further evidenced their status to the world by the elegance of their attire. The pains they took to adopt the latest court styles appear in their elaborate orders to English tailors and the loud complaints over the pattern, fit, or color of the articles commissioned. Washington, for one, cautioned his London agent, "Whatever goods you may send me, let them be fashionable, neat and good of their several kinds." William Eddis wrote in 1771 after a few years in Annapolis that he was "almost inclined to believe" that a new mode spread more rapidly among "polished and affluent Americans" than among "many opulent" Londoners. Subject to the season's vagaries in matters of detail, gentlemen wore cocked hats, white ruffled silk shirts, and embroidered broadcloth frock coats, with knee breeches of fine texture and gorgeous hues, silk hose fastened with ornamental garters, and pumps displaying gold or silver buckles. Never since has the male of the species so closely rivaled the female in the brilliance of his plumage. Powdered wigs, an added adornment, began to lose favor about 1754, when George II discarded his, to be followed by the vogue of letting one's natural hair grow long and powdering and queuing it behind or tying the tail in a small silk bag. Men of all ranks, however, went smooth shaven.

Gentlewomen on festive occasions tripped about on dainty high-heeled slippers in rustling gowns of imported brocade, bombazine, sarsenet, shalloon, damask, velvet, taffeta, and other expensive fabrics. They stiffened their bodices with whalebone stays and stretched their skirts over great hoops of the same material. They kept abreast of the latest English dress designs by means of clothed dolls sent over from London, and shortly before the Revolution they had the additional help of engraved pictures. Indicative of the irresistible sweep of style, the Yearly Meeting of Friends in 1726 at Philadelphia futilely decried the "immodest fashion of hooped petticoats" and such improprieties as "bare necks" and "shoes trimmed with gaudy colors." An object of special pride was milady's coiffure, a structure painstakingly erected on a concealed crepe roller or cushion. In preparation for a ball or party she would have her hair dressed the day before and perhaps sleep in a chair that night to keep it in condition. Children, for their part, were sartorially small copies of their elders.

When the umbrella, or "imbrillo," was introduced into England from India toward the middle of the eighteenth century, its use quickly spread across the Atlantic. These portable covers against rain and sun consisted of linen or silk tops over rattan sticks, which could not be lowered. In 1744 the Scottish traveler Alexander Hamilton observed New York ladies carrying them "prittily adorned with feathers and painted." Too costly for the average purse, they constituted another badge of gentility. So also did pocket timepieces—bulky objects each separately fabricated and enclosed in gold or silver cases. For going about outdoors the first families maintained their own carriages, stylish vehicles variously called chaises, calashes, chairs, and landaus, or, still more grandly, they traveled in coaches-and-four and berlins attended with liveried drivers and footmen.

The dress of the simple folk similarly expressed their status. The men, their hair short-cropped, typically wore caps, coarse linen shirts, leather coats and aprons, homespun stockings, cowhide shoes, and either long or short buckskin breeches, while the women's garments were of equal cheapness and durability. The French Revolution's impact on America was in the years ahead to go far toward removing class differences in male apparel, but portents of what awaited revealed themselves in unexpected ways in the events leading up to the rupture with Britain. Thus, to conceal their participation in the Stamp Act violence at Boston in August, 1765, "there were fifty gentlemen actors in this scene," Thomas Hutchinson relates in his *History*, "disguised with trousers and jackets on." Their motive was doubtless to escape the possible legal consequences of their connivance, but it was probably only a desire for sheer comfort which caused the South Carolina Assembly in 1769 to permit the members to forgo wigs and knee breeches in order to transact committee business in caps and trousers—like "so many unhappy persons ready for execution," complained a newspaper commentator.

For those on top, the Anglican Church held a compelling attraction. Just as it was the allegiance of the upper class at home, so it was that of the Crown officials sent to America. The dignified ritual of the Book of Common Prayer, with its setting of fine music, exerted an undoubted appeal, but the social prestige of membership probably formed the greater magnet. At any rate hundreds of Congregationalists, Presbyterians, Quakers, Lutherans, and others, as they moved upward in the world, forsook the faith of their fathers for the more stylish communion.

Other evidences of snobbishness were even clearer. An English nobleman passing through the colonies never failed to ruffle the social waters. Lord Adam Gordon, one of the few members of Parliament ever to visit America, conquered all before him as he journeyed from Charleston to Boston in 1765; and Lord Charles Hope on a similar excursion in 1766 met with a like reception. Four years later Sir William Draper crowned his New York stay by marrying Susannah De Lancey. The convict servant Sarah Wilson merely traded on this weakness for titles when fleecing her hosts as the pretended sister of Queen Charlotte.

Two crucial moments in life—marriage and death—afforded particular opportunities for conspicuous display. Weddings were celebrated with banquets, innumerable toasts and festivities, extending sometimes over several days. A funeral obliged the bereaved family to provide the assemblage with such souvenirs of the occasion as mourning gloves and scarves and gold rings, as well as quantities of food and drink. At the burial of John Grove of Surrey County, Virginia, in 1673, the liquor consumed equaled the cost of a thousand pounds of tobacco. Governor Jonathan Belcher of Massachusetts in 1736 distributed more than a thousand pairs of gloves in memory of his wife, but Peter Faneuil two years later overtopped him with three thousand at the services for his uncle Andrew. In addition, the grief-stricken friends would don appropriate attire for a given period at their own expense; according to a shopkeeper's advertisement in the *Virginia Gazette*, March 1, 1737, this included items like "Bombazeens, Crapes, and other Sorts of Mourning, for Ladies; also Hat-bands, and Gloves, for Gentlemen."

As this extravagant fashion seeped downward in society, it placed an excessive burden on families who, desiring to do as great honor to their own departed, could ill afford the means. To ease their plight the Yearly Meeting of Friends at Philadelphia in 1729 recommended that "wine and other strong liquors" be furnished "but once." The Massachusetts legislature went so far in a series of statutes between 1721 and 1741 as to prohibit under heavy fine the "Extraordinary Expense" of gloves, scarves, rings, rum, or wine. But custom proved stubborn; and no real change came about until the colonists, provoked by the Sugar Act of 1764 and its successors, saw a chance to strike back at Britain by disusing (among other things) the mourning materials they had hitherto imported. Public meetings from New Hampshire to Georgia urged "the new mode." The *Boston News-Letter*, March 9, 1769, observed with special gratification that the rich Charlestonian Christopher Gadsden had worn simple homespun at his wife's obsequies and that "the whole expense of her funeral, of the manufacture of England, did not amount to more than £3.10s. our currency." At another South Carolina funeral the people in attendance declined to accept the gifts that the family had provided. The First Continental Congress, in 1774, climaxed these efforts by subjecting to boycott all persons who distributed scarves or went "into any further mourning-dress, than a black crape or ribbon on the arm or hat, for gentlemen, and a black ribbon or necklace for ladies." From this blow the practice never recovered.

Class differences followed the deceased even to the burial ground. Table monuments and imposing family vaults, often of marble, dignified the final resting places of the wellborn, lording it over the flimsy freestone and slate slabs of the common run. Yet these simple markers sometimes had a quiet charm of their own, with perhaps the winged head of a cherub on the gravestone of an infant and a rudely carved hourglass to warn the passerby of the brevity of the mortal span. An inscription frequent on the headstones of the humble slyly mocked the worldly posturings of gentlefolk:

> Stop here, my Friend, and cast an Eye,
> As you are now so once was I.
> As I am now so you must be.
> Prepare for Death and follow me.

One aspect of Old World patrician life the Americans did not achieve or even seek to achieve. Perhaps because of a generally more humane disposition, they recoiled from the settlement of disputes by personal combat. Although occasional duels took place during the century and a half, these typically involved royal officers on overseas assignment or recent comers not yet fully Americanized, unless they partook of the shabby character of the encounter between the Charleston youth and a sea captain over what the *South-Carolina Gazette,* September 6, 1735, termed their "pretensions to the Favours of a certain sable Beauty."

The few cases involving colonial aristocrats shocked public sentiment and, if death resulted, brought on criminal prosecutions. What was apparently the earliest such affair cost the life of Dr. John Livingston of New York in 1715 at the hands of Governor Dongan's nephew Thomas, whom the court two days afterward adjudged guilty of manslaughter. In 1728 occurred a sword fight between two Boston young men in which Henry Phillips killed Benjamin Woodbridge over differences not then or since revealed. Before the grand jury could bring in an indictment for murder the victor fled to France with the help of Peter Faneuil, a kinsman by marriage. Some years afterward, in 1770, Dr. John Haly of Charleston fatally shot Peter De Lancey, the deputy postmaster, in a duel in the candlelit parlor of a tavern. Although he, like Dongan, was convicted of manslaughter, he escaped the consequences through the pardon of the governor. In 1775 came the last instance, also between two South Carolinians, but this one differed markedly from the earlier clashes in that Henry Laurens, while willing to accept the challenge of John Grimké, declined as a matter of principle to fire on him. Happily he escaped unscathed. No one could have foreseen as the colonial period ended that the discredited practice would under altered circumstances find a new life on the frontier and wide favor in the next generation.

The continuous recruitment of the top stratum of the community reveals sharply the basic aspect of colonial society: its fluidity, the incessant movement of people upward. The American aristocracy, however undemocratic once it took form, was undeniably democratic in its method of forming. The only class struggle in that far day was the struggle to climb out of a lower class into a higher one, for, as Nathaniel Ames put it in his 1762 almanac:

> All Men are by Nature equal,
> But differ greatly in the sequel.

The self-made man thus began his career in America, to become in time a folk hero. In the absence of England's officially prescribed ranks it was, above all, the acquisition of wealth that elevated a family to social heights. Extensive land grants and other perquisites from the government, obtained perhaps through favoritism or fraud, might expedite the process. Further help could and often did come from lucrative marriages. Newspapers, with no thought of impropriety, would describe a bride as "a most amiable young Lady with a handsome Fortune," sometimes stating the amount, although, of course, the unions not infrequently joined couples already well-to-do. But, for the most part, it was industry and ability applied imaginatively to beckoning opportunities that ensured the outcome.

As early as 1656 John Hammond, a Briton who had spent many years among the Virginia and Maryland settlers, wrote that "some from being wool-hoppers and of as mean or meaner imploy-ment in England have there grown great merchants, and attained to the most eminent advancements the Country afforded." And a century later, in 1765, the scholarly officeholder Cadwallader Colden similarly said of New York that "the most opulent families, in our own memory, have arisen from the lowest rank of the people." If a writer in the *Pennsylvania Evening-Post*, March 14, 1776, is to be credited, half the property in the city of Philadelphia belonged to "men whose fathers or grandfathers wore LEATHER APRONS." Indeed, Colden believed that "The only principle of Life propagated among the young People is to get Money and Men are only esteemed according to . . . the Money they are possessed of." And even the *New-England Primer* taught:

> He who ne'er learns his A, B, C,
> Forever will a Blockhead be;
> But he who learns his Letters fair,
> Shall have a Coach to take the Air.

Some examples of nobodies becoming somebodies will make the matter more concrete. Henry Shrimpton, a London brazier, so expanded his interests and activities after settling in Boston in 1639 that he left an estate of nearly £12,000 twenty-seven years later, and with this nest egg his son Samuel (who in filial gratitude displayed a brass kettle on his "very stately house") succeeded before his death in 1698 in making himself the town's richest citizen. The Belcher family of Massachusetts progressed in three generations from the vocation of innkeeping at Cambridge to mercantile greatness in Boston and then to the officeholding eminence of the grandson Jonathan, who served as royal governor of Massachusetts and New Hampshire from 1730 to 1741 and of New Jersey from 1747 to 1757. In a like number of generations the Reverend John Hancock, an impecunious Lexington minister, apprenticed his son Thomas to a Boston bookseller; and Thomas, opening his own establishment in 1723 and later branching out into more profitable lines, amassed a fortune of £ 100,000 sterling, which at his demise in 1764 he willed to his nephew John, making him the Croesus of the patriot movement in Massachusetts. John Singleton Copley of Boston, the foremost colonial painter, who was to add to his substance and laurels in Britain, likewise came from simple beginnings, his father being an immigrant tobacconist from Ireland. Connecticut's Roger Sherman, another signer of the Declaration of Independence, started out as a shoemaker's apprentice and, after following the trade on his own for some years, turned to surveying, the law, and other fields that won him independent means.

In the Middle colonies Robert Livingston, son of a poor parson in Scotland and founder of the renowned New York clan, began his American career in 1673 at the age of twenty-one as town clerk in the frontier village of Albany and within another twenty-one years owned a princely domain of 160,000 acres. The great Manhattan merchant John Lamb, an associate of Livingston's descendants in Revolutionary days and a general in the Continental Army, was the American-born child of a Londoner who in 1724 had escaped hanging for burglary when his sentence was commuted to indentured service overseas. Isaac Norris, the progenitor of the notable Pennsylvania family, arrived in Philadelphia from England in 1691 with a little more than £ 100 and in less than a quarter-century became the colony's principal landholder. George Taylor, coming as an indentured servant from Ireland in 1736, first worked at an iron furnace in Chester County, then, setting up in the trade with a partner, accumulated his comfortable fortune. He was another man of humble pedigree to sign the Declaration of Independence. The meteoric rise of Benjamin Franklin, the runaway apprentice from Boston, has become a legendary American success story.

Although the economic situation of the Southern colonies differed markedly from that of the North, the outcome there was also the same. Thus the Irish-born Daniel Dulany, talented lawyer and political leader in early eighteenth-century Maryland, commenced his American years in 1703 as a penniless eighteen-year-old lad under indenture. In neighboring Virginia, John Carter, an English newcomer in 1649 of obscure antecedents, laid the material basis of one of that province's first families; his son Robert of Nomini Hall, known to his contemporaries as "King" Carter, owned some 300,000 acres, 700 slaves, and over 2,000 horses and other livestock at the time of his decease in 1732. William Byrd, the forerunner of another Virginia dynasty, came from England in 1671 at the age of nineteen with the bequest of some land from an uncle, which he made the springboard for a great fortune in tobacco culture and trading before his death in 1704. Philip Pendleton, grandfather of Edmund Pendleton, the Revolutionary patriot and noted jurist, had migrated from England in 1682 as an indentured servant.

In South Carolina the Manigaults, Allstons, and Laurenses, among others, conformed to the familiar pattern. The first American Manigault, a French Huguenot emigré from London in 1695, originally tried farming, then made good at victualing and more remunerative ventures, and in 1729 he bequeathed an estate that his son Gabriel by the mid-eighteenth century built into the largest fortune in the province. By contrast, Jonathan Allston was "a gentleman of immense income, all of his own acquisition," according to Josiah Quincy, Jr., who visited his plantation in 1773. Henry Laurens, like Gabriel Manigault, owed the silver spoon in his mouth to his father, a Charleston saddler who had amassed riches in that trade and other undertakings.

But only a few Americans ever achieved the accolade of English noble rank, and this came about under circumstances so fortuitous as to make it the despair of other colonists. William Phips, who had risen from shepherd boy and shipwright's apprentice on the Maine frontier to prosper as a shipbuilder in Boston, was knighted in 1687 for raising in Haitian waters a Spanish galleon laden with £300,000 of treasure, of which the Crown granted him £16,000 as well as the title. John Randolph, a distinguished Virginia lawyer and planter, obtained his knighthood in 1732 for statesmanlike skill in negotiating certain differences between the London government and his colony. William Pepperrell, a business leader and landholder in Massachusetts and Maine, won the status of baronet in 1744 in return for commanding the victorious American forces against the French fortress of Louisbourg. A more dubious case was that of the well-to-do New Jersey officeholder William Alexander, who on the basis of tenuous evidence laid claim to being the sixth Earl of Stirling. Ignoring the rejection of his contention by a House of Lords committee in 1762, he continued to profess the title, and it was as Lord Stirling that he rendered valuable service to the American cause in the War for Independence.

In a special category was the Cinderella-like story of Agnes Surriage. This comely sixteen-year-old maiden, a barefoot servant in a Marblehead tavern in 1742, so captivated Charles Henry Frankland at first sight that the English-born revenue officer from Boston sent her to school at his own expense. Then he kept her as his mistress in an elegant mansion he had built for her in nearby Hopkinton. Even his inheritance of a baronetcy did not change the relationship. But something that occurred when the couple were abroad in 1775—according to tradition, it was her daring rescue of him during the Lisbon earthquake—had this effect: Sir Henry at long last made Agnes his wife. Boston society, hitherto scandalized, now forgot the past and received her as Lady Frankland with open arms. Warmhearted by nature, she had by all accounts become through the years a person of cultivation and charm. Her unusual tale has fascinated numerous chroniclers, including Oliver Wendell Holmes, who recounted it in ballad form in *Songs in Many Keys* (1865).

Governor Francis Bernard of Massachusetts, seeing in the creation of an American peerage an opportunity to "give strength and stability" to supporters of Britain, urged the proposal on the Ministry in 1764 soon after the difficulties with the colonists arose. "Although *America*," he conceded, "is not now (and probably will not be for many years to come) ripe enough for an hereditary *Nobility;* yet it is now capable of a *Nobility* for life." Indeed, in men like Thomas Hutchinson, Philip Livingston, Franklin and Henry Laurens (to name no others) the colonies possessed personages who by Old World standards could qualify for even heritable rank. But whatever fate might have befallen the scheme if it had been put forward and adopted earlier, it could hardly have succeeded at so late a juncture. With the colonists already fearful of British designs for other reasons, anybody who accepted an honorific dignity at this stage would have marked himself indelibly as one who had sold out to the government. But the matter never came to a test, for the Ministry quietly shelved the suggestion.

By 1776 the colonial aristocracy had endured for more than a century and a half in the oldest regions, for over a century in others, and had sunk deep roots elsewhere. With the passage of time it had consolidated its position and constantly replenished its vitality with transfusions of new blood. Its members had not, moreover, used their station exclusively for self-aggrandizement and worldly display but, as a class, had considered themselves trustees for the common good, identifying their welfare with that of the community at large. In the case of the Southern gentry the need to superintend the lives of hosts of slaves served to heighten this theory of stewardship, making them feel as fit to rule as were those guardians to whom Plato had entrusted his republic.

In all the colonies men of quality occupied responsible posts in every sphere of official activity: the executive department, the provincial and local lawmaking branches, the armed forces, the judiciary. True, the alternative would have been to allow ill-prepared and possibly rash underlings to seize the reins, but the deeper reason lay in the conviction that only the rich and wellborn possessed the required wisdom and capacity. In no less degree they provided the cultural leadership. They not only exemplified for all to see the refinements of living, but they also set standards of tasteful architecture and well-kept grounds and through their patronage enabled portrait painters to pursue their calling. They assembled the best private libraries and afforded their sons superior intellectual advantages. And from their largess came the principal benefactions to religion and education, to charity and projects of community improvement.

Nor did their role in any of these respects excite resentment. Men in every walk of life not only accepted the reality of a layered society, but also believed in its rightness. The clergy preached it; all classes practiced it. Whatever might be the shortcomings of the English aristocracy—and colonial editors repeated lurid accounts from the London press of its immoralities and profligacy—the American variety was no privileged group living off the unearned increment of ancestral achievements. By and large, they had mounted the heights through shrewdness and ability and stayed there by the continued exercise of those faculties. The ordinary citizen deemed it only proper to accord them deference. Very rarely did their real or alleged abuses of power provoke popular opposition; and such occasions hardly ever lasted long.

The quarrel with the mother country had nothing to do with the stratified character of British society, only with the objectionable actions of certain high officials. Not even the fiery Tom Paine condemned the class system in his tract *Common Sense,* when blasting the titular head of the system as "the royal brute." Nor did the framers of the Declaration of Independence do so later that year. Although they proclaimed that all men are created equal, they merely rebuked their brethren at home for suffering George to act the "tyrant" toward his American subjects. To be sure, in the events foreshadowing this final crisis the colonial gentry betrayed divided sympathies, notably in New York and Pennsylvania, some siding ardently with Britain or at least seeking to prevent an irreparable break. But the well-informed Thomas McKean, himself a signer, stated in retrospect that upwards of two thirds of the country's "influential characters"—that is, the overwhelming majority—had favored the American cause.

The heritage of a common history and culture bound the upper-class patriots to the homeland no less than it did the loyalist minority; but, unlike the latter, they had developed a passionate attachment to colonial self-government, a fierce jealousy of any encroachments on the authority they had so long and capably wielded. Besides, the new taxation and trade legislation, falling heaviest on the well-to-do, supplied a potent economic motive that was intensified by the conviction that, if the present enactments went unchallenged, worse ones would follow. The phenomenal progress of the colonies during the many years that London had permitted them virtual autonomy thoroughly justified in their minds implacable resistance to the ministerial innovations.

To counteract the measures, however, the members of the aristocracy required the support of the humbler elements; but this they were accustomed to get. Sometimes to their alarm these allies threatened the orderly course of opposition by gratuitously resorting to riot and violence, but the men of quality were invariably able to regain control. In recognition of their role the Continental Congress, when the war broke out, unanimously chose a Virginia aristocrat as commander in chief of the armed forces, and in due course a grateful Republic named him its first President. The revolt against upper-class dominance was to come in later times.

CHAPTER X

The Mind of the People

Nothing perhaps was more surprising in 1776 than the varied and vigorous intellectual life of the Americans. The founders of the colonies had feared that distance from the centers of Western civilization would reduce the settlers to a state of savagery; and wilderness conditions did in fact pose formidable obstacles. The necessity of wresting a living from untamed nature, the scattered population, and the absence or feebleness of tax support for popular education all tended to distract attention from the importance of learning, while the presence of immigrant groups from non-British countries interposed a language barrier.

Yet the colonists were never in serious danger of lapsing into barbarism. Counter influences were too strong. The transplanted people, whether from England or other lands, had no thought of leaving civilization behind. They cherished their ancient heritage. Moreover, the desire to arm the young with a knowledge of the Bible for the inevitable contest with Satan encouraged literacy; and the concern of parents to help their offspring advance in the world provided a potent additional incentive. In the case of the followers of John Calvin, as has been seen, the two aspirations worked with combined force.

Education characteristically began in the colonial home. The family imparted the rudiments of spelling, reading, and writing; or, if the parents lacked sufficient knowledge or time, a neighbor, usually an indigent widow, would assume the task for a fee, using her kitchen as a classroom. This practice, commonest in New England, was dignified with the name of dame school. Along with these formal exercises, influences of a more informal kind helped shape the child's development. The incessant performance of chores on the farm or about the shop instilled self-reliance and probably fostered more sturdiness of character than the sermons to which children were exposed every Sunday at church. They also learned mechanical skills as well as a knowledge of the fauna and flora of the vicinity that they could not have gained from books. Boys along the seaboard often picked up the elements of navigation by accompanying their elders on fishing and trading expeditions.

For the children of the poor the apprenticeship system provided a more specialized form of vocational training. It did not stop with this, however, as it normally did in England. Colonial law as a rule obligated a master to teach his charges reading and writing as well as a particular trade, and not infrequently the articles of indenture added ciphering, or numbers. To comply with these conditions some masters paid for the instruction in daytime or evening classes off the premises. In either case the arrangement typically required that the lessons be given from three to nine months annually over a period of at least three years.

These two methods—the home or the dame school, and the apprenticeship plan—introduced the great majority of colonial children to learning. Neither method, to be sure, worked perfectly. Families might on occasion ignore their duty; and everywhere there were masters who violated their obligations and had to be haled into court. In Massachusetts, indeed, where the official zeal for education was unsleeping, tendencies toward parental neglect in the beginning so alarmed the authorities that they resorted after a time to legal coercion, an example which neighboring Connecticut and New Hampshire followed. As a result, these infant colonies, while still struggling for survival, devised the nearest approach to the modern American system of free public education then known in the English-speaking world. Acting not on theory but to meet a specific need, they strictly limited the part the government should play. Although they legislated schools into being, they did not require attendance, and they allowed each community to decide for itself whether to levy the cost of teaching on the taxpayers collectively or only on the pupils' families.

Massachusetts, as the leader in this educational departure, best illustrates the measures adopted. In 1642, it merely set fines for parents who failed to teach their children to read. Five years later, disappointed with the results, the legislature shifted the obligation in the more settled areas from the home to the communities and required them additionally, as they grew in population, to furnish instruction of a more advanced character. Specifically, the statute of 1647 provided that when any town (that is, township, in the common American sense) attained fifty householders it must on pain of fine appoint a teacher of reading and writing for "all such children as resort to him" and that towns with a hundred families and upward must further maintain secondary or "grammer" schools "able to instruct youths so farr as they shall be fitted for the Universitie." The act left optional who should foot the bill— "the inhabitants in genrall" or the students' parents—and in practice both methods, sometimes in conjunction, were used in Massachusetts down to the Revolutionary War and after.

Carrying out the law, however, presented continuing problems, and the intention of the framers was never wholly realized. Towns, notably in the interior, sometimes felt too poor or simply refused to comply, finding it cheaper to pay the fines. Boston, the chief population center and seat of the government, was in fact one of the few places to abide by all of the regulations all of the time. In Connecticut and New Hampshire the legislation encountered similar obstacles. However, despite the difficulties of enforcement, the children in these New England colonies enjoyed more abundant educational facilities than those in any other part of America.

Under the system as fully in effect, the youngsters, usually at the age of seven, progressed from the dame school or its equivalent to the grammar, or "Latin," school, or "academy." Only those heading for college and presumably for future prominence were expected to stick out the course. At this upper level the boys for seven grueling years concentrated on Latin, the traditional language of religion and learning, supplementing it mainly with Greek, mathematics, rhetoric, and ancient history. A larger proportion of youths than in the more stratified society of Britain went on to grammar school, but public pressure nevertheless caused the authorities over the years to establish an alternative and less difficult institution for children not aiming at college. The writing, or "English," school, as it was called, offered intensive drill in spelling, reading, penmanship, and arithmetic in a matter of only months or a year. That these more practical subjects met a popular need is reflected by the fact that the students at writing schools in Boston in 1773 outnumbered those in the Latin grammar schools by more than four to one.

Private schools, though very much the exception in Massachusetts, Connecticut, and New Hampshire, were elsewhere virtually the only formal means of education. In Rhode Island and the Middle Atlantic region, for instance, the churches dominated elementary education. The English as well as the German and Dutch denominations sought in this manner to assure themselves a steady flow of juvenile recruits, charging tuition or not according to their parents' financial ability. The Society for the Propagation of the Gospel in Foreign Parts was especially active. Paralleling its endeavors to bring the three R's to Indians and Negroes, this Anglican agency established charity schools for indigent white children at Newport, New York, Philadelphia, and other places.

Secondary education in this central seaboard section, however, was the product of lay initiative. These schools depended on tuition fees for support and, even when aided in a few cases by the government, existed only in communities large enough to provide sufficient patronage. The instruction, which generally had no fixed length, was typically utilitarian, though usually emphasizing more exacting subjects than those taught in the Yankee writing schools. The curriculum of the New York grammar school, founded in 1732 with legislative help, included, for example, navigation, bookkeeping, and geography; and Benjamin Franklin devised for the Philadelphia Academy, which opened in 1751 with municipal assistance, an even broader program, if one that was never fully realized. Supplementing such formal educational facilities were miscellaneous courses offered for pay by self-advertising instructors, who also operated to some extent in New England centers. Persons wanting to increase their earning power might so study

surveying, accounting, marine astronomy, and the like. Those
seeking social polish could learn fencing, horsemanship, and the
"elegant" language of French among other graces. The abundance of the newspaper notices indicates that these specialized
efforts, appealing to both old and young, attracted extensive and
continuing support, although they too were confined to city
dwellers.

The Southern colonies did the least to extend educational
opportunities. The sharper class lines, the rural style of living, and
the weaker religious interest in promoting knowledge all stood in
the way. In widely scattered places, however, there were elementary schools for destitute children, established sometimes by
the local authorities but more often through private means. The
Virginian Benjamin Syms, for instance, endowed a charity school
in Elizabeth City County in 1635; and George Whitefield's
Orphan House, located on grounds granted by the Georgia government and supported by popular contributions, affords an example in the 1740's. Secondary education in the South was in an
even worse plight, falling mainly to a handful of tuition-charging
schools in and about Charleston and Annapolis. As in the North,
however, the people in these and a few other towns could pay for
lessons from self-appointed teachers. Hundreds of such advertisements appeared in the Charleston papers over the years.

The inadequacy of popular facilities, however, did not worry
the gentlefolk, who had money enough to make the special arrangements that their position in society demanded. They generally educated their children at home either by engaging a tutor
from a Northern colony or from Britain or by confiding the duty
to a competent indentured servant. John Carter, indeed, left
orders in his will in 1669 to procure a qualified servant to teach
his six-year-old son, the later "King" Carter; and the young
George Washington likewise received his first lessons at the hands
of a servant whose time his father had purchased. Still other
parents sent their boys overseas to Eton or some other respected
English school. The *South-Carolina Gazette* in 1765 estimated
that an annual £2,000 sterling was drained from that province
alone in this fashion. In no other part of America were upper-class
lads as a rule so well educated or lower-class ones so poorly.

Whether in the North or South, girls received but scant attention. By general consent the simplest elements of learning sufficed for their predestined role of wives and mothers or for such jobs outside the home as ill chance might allot them. In fact, it was even doubted that they had the mental capacity for more. Girls who secured any regular education at all rarely had more than two or three years, and sometimes only a few months. A few managed to go on to secondary schools, either separately or in the company of boys; but none, however richly deserving, could go on to college, where men alone were admitted. City women, if merely seeking stylish graces, might acquire them at will from preceptors advertising in the press. These "polite Accomplishments" varied in nature from fancy needlework, "flourishing" (ornamental penmanship), painting on glass, and the art of making artificial flowers to dancing, vocal and instrumental music, and a knowledge of French.

Only the most self-assured rebelled at the discriminatory treatment. Abigail Adams, for one, keenly resented the fact that she "never was sent to any school," and the future President's wife feelingly shared the irritation of her friend, the author Mercy Otis Warren, over the belittling of feminine brains. With some asperity Mrs. Warren insisted that "the Deficiency lies not so much in the Inferior Contexture of Female Intellects as in the different Education bestow'd on the Sexes, for when the Cultivation of the Mind is neglected in Either, we see Ignorance, Stupidity, & Ferocity of Manners equally Conspicuous in both." Such sentiments, however, were expressed only in private and in any case would have too far outrun the times to shake male certitudes.

Schoolhouses were generally built of rough-hewn logs loosely wedged with mud. By modern standards they lacked everything but ventilation, which in winter the chinks in the walls rendered all too insistent. Coarse board shelves edging the interior of the single room answered for desks; blackboards, maps, and pencils were unknown, while goose quills served for pens and birchbark often for writing paper. An important duty of the schoolmaster and the older scholars was to cut the quills and keep them constantly in repair.

As befitted so Spartan an environment, discipline was harsh

and swift, with the whipping post frequently in use. True, the
veteran Pennsylvania Mennonite educator Christopher Dock
counseled in his *Schul-Ordnung* (1770) that gentleness and appeals to children's pride yielded better results; but his book, the
earliest known American text on pedagogy, reached few beyond
his German compatriots. Here and there, however, schoolmasters
discovered the same principles on their own. Young John Adams,
for instance, doubling as a teacher when reading for the bar,
found for himself that "incouragement and praise" worked better
than "punishment, and threatning and Blame." Such heretics,
however, proved too exceptional to affect the established practice.
Had not the Bible itself sternly warned against sparing the rod?

A single master taught all subjects, even in the secondary
schools; and the pupils after memorizing their lessons went separately to their desks to recite. This method, however mechanical,
had at least the merit of allowing each child to progress according
to individual ability and application—an advantage that the nineteenth century sacrificed when mounting enrollments led communities to group the children into grades. The standard manual
for beginners was the *New-England Primer*. Based on an English
prototype and first published in Boston around 1690, this little
reader found favor throughout the colonies, continuing in use
with slight revision until long after the Revolution. Its total sales
have been estimated at over six million. The unknown compiler,
to quicken juvenile interest, often presented his somber religious
themes in rhyme and accompanied them with rude woodcuts. The
illustrated alphabet, which began with "In Adam's Fall/We
sinned all," made timely application of the couplet under letter
"F": "The idle Fool/is whipt in School." In the Latin grammar
schools the mainstay for seventy years was *A Short Introduction
to the Latin Tongue* (1709), by Ezekiel Cheever, a famous
pedagogue in Connecticut and Massachusetts, who numbered
young Cotton Mather among his charges. This handbook similarly
outlasted the colonial period.

The settlers from Continental Europe went their own way. By
and large they chose to give their offspring merely the rudiments
of an education, basing instruction, like the Anglo-Americans, on
pious subject matter. They conducted their schools, however, in

the foreign tongues in the hope of perpetuating their Old World identities. This held back their children from entering the mainstream of colonial life and retarded the adoption of English as the universal speech. The provincial governments, always eager for manpower, nevertheless condoned the separatist practice; and the Society for the Propagation of the Gospel, valuing a common Protestantism above a common vocabulary, actually aided immigrant groups on occasion with schoolmasters, pastors, and reading materials in their respective languages. The groups most resistant to change were the two largest and most isolated: the Germans in Pennsylvania and the Dutch in New York.

The Germans not only instituted their own schools but also supplied their communities with books, tracts, almanacs, and newspapers in their own tongue. Like the colonists of English stock, they aimed to establish a permanent overseas extension of their fatherland. It has been noted that by 1751 Franklin came to fear that they would "Germanize us instead of our Anglifying them," and Provost William Smith of the College of Philadelphia considered them so wanting in loyalty to Britain that they might side with France in the event of another war. Consequently, in 1754 Franklin and Smith united with others of similar mind in seconding the program of the Society for Promoting Christian Knowledge among the Germans in America. This body, newly formed in London, set up in the next few years a dozen or so free elementary schools in Pennsylvania, which taught English to the pupils as a second language and acquainted them with "the Constitution and interest of the Colonies." But the German leaders rightly perceived in the project an insidious attempt to wean the young from parental beliefs and through unremitting opposition closed the last of the schools within a decade.

Insensibly, however, circumstances helped to bridge the gap. The most rapid assimilation occurred in the more thickly settled coastal region. There, as the years went by, more and more German children attended private bilingual schools in Philadelphia, while their elders learned the strange tongue and ways through association with their English neighbors. The institution of bond labor also helped by requiring apprentices and indentured servants to learn enough English to follow their masters' orders.

Above all, the exclusive use of English as the language of the government had an inevitable effect. Increasingly, intermarriage took place, and German families anglicized their names (Schmidt to Smith, Müller to Miller, and so on). The process fell short of completeness, notably in the back country, where most of the newcomers lived, but even these people used occasional English words and grammatical constructions and otherwise modified both their idiom and their customs.

The Dutch story was much the same. Like the Germans, they dwelt for the most part on farms, safe from unsettling urban influences. The Dutch, however, had been firmly established in New Netherland before the English ever came on the scene; and in their eyes the Anglo-Americans were the intruders. They differed further in relying chiefly on passive resistance rather than on concerted opposition to meet the threats to linguistic and ethnic identity. Yet basically the same anglicizing forces were at work. The Swedish traveler Peter Kalm, visiting New York province in 1748, noted that although the elderly still generally spoke the mother tongue even they had discarded many of their ancient ways, while the young talked "principally *English* . . . and would take it amiss if they were called *Dutchmen* and not *Englishmen*." In the case of both the Dutch and the Germans, however, enough remained faithful to the ancestral tongue to oblige the patriots early in 1776 to seek their support for Independence by circulating translations of Paine's *Common Sense*.

In sum, the education of the colonial youth was the product of many factors, some adopted or adapted from the Old World, some due purely to American conditions. The result, though affecting children differently and unequally, was to bring literacy—the key to further knowledge—to a greater proportion of the people than anywhere else on the globe. New England, with its statutory schools and largely homogeneous population, achieved the best record. While no contemporary figures exist, a historian's painstaking examination of the relative frequency of signatures as contrasted with marks on official documents indicates that in Massachusetts and Connecticut the illiterates in 1700 numbered only one out of twenty. John Adams in 1765 could observe that such hapless New Englanders were "as rare a Phenomenon as a

Comet." A similar but narrower investigation of wills in Virginia, where educational opportunities were fewer, places the ratio during the first half of the eighteenth century at roughly one illiterate in four, also surprisingly low for the age. Even when it is taken into account that many illiterates had no need to sign legal papers and that scrawling a signature in any case implied no general proficiency in reading or writing, the showing still represents a considerable achievement on the part of a people living on the fringes of civilization.

Observers from the homeland uniformly praised the speech of the colonists. Lord Adam Gordon around the time of the Stamp Act went so far as to say that "the English tongue being spoken by all ranks" in the region between Philadelphia and Virginia surpassed in purity that of "any, but the polite part of London"; and Dr. John Witherspoon, president of the College of New Jersey from 1768 to 1794, observed from longer and wider experience that the language of "the vulgar" throughout America was "much better" than that of their like in Britain. The Scottish educator, noticing fewer differences of usage between colony and colony than between county and county in the mother country, ascribed this superiority to the colonists' "moving frequently from place to place" and thus being "not so liable to local peculiarities either in accent or phraseology." Undoubtedly an equal factor was the widespread literacy.

The English language, though, did not stand still upon crossing the ocean. Witherspoon himself coined the expression "Americanisms." The American language first grew out of the need of the settlers to designate strange plants and animals. For this purpose they invented such names as *Jimson* (that is, Jamestown) *weed, eelgrass, eggplant, mudhen, copperhead,* and *groundhog.* From ignorance or carelessness they also sometimes used familiar words in new senses. The outstanding instance was *corn,* which signified wheat in the Old World but maize in the New. They adopted still other terms from their non-English-speaking neighbors. The Dutch supplied, for example, *sleigh, boss, cruller,* and *Yankee* (apparently from *Janke,* a diminutive of the common Dutch name *Jan* or John); the Germans, *sauerkraut* and *pretzel;* the French, *prairie* and *portage.* How differently United States history would

read without *Yankee* and *prairie* and the post-Revolutionary
French contribution of *frontier!* But the Indians, by reason of
their long-continued presence, enriched the language the most. On
the one hand, they provided a wide range of expressions, like
tomahawk, canoe, raccoon, and *hickory;* on the other, such geographic names as *Massachusetts, Potomac,* and *Susquehanna.* By
contrast, the Negroes probably had their main impact less on
language than on diction. This rising tide of Americanisms pre-
saged the far greater liberties that succeeding generations would
take with the ancestral tongue.

Of informal instruments of education, the most important was
doubtless printing. The primitive wooden presses hardly differed
from Gutenberg's original in Christopher Columbus's youth, and
these as well as all of the type came from England until nearly the
end of the colonial period. With few or no assistants, the printer
assembled the letters by hand, word for word and line by line, and
then with muscular power worked the pages through the press.
However great his pride in performing an indispensable community function, his arduous employment seldom yielded more
than a bare living. Although Cambridge, the seat of Harvard
College, acquired a press as early as 1638, other communities
followed so slowly that printing facilities did not become widespread until well into the next century. On the side the printer
usually dealt in general merchandise—stationery, books, soap,
tea, patent medicines, compasses, mirrors, and fur hats. If he
stood well with the royal authorities, he might further add to his
income by serving as local postmaster. As printer, he relied on
selling commercial and legal blanks, on such government work as
he could obtain, and on issuing from time to time flyers, pamphlets, and books. As the years went on, an increasing number of
printers brought out almanacs and newspapers. By exploiting all
these opportunities Franklin, who missed no chance to turn an
honest penny, acquired early a financial competence.

The first almanac was a product of the earliest American
press. Though a secular document, it came out in Puritan Massachusetts in 1639, a year before the famous Bay Psalm Book. This
tells something of the place these annual paperback compilations
occupied in the beginning as well as why they leaped in number as

the population grew. They were as necessary to the colonists for the life at hand as the Bible was for their life to come. Costing but a few pennies, they went into homes where, as an editor in 1776 said, "the studied ingenuity of the Learned Writer never comes." Of the more notable undertakings Franklin's *Poor Richard's Almanack,* starting in 1732 in Philadelphia, reached a circulation of over ten thousand, only to be outstripped by Nathaniel Ames's in Boston which from 1726 to 1764 reputedly averaged a yearly sixty thousand.

Besides meteorological data and weather predictions the booklets offered an abundance of miscellaneous matter: medical advice, notes on farming, cooking recipes, public documents, excerpts from historical works, poems, anecdotes, aphorisms, and jokes. As the troubles with Britain heightened, editors devoted increasing space with increasing fervor to the patriot cause. The tax the Stamp Act levied on almanacs no doubt gave the effort a special incentive. Thus Nathaniel Ames, Jr., successor to his father, enjoined his readers in his 1766 edition that "above all things" they should trust Heaven to rebuke "those who would oppress and tyrannize over us," and after a decade of mounting friction he bluntly avowed in 1775 that the execution of Charles I set a precedent for *"Tyrants"* and pointedly supplied practical directions for the making of gunpowder. These well-thumbed annuals, reflecting as well as directing popular sentiment, had an incalculable effect in preparing the rank and file for the final break with England.

Daily newspapers wielded a more continuing influence in these climactic times. The fourth estate, however, was a tardy arrival, in the Old World as well as the New. The great city of London itself had no regular journal prior to the semiweekly *Gazette* in 1665—over half a century after the founding of Jamestown—and it lacked a daily until the *Courier* appeared in 1702. In both Britain and the colonies the government frowned on the development of the press from fear of its political power, and in America the scarcity of towns posed a further obstacle. Thus weeklies were the rule, with merely fleeting attempts at semiweeklies or triweeklies.

Boston, the first to enter the field, attempted a monthly news-sheet in 1690, but it lasted only a single issue. The editor, Benjamin Harris, had failed to obtain the advance official approval then required, and, worse, he had rashly censured the barbarities of Britain's Indian allies toward French captives in the current war. Consequently, the real beginning of the American press occurred in the new century, when the weekly *Boston News-Letter*, "Published by Authority," was established in 1704 by John Campbell, the local postmaster. It enjoyed the longest life of any colonial journal, continuing to 1776. Meanwhile, other towns launched papers: Philadelphia in 1719, New York in 1725, Annapolis in 1727, Charleston in 1730, Newport in 1732, and Williamsburg in 1736, until every province but New Jersey and Delaware possessed at least one weekly. These two, however, depended on sheets from New York and Philadelphia.

The rise of the newspaper reflected the heightened interest in news as the population expanded, as well as the need of merchants and land salesmen to advertise their offerings and of colonial administrations to announce acts and regulations. Franklin was a particular patron of journalism. With his characteristic blend of altruism and practicality he readily perceived how to extend popular enlightenment at the same time he lined his pocketbook. Starting out in 1729 by acquiring the moribund *Pennsylvania Gazette* for a song and making it a civic-minded and lucrative sheet, he went on to subsidize newspaper ventures from Rhode Island to South Carolina, indeed even in three West Indian islands, in return for a temporary share of the profits. Moreover, a succession of printers he had trained went into the business for themselves. No other individual left so deep an impress on colonial journalism.

By 1776 thirty-two journals were in existence, published mostly at the principal seaports and provincial capitals, whence they circulated far and wide through the countryside. This "incredible number," according to a *Pennsylvania Packet* article, February 12, 1776, exercised an influence which "could never have been so great in any community, yet known, as in these *pantoplebeian* colonies." With a yearly cost of from six and a half to ten shillings, local currency, most people could afford to subscribe, and those who could not borrowed their neighbors' papers or read copies at the taverns. The *Boston News-Letter,* when it was New England's only paper early in the century, had fewer than three hundred subscribers, but by the 1750's, despite the multiplying competition, an editor could count on five hundred or six hundred, and the dramatic events from the Sugar Act onward raised the figure for the major newspapers to between 1,500 and 3,600.

The typical journal consisted of four small pages of fine print three or four columns wide, unrelieved with either headlines or pictures. Shears and paste furnished the bulk of the contents, the publisher generally clipping his overseas reports from the British press and the news of other colonies from their respective papers. The lapse of time—six weeks or more in the case of Europe—did not at all dampen the reader's interest, for the accounts were still fresh to him. Local happenings received slight notice on the well-warranted assumption that the residents already knew the facts. On occasion the paper also ran pieces by contributors on religious, economic, and social topics and, as the Anglo-American crisis intensified, gave ever greater attention to political and constitutional issues. There was sometimes, too, original or copied verse in a "Poet's Corner." Advertisements commonly occupied a quarter or more of the space.

The publisher led a harried existence. With such journeymen and apprentices as he could afford, he not only set the type and printed the sheet but also did everything else. Besides selecting and scissoring out-of-town news, he gathered local items, solicited ads, addressed and mailed the out-of-town copies, and all the while worried constantly over the circulation. Many a newspaper went to the wall through the years. In the 1770's, according to the proprietor of the *Massachusetts Spy,* at least six hundred subscribers "with a sufficient number of advertisements" were required to keep afloat. Even the papers that made good faced endless difficulty in collecting unpaid obligations. The *New-Hampshire Gazette,* January 15, 1768, in a typical plea plaintively reminded its readers and advertisers that "it is not possible to print News Papers without a Stock of Paper, Ink, Hands, and in

Winters a good Fire." To counter the excuse that no cash was to
be had, hard-pressed editors would offer to accept the equivalent
in food, wool, or firewood.

Criticism of public men or affairs created an additional problem. As in Britain, this exposed journalists to the severities of the
law—a danger they also ran in their related capacity as printers of
controversial pamphlets and broadsides. Until nearly the end of
the seventeenth century, in fact, all publications were supposed to
obtain a prior government license. Although this system of advance censorship thenceforth lapsed, it was replaced on both sides
of the Atlantic with a hardly less repressive censorship after the
fact. Now the resentful branch of the government could prosecute
the offending printer or author for seditious libel under the common law.

This method seemed fairer to an accused, for it customarily
assured him the safeguard of being indicted by the grand jury
before his case could go to the petit or trial jury. At neither stage,
however, did the truthfulness of the comment constitute a defense:
the jurors' sole function was to determine whether the defendant
was responsible, leaving the trial judges to declare the punishment
for his misdoing if they decided he had acted with malice. The
penalties, unregulated by statute, ranged from such relatively
minor ordeals as an official reprimand and the public burning of
the obnoxious composition to such harsher ones as a fine, the
exaction of a bond for future good behavior, and detention in the
pillory or prison, with these sentences on occasion variously
combined. In addition, the legislature, proceeding through either
or both houses, retained its traditional right, independent of the
judiciary, to punish at will an offender for contempt or breach of
its authority.

In the great Blackstone's words, liberty of the press thus
consisted solely in the absence of *"previous* restraints upon publications, not in freedom from censure for criminal matter when
published." Not unlike Jonathan Edwards expounding the relation
of the divine authority to man, the English jurist maintained that
"the will of individuals is still left free; the abuse only of that free-
will is the object of legal punishment." The "bad sentiments" did
not need, in the modern phrase, even to involve a clear and

present danger; the words in themselves were enough. The effect of this system in daunting the typographical fraternity is understandable.

A printer who nevertheless braved the consequences was John Peter Zenger, the German-born publisher of the *New-York Weekly Journal*. Although he was not the only one to risk official reprisal, the unexpected outcome of his hardihood has made him a permanent symbol in the American struggle for unfettered expression. Zenger stubbornly believed it was a newspaper's duty to scrutinize the actions of public figures, since "the best defense we have against their being knaves is to make it terrible for them to be knaves." Backed by the political foes of the royal governor, William Cosby, he loosed a series of vitriolic attacks in 1734 on that unprincipled and arbitrary executive. The enraged official, resolving at all costs to stop the barrage, first tried on his own motion to get the grand jury to indict the editor, then attempted to persuade the two branches of the legislature to join him for the purpose; and when these efforts failed, he and the appointive upper house circumvented the grand jury and took the case directly to the petit jury by means of the rarely used legal process known as an information.

Unable to furnish the exorbitant bail, Zenger remained in jail for ten months until he came up for trial in August, 1735, meanwhile bringing out the *Journal* with the help of his wife and political associates. Andrew Hamilton, a Philadelphia lawyer of intercolonial prestige, served as his principal counsel. Although Hamilton himself as a member of the Pennsylvania upper house had earlier supported legislative penalties on the press, he viewed very differently the power exercised by the judiciary under the common law. With rousing eloquence he maintained the jury's exclusive right to determine the truth as well as the source of an alleged libel and to exonerate the defendant if his comments were found valid. The jurors, flouting the court's contrary instructions, jubilantly acquitted Zenger. That night Hamilton was honored at a civic banquet; vessels in the harbor boomed their cannon upon his departure for Philadelphia; and the Board of Aldermen sent after him the keys of the city in a gold box.

The verdict, though widely acclaimed, actually wrought no

change in the legal concept of seditious libel. The acquittal indeed afforded no assurance that Zenger himself might not again be called to account for a repetition of his temerity. Nor had Hamilton even contended that false accusations of officials should escape punishment, simply that the jury alone should judge the veracity. The idea that grossly partisan charges made in the heat of public controversy should be permitted broad latitude—Franklin's view that "when Truth and Error have fair Play the former is always an overmatch for the latter"—found no judicial or statutory sanction in America until well after the Revolution. Nevertheless, the case, while not altering the common-law doctrine, did in a practical sense advance the cause of journalistic independence. It showed dramatically that when community opinion was aroused against misrule a jury of the citizens would take the law into their own hands to vindicate an independent press. This demonstration nerved printers to greater fearlessness thereafter and correspondingly deterred the authorities from seeking legal measures of restraint.

That, then, was the situation when the Stamp Act in 1765 imprudently imposed British duties on all newspapers, advertisements, and virtually everything else printed in the colonies and so gave the typographical craft a personal interest in popular resistance. Articles proliferated in the press flaying the act as unconstitutionally denying the principle of no taxation without representation and as an economic death sentence. Rather than comply, the editors defiantly continued to publish without the "Symbols of Oppression" or suspended publication until the American opposition forced repeal.

At each successive stage, the newspapers advanced almost as one; no more than a handful ever sided with Britain. For the war of words they drew heavily on leading patriots, who, according to the custom of the age, generally wrote anonymously. Vigorous controversialists leaped into the fray in every part of America—among them, James Otis and the Adamses in Massachusetts, William Livingston and Alexander McDougall in New York, John Dickinson and Benjamin Rush in Pennsylvania, George Mason and Arthur Lee in Virginia, Christopher Gadsden in South Carolina. Many were lawyers who now employed in the political arena the weapons of special pleading they had developed in the courtroom. Understandably, the New York Tory Cadwallader Colden bitterly observed that "the Press is to them what the Pulpit was in times of Popery." Meanwhile, Benjamin Franklin missed no opportunity as a colonial agent to forward the cause in the London papers.

Boston and New York were the focal points of the contest, and there the Crown officials, fearing a repetition of the Zenger fiasco, freely berated their assailants but hesitated to invoke legal penalties. Gross provocations, however, stung them on a few occasions into seeking redress, but, not surprisingly, these efforts, whether directed at the grand jury or at the popularly controlled branch of the legislature, miscarried; and only once did the upper house itself respond favorably. Then, at the instigation of Governor Hutchinson, the Massachusetts Council in 1771, though unable to obtain the indictment of the editor of the *Massachusetts Spy,* dismissed on its own motion one of his contributors from a local provincial post for declining to appear for questioning. Indeed, even the suspicion that coercive measures were contemplated promised to bring the mob down on the authorities. The "present temper of the People" will not tolerate a prosecution, the New York governor confessed to the Ministry late in 1765. And in like vein the Massachusetts executive reported in 1768: "The Time is not yet come when the House is to be moved against Popular Printers however profligate and flagitious." Occasional clashes also occurred in other colonies, but in these years no editor anywhere in America suffered the legal consequences of his daring.

The editors, for their part, justified their actions both as personal right and public duty. Week after week the *Pennsylvania Chronicle,* quoting in capital letters from the Latin original of Tacitus, paraded as its motto: "Happy the age in which one can think what he pleases and say what he thinks." In like manner the *Boston Gazette* in one of its many screeds on the subject proclaimed, "Freedom of Speech is the great Bulwark of Liberty; they prosper and die together." As the controversy waxed ever fiercer, however, the printers and their writers in their partisanship came to assert this freedom only for their own cause. Liberty of the press, they now declared, belonged solely to those who pressed for liberty. And the community, lacking the machinery of the law for enforcement, nevertheless found potent extralegal means in boycotting opposition publications, threatening bodily harm to editors and, when necessary, assaulting their persons and equipment. Only two sheets—the *Boston Chronicle* during the period of the Townshend Acts and the *New-York Gazetteer* in the wake of the Intolerable Acts—stubbornly stood their ground. In both instances the proprietors were in the end driven out of the business and out of the country.

Thus the vaunted ideal of a free and unfettered press became itself a casualty of the decade of disputation. Yet that very fact, inconsistent as it was with principle, enabled the patriots to put their own case with the utmost completeness and vigor, mingling blatant appeals to prejudice and passion with carefully wrought intellectual expositions. In Franklin's words, newspapers by presenting the same "truths" in ever "different lights" could "strike while the iron is hot" as well as "heat it continually by striking." In their reasoned discussions they not only paralleled and underscored but also sometimes anticipated the anti-British arguments in the revolutionary pamphlets. Except for this sustained and well-directed offensive it is difficult to see how the people could have been sufficiently aroused to hazard the fateful step of Independence.

By contrast, magazines made very little impression on either politics or culture. Indeed, none ever actually took hold in the colonies. The few attempts had to compete for popular support with the literary fare strewn through newspapers and almanacs, or, if they sought a more cultivated audience, to rival the finished compositions in the *Gentleman's Magazine,* the *London Magazine,* and other English publications. No monthly was even tried until 1741, and the speedy demise of this Philadelphia offering foreshadowed the fate of the eight that followed in the colonial era. The most successful, Boston's *American Magazine and Historical Chronicle,* barely survived the three years from its birth in 1743. Nor did the Anglo-American crisis effect much change, for the journals then in existence considered themselves as primarily cultural vehicles. The principal exception, the *Pennsylvania Mag-*

azine, founded in January 1775 with Tom Paine as contributing editor, might, however, have endured but for the disruptive effect of the Declaration of Independence on publishing. With no sign of regret, though, the periodical printed the full text of the great document in its farewell number, July 1776.

If the colonists by and large spent their idle moments on almanacs and newspapers, an increasing number also cherished reading of a more solid and more permanent character. This bespoke growing intellectual maturity. As a writer pointed out in the *New-York Gazette and Weekly Mercury,* November 7, 1774, "Books are standing counsellors, always at hand . . . they are ready to repeat their lessons as often as we please." Three decades before, Franklin had written an English friend, "Your authors know little of the fame they have on this side of the ocean. We are a kind of Posterity in respect to them." By way of confirmation the Philadelphia cleric Jacob Duché asserted in 1771, "You would be astonished, my Lord, at the general taste for books, which prevails among all orders and ranks of people in this city."

Books accompanied the first arrivals and afterward became a symbol of the style of life the transplanted people desired to cultivate in the wilderness. During the seventeenth century they came mostly from Britain, but by 1755 the twenty-four presses operating in ten of the colonies published an estimated twelve hundred different titles in the single year. This amounted to no less than one for every thousand Americans, including infants, Negroes, and illiterate white adults (as against about one for every ten thousand Americans in 1965). In variety the output ranged from government documents—a financial plum coveted by all printers —to miscellaneous native writings and foreign volumes reprinted in America.

Pilgrim's Progress, for example, was republished in 1681 in Cambridge, Massachusetts, only three years after it came off the press in England; for the common folk it was a sort of second Bible. The eighteenth century, with its accent on secular literature and its enlarged colonial reading public, stepped up the number of reprints. They now embraced such writings as Richardson's *Pamela,* Johnson's *Rasselas,* Pope's *Essay on Man,* Addison's *Cato,* Sterne's *Tristram Shandy,* Robertson's *Charles the Fifth,* and Goldsmith's *Vicar of Wakefield* and *She Stoops to Conquer*. Indeed, they even included a legal treatise. In 1771 Philadelphia's Robert Bell published one thousand sets of Blackstone's *Commentaries on the Laws of England* after having tested the American demand with one thousand copies he had imported.

The reprints ordinarily cost less than the originals, thanks to the saving of transportation and middleman charges and the denial of royalties to the overseas owners of the rights. American underselling reduced importations over the years but never actually stopped them, since customers in out-of-the-way places sometimes found it easier to order direct from Britain. In any case, cheapness had no effect when interest was too slight to warrant American republication. In 1773, according to John Dunlap, a Philadelphian in the trade, printers had to sell three thousand copies of a sizable volume to recover the expenses of presswork, paper, and binding. Consequently, to play safe, they generally signed up a big enough list of subscribers in advance. The failure to reprint the Scriptures, however, arose not from want of demand but from lack of suitable type, and that deficiency was not fully repaired until 1782, when war cut off the flow of Bibles from the mother country. Then an edition was finally undertaken with the encouragement of the Continental Congress.

As the population and literacy grew, shopkeepers in the major towns found it profitable to go into the book business. They imported books from England and also handled American reprints of English works as well as writings by colonial authors. Some dealers mixed the intellectual fare with general merchandise; others made it their exclusive occupation. From the advent of the first booksellers in Boston in the 1640's the number multiplied so that no fewer than 135 entered the business in Philadelphia, Boston, and New York alone in the decade and a half before Independence, surpassing the total for the sixteen principal English cities apart from London. Newport had ten dealers and Charleston six. Robert Bell, the leading Philadelphian in the trade, advertised his stock in newspapers from New Hampshire to Georgia. Country folk, moreover, could buy assorted volumes at their doors from peddlers who sold them along with household articles.

The craving for writings of durable worth meanwhile led men of means to build up impressive private libraries. Thomas Jefferson, for example, inheriting a mere 40 volumes from his father in 1757, avidly added to them until by 1773 he owned 1,250 and a decade later 2,645. Even larger were the libraries of James Logan in Philadelphia and Cotton Mather in Boston, containing over 3,000 books each, and the collection of William Byrd II in Virginia with more than 3,500. That these three men were respectively a businessman, a theologian, and a large-scale planter indicates that no single background had decreed their interest.

The idea of multiplying the usefulness of a book by making it available to many readers dawned accidentally when a Boston merchant in 1656 bequeathed a small collection to the town authorities for a public library. Later, the South Carolina legislature in 1698 founded a similar institution for the whole province, and New York City followed in 1730 with one for its residents. But these libraries, even in their own areas, fell sadly short of the need, for the holdings were small in quantity as well as excessively devout in character and, in addition, were not regularly kept up. Much the same proved true of the occasional nongovernmental enterprises, notably the most ambitious of the projects, a group of thirty-some libraries formed around the turn of the eighteenth century with funds solicited by Thomas Bray, an Anglican churchman in England. They extended to nearly every parish in Maryland and to scattered places elsewhere; but the books were mainly for the established clergy and, even so, the largest collection, that at Annapolis, contained less than eleven hundred volumes. However, two libraries created late in the colonial period by individual philanthropy did function on a free general basis: that at Newport, based on a gift to the town of £500 sterling from the merchant Abraham Redwood in 1747, the other at Philadelphia, arising from James Logan's legacy of a building and his books to the municipality in 1751. But these collections, too, although Logan's exceeded three thousand volumes, had only a limited range of subject matter.

The colonial taxpayer, backward in supporting free schools and other needed public projects, understandably shrank from supplying the common herd with reading material out of his purse.

Interested citizens therefore had to devise their own means. The resourcefulness that had distinguished Americans in so many other respects served them well in this instance. The outcome was the subscription, or social, library, started by Franklin with a number of artisans and tradesmen of Philadelphia in 1731. Soon copied elsewhere, this arrangement enabled the members for a modest fee to borrow writings of the most varied kind: vocational, political, scientific, literary, historical, with usually only a sprinkling of pious works. It was the interests of the patrons that determined the make-up of the collections. Generally, voluntary groups conducted the undertakings on a nonprofit, divided-cost basis. Sometimes, however, canny booksellers organized them for personal gain.

By 1776 sixty or more subscription libraries had sprung up in towns, large and small, all the way from Falmouth (now Portland, Maine) to Savannah, though with the fewest, as usual, in the agrarian South. While they differed in the size as well as the quality of their holdings, probably none failed to widen the horizons of their users. Charleston's Library Society in 1760 had nearly three thousand volumes on its shelves. In 1774 the Union Library Society of Philadelphia, a merger of earlier organizations, housed as many as eight thousand. Franklin, thinking back in 1771 over the forty years since he had first introduced the idea, could only marvel at the results. "These libraries," he believed, "have improved the general conversation of the Americans, made the common tradesmen and farmers as intelligent as most gentlemen from other countries, and perhaps have contributed in some degree to the stand so generally made throughout the colonies in defence of their privileges."

Fortunately, the period of colonization coincided with the most glorious age of English letters. Shakespeare composed his tragedies and Bacon his *Essays* and *The Advancement of Learning* at about the time the colonists arrived at Jamestown, and Milton wrote *Paradise Lost* while the Carolinas were being settled. Bunyan published *Pilgrim's Progress* shortly before William Penn founded his province, and John Locke brought out his *Treatises on Government* not long before Salem's witchcraft delusion. Besides, there were such giants of a former era for the Americans to turn to as Chaucer and Spenser, while the literary flowering of the eighteenth century brought them the novelists Richardson, Sterne, Smollett, Defoe, and Fielding, the historians Hume and Robertson, not to speak of the poets, playwrights and essayists: Pope, Goldsmith, Addison, and Steele. More than their nineteenth- or twentieth-century descendants, the colonists also read in the original or in translation classical authors like Homer, Plutarch, Cicero, and Virgil; and many, too, knew celebrated Continental writers: Voltaire, Fénelon, Montaigne, Rabelais, Machiavelli, Cervantes, and others. Even George Washington, no great reader, acquired in manhood sets of Shakespeare, Smollett, Sterne, and Swift, as well as Homer's poetry and *Don Quixote*. Such commanding names appeared again and again in booksellers' announcements and in the entries of personal and circulating libraries. The colonists, despite their geographic remoteness, thus shared the creative imagination of the West.

As grateful partakers of the mother country's treasury of letters, the transplanted Britons, accepting a sort of imperial division of labor, felt little need for a separate literature of their own. In any event, as a correspondent observed in the *Rhode-Island Gazette,* October 25, 1732, "In the Rise of States the Arts of War and Peace, Agriculture, and the like, are of Necessity more attended to than Erudition and Politeness, that comes of course afterwards, when the *Golden Age* succeeds the *Iron*." The creative impulse nevertheless existed, though not with the urge to take published form. The authors in their solitude did not look beyond the unsung rewards of self-expression. Hence the products of their pen at most passed simply from hand to hand, none indeed seeing print until after the end of British rule, in some cases long after. Accordingly, what they wrote could not inspire others to emulate and so nourish a general tradition of American letters. The writers, to be sure, did not essay the whole gamut of English authorship. They attempted no romances or stage plays and, with a single exception, no poetry of originality. Instead they descanted autobiographically on their own doings and the life about them, recording their experiences with fidelity, insight, and native literary skill. Unlike writers abroad they did not have to tax their imaginations for the interesting and unusual. As men of the strange New World it sufficed for them to set down merely what they themselves had seen and felt.

The first examples of these closet writings were Governor William Bradford's account "Of Plimoth Plantation" and Governor John Winthrop's "Journal" of the beginnings of the Massachusetts Bay Colony. Among other works by New England Puritans in the seventeenth and early eighteenth centuries were the "Diary" kept for over fifty years by Judge Samuel Sewall, the American counterpart to Samuel Pepys, and the verse of the Reverend Edward Taylor, whose spiritual intensity and delicate imagery made him colonial America's only distinguished poet. Taylor, who expressly forbade his heirs to print his poems, had to wait longer than any of his fellow writers for posthumous recognition. His poetry in fact continued unknown until it was rediscovered and published in 1939.

As the eighteenth century advanced and the temper of the times changed, the manuscript performances took on a secular character. Outstanding now were the sprightly "History of the Dividing Line betwixt Virginia and North Carolina" with other contributions of the Virginia planter William Byrd II, and the engaging "Journal" penned by the Princeton-educated Philip Fithian while tutoring the great-grandchildren of "King" Carter in the Old Dominion. Franklin's inimitable "Autobiography," begun and in large part finished before the break with England, also remained in longhand for many years. Possibly other writings of equal quality arc permanently lost to posterity. But those which have survived provide ample evidence of the workings of the creative spirit among the colonists in their private lives.

Writings of more utilitarian purpose flowed from the press in a mounting stream over the years. These authors, far from hiding their lights under a bushel, hurried into print to promote some cherished cause—religious, political, or economic. Only now and then did any of them seek to delineate what had gone on before, and this too was usually with the hope of influencing current actions. Yet if their writings today possess little more than scholarly interest they nevertheless made a mark on their times.

The principal religious outpourings occurred in New England, chiefly in the form of sermons and expository or polemic tracts.

The Puritan clergy, the most articulate as well as the most learned in the colonies, were quick to carry their warfare with Satan and sectarian foes beyond church walls to the public at large. Although they generally discoursed in austere intellectual terms, some smote the emotions directly in their concern for human souls. The Reverend Michael Wigglesworth, the outstanding instance, frightened and fascinated his readers with *The Day of Doom* (1662), a grim and grisly epic of the Last Judgment. Though written incongruously in doggerel verse, the little book struck a chord which made it a best seller in New England for the next hundred years. By contrast, Wigglesworth's genteel contemporary, the poet Anne Bradstreet, fused a love of nature with religiosity in her lines, and her work, reflecting a European manner, lacked all popular appeal. The most erudite and prolific of the theological authors were the Mathers, father and son, whose combined output totaled over six hundred titles. Yet the only treatise to outlast the colonial era was Jonathan Edwards's masterpiece *On the Freedom of the Will*.

Historical writing, on the other hand, aside from personal and private memoirs, received little attention. Through the pages of history a people relives the past, and for many years the colonists were too occupied with living the present. Save for some depictions of early Massachusetts days, piously attesting God's hand in what had befallen, there was little historical writing in the seventeenth century. The next century, however, with its relaxed religious outlook, brought accounts that sought to record the facts from a more secular perspective and as accurately as available source materials permitted. Even so, the number of authors remained small, and with one unimportant exception they confined their narratives to single colonies. Obliged, moreover, to steal time from other pressing duties, they gave little thought to how they wrote. Nonetheless their histories, however faulty by modern standards, gave their readers a keener pride in bygone achievements that were distinctively American and helped the emergent sense of national identity.

The most scholarly and judicious work was the two-volume *History of the Colony and Province of Massachusetts-Bay* by Thomas Hutchinson, published in Boston in 1764 and 1767, which recited the story from the first settlements to the year 1750. Hutchinson, then Lieutenant Governor and soon to be Governor, had inherited a large body of manuscripts from progenitors who for four generations had, as he properly described them, been "principal actors" in Massachusetts affairs; but his work was no mere filiopietistic performance. For instance, he ascribed the heretical conduct of his original American ancestress Anne Hutchinson to her immoderate vanity. A third volume, however, written in England and appearing posthumously in London in 1828, carried the account in an increasingly partisan spirit to 1774, when Hutchinson, having lost credit as a Crown official, sailed for the mother country to report on his actions. From the Stamp Act onward he had stoutly upheld British authority against the swelling popular opposition, and his pages exhibit the scars of that ordeal. To the present-day reader, however, they also show that he was not the unconscionable villain the patriots had deemed him, but a man who, while personally disliking many of the imperial measures, nevertheless insisted on their constitutionality and on his own duty to carry them out.

Political pamphleteering—a reflection of history in the making—began with the early settlers. By dint of temperament as well as inheritance, the Americans were a disputatious lot who neglected no opportunity to inveigh against objectionable governors and lawmakers. The quarrel with the motherland, affecting the colonies collectively, called forth this propensity in combined strength. Every ministerial move begot immediate answers. The authors, fortified with extensive reading, not only cited the palpable economic grievances, but summoned cogent theoretical and constitutional arguments from English and classical history, the provincial charters, and the writings of John Locke and the natural-rights school. With the equally well-grounded framers of legislative remonstrances, they thus made it possible for the law-abiding to oppose the law in the very name of the law or, at least, of the higher law. They did not formulate a new political philosophy. They had no reason to. It sufficed to adapt to their needs principles long cherished in the homeland.

By the time the pen yielded to the sword, moreover, they enjoyed the enormous advantage of occupying the field almost unopposed. The King's adherents as obedient subjects blindly trusted to the British authorities to handle the situation. No formidable Tory pamphleteer took up the cudgels until 1774, following the Intolerable Acts and the holding of the First Continental Congress, and by then it was too late. Few printers even when so disposed dared bring out the tracts for fear of mob reprisals, and public gatherings angrily consigned the writings to the flames. As in the case of the newspaper press, the right of free discussion did not at that stage embrace in patriot eyes the privilege of dissent. At any rate ten years of mounting acerbity had closed most men's minds to counterarguments.

Of the patriot pamphlets two in particular proved landmarks, for each directed the American philosophy of imperial relations toward more extreme goals. At the very beginning of the difficulties the assailants of the Stamp Act had generally gone no further than to reject Britain's constitutional right to levy internal taxes, this power in the past having resided in the colonial legislatures. But when the Townshend Acts removed that objection by prescribing merely external duties, that argument became vulnerable. The writers had not made clear that the popular slogan of no taxation without representation actually applied to port levies as well as every other form.

To establish this point beyond peradventure John Dickinson of Philadelphia made his signal contribution to the colonial position. In his *Letters from a Farmer in Pennsylvania to the Inhabitants of the British Colonies,* published early in 1768, he argued with dispassionate power that Parliament as the central organ of the Empire could properly regulate the over-all trade but that this in no sense justified it in exacting an American revenue, as the Townshend Acts provided. Such an exercise of power was without precedent and blatantly illegal. According to this uncompromising formula each provincial legislature thus held the same relation to the King in fiscal matters as did Parliament itself. The doctrine won immediate acceptance. The people indeed seized on it, so the Massachusetts Tory governor wrote in dismay to the Ministry, as "a Bill of Rights."

Then events in due course pushed the colonial theory to a final stage. Thomas Paine's *Common Sense,* appearing in January

1776, tore every shred of authority from both King and Parliament. The two years or so preceding had piled crisis upon crisis. The Bostonians had sunk the tea; Parliament had retorted with the Intolerable Acts; the First Continental Congress had instituted a program of intercolonial economic resistance; war had erupted on Lexington Green; and an American army under the Second Congress had shut up General Gage and his regulars in Boston. In stirring and violent rhetoric the English-born Paine, who had recently settled in Philadelphia with a heart full of rancor for his native land, addressed the emotions as well as the minds of his readers. The "period of debate is closed," he concluded, " 'TIS TIME TO PART." Although a half year was to elapse before Congress complied, Paine's trumpet call was a mighty factor in influencing the public as well as the delegates themselves to adopt the fateful step. No other work written in America, save perhaps *Uncle Tom's Cabin,* has ever had such crucial repercussions.

Although most of the propaganda was grimly earnest, now and then writers employed satire and mockery. In particular they liked to parody Britain's behavior in the antique phraseology of Holy Writ—a method calculated to delight a people accustomed from childhood to the Scriptures. The most successful effort was *The First Book of the American Chronicles of the Times* (1775), which attracted "upwards of 3,000" purchasers upon its publication in Philadelphia and was quickly reprinted in other colonies. The unknown author recited in burlesque Gospel style the woes visited by "the Lord the King" and "Thomas the Gageite" on "the Bostonites" for refusing to sell their birthright "for a dish of TEA." Of like Philadelphia origin was Francis Hopkinson's *The Prophecy* (1776), which seconded Paine's summons to Independence. Diverging from the Biblical pattern, the youthful New Yorker Philip Freneau also entered the lists, shooting derisive verses at divers officials and policies. As Franklin, himself a master of the game in the London press, observed, "Odd ways of presenting Matters to publick View sometimes occasion them to be more read, talk'd of, and more attended to." To jeer at the long-venerated parent nation was a particularly adroit means of sapping filial affection. That was the special contribution of the satirists to the molding of opinion.

The American mind in 1776 was well-stocked. The system of education, open in some degree and kind to all levels of society, had made the people probably the most literate on the globe. Not only did they read almanacs and newspapers as well as pamphlets on many subjects, but a surprising number also knew the major writings of ancient and modern times. And beyond mere booklore those participating in public affairs as voters and officeholders possessed a practical grasp of the workings of government. A Tory growled in the *Boston Evening-Post,* May 22, 1769, that even "the peasants and their housewives in every part of the land . . . dispute in politics"; and to like effect the Reverend Jacob Duché in Philadelphia remarked a few years later, "The poorest labourer upon the shore of Delaware thinks himself entitled to deliver his sentiments in matters of religion or politicks with as much freedom as the gentleman or the scholar."

The rulers in far-off London, though, had little comprehension of these developments. Edmund Burke, one of the few statesmen who understood, solemnly warned the House of Commons shortly before the Lexington hostilities: "This fierce spirit of liberty is stronger in the English colonies probably than in any other people on earth." Unhappily for the maintenance of the British Empire, however, he addressed deaf ears.

CHAPTER XI

The
March of Knowledge

THE MIND of the people was responsive not only to the immediate claims of religion and politics but also, if more hesitantly, to the long-run obligations of knowledge for its own sake. From the first there had been a desire to protect and transmit the accumulated learning of the past lest the precious heritage be lost in the perils of wilderness life; and this had found expression above all in the founding of institutions of higher education. In the first century of settlement, the colonists established three colleges; and by 1776 they could choose among nine in as many provinces.

The Puritans founded Harvard at Cambridge, near Boston, in 1636, just six years after their initial migration to Massachusetts. The Anglicans in Virginia, undeterred by several false starts, succeeded in 1693 in opening the College of William and Mary at Williamsburg, although the faculty did not offer true college instruction until about twenty years later. In 1701, a conservative wing of the New England Congregationalists, alarmed by the growing theological liberalism of Harvard and its vulnerability to the worldly temptations of Boston, set up Yale in Connecticut, ultimately at New Haven, as a refuge for the orthodox.

Then, as the colonies continued to fill up and the religious impulses generated by the Great Awakening promoted interest in higher education, six new institutions followed. These, too, were all denominational, excepting the College of Philadelphia (later the University of Pennsylvania), initially established in 1755 by laymen, though soon to fall under Anglican control. The College of New Jersey (later Princeton) was founded in 1746 by Presbyterians; King's College (later Columbia) in New York City in 1754 mainly by Anglicans; the College of Rhode Island (Brown) at Providence in 1764 by Baptists; Queen's College (later renamed Rutgers) at New Brunswick, New Jersey, in 1766 by members of the Dutch Reformed Church; and Dartmouth, at Hanover, New Hampshire, in 1769 by Congregationalists.

Despite the sectarian ties, none of the nine institutions was in a precise sense a theological seminary. The need in a fast-growing society for trained minds in profane fields was too urgent to confine instruction to a single skill, even that of preparing young men to save souls. The colleges therefore accepted students regardless of creed, though of course with the hope of inoculating them against error. Following English example, the schools sought to equip the youths for their lifework, whatever it might be. Thus Harvard's president in 1711 noted that its alumni had served the community as judges, teachers, merchants, physicians, soldiers, and farmers as well as divines. And in 1777 Yale's president declared a little ostentatiously that more than three fourths of its graduates "return home, mix in with the body of the public, and enter upon Commerce or the cultivation of their Estates."

The colleges had a further role—one expressed by George III in 1762 in sponsoring a joint appeal by the College of Philadelphia and King's College for British contributions. "The continual Accession of People" to the Middle colonies "from different Parts of the World," the king said, presented dangers should "so mixt a Multitude" be left "unenlightened in Religion, uncemented in a common Education, strangers to the Humane Arts, and to the just use of rational Liberty." Schooling was thus also counted on to expedite the operation of what Americans had not yet learned to call the melting pot.

Financial problems worried the colleges incessantly. They tapped sources both in and outside America and somehow, in every case, despite times of want and crisis, managed to survive. Governmental assistance proved a frail reed, although six of the colleges, including the three oldest, received modest provincial grants with more or less regularity. On occasion, government support took eccentric forms. In 1688, for example, the Privy Council freed three pirates captured by a British frigate at the mouth of the James River upon their giving £300 and a quarter of their booty toward the founding of William and Mary. (Unlike piratical benefactors of later days, they did not receive honorary degrees.) King's College, Yale, and the Colleges of New Jersey and Philadelphia resorted to lotteries. In addition, all colleges charged for tuition, board, and lodging and fined undergraduates for misconduct, although these payments, as the Harvard records show, could be commuted in case of need into wheat, lumber, dry goods, nails, fish, malt, and other approved commodities.

Individual gifts, however, while seldom large, constituted the main support from American sources. Coming from people high and low, these contributions revealed strikingly the colonial faith in academic training. Besides money, the subscriptions included real estate, buildings, books, scientific instruments, and physical labor. The greatest single benefactor appears to have been the New York lawyer Joseph Murray, who in 1757 bequeathed £5,555 to King's College.

The principal aid from outside the colonies came from the British Isles, with the remainder chiefly from Holland and the British West Indies. Sometimes the contributions resulted from organized drives, as in the case of the 1762 solicitation, which yielded £16,200 from over eight hundred Britons, but more typically they stemmed from individual benevolence. The givers included such eminent figures, lay and religious, as Sir Isaac Newton, Edmund Halley of Halley's comet fame, the hymnologist Isaac Watts, Bishop George Berkeley, and England's foremost actor, David Garrick. Berkeley, for instance, sent valuable collections of books to both Harvard and Yale, besides presenting the latter with the deed to his Rhode Island farm; and Garrick gave a benefit performance at Drury Lane in behalf of Philadelphia College. Unfortunately, no complete roster of the countless benefactors in America and abroad has been preserved. Two, however—the English-born clergyman John Harvard of Charlestown, Massachusetts, and the Boston-born London merchant Elihu Yale —are known to posterity, thanks to the good luck of having their names attached to the institutions they assisted.

As at Oxford and Cambridge, admission everywhere required a knowledge of Latin and Greek. The curriculum, continuing with little change from the Middle Ages, stressed the so-called liberal arts. Every student took the same course, and except at Harvard after 1766 a single instructor taught all of them to a given class through to graduation. Apart from further study of the classics, the regimen ordinarily consisted of advanced mathematics, ancient history, Hebrew, logic, rhetoric (the art of persuasion), moral philosophy (ethics), mental philosophy (metaphysics), and natural philosophy (an introduction mainly to physics and astronomy taught without benefit of laboratory or observatory). The word "philosophy," as then used, meant learning in general, with the adjectives designating the particular fields. The College of Philadelphia, in whose founding Franklin was active, alone aimed to alter the pattern, but the broader and more utilitarian program which he envisaged never was realized.

Only a small proportion of American youths received a higher education. At the eve of the Revolution, the nine colleges did not enroll more than 750. Harvard and Yale led with about 175 each, and the others tailed off from New Jersey College's 100 to the 20 at Queen's. While boys from upper-class families comprised the great majority, the authorities, mindful of the ceaseless upward movement in colonial society, took pains to encourage also the attendance of sons of shopkeepers, artisans, small farmers, and the like. One method was through scholarships; another, a reduction of fees in return for performing tasks like ringing the college bell and waiting on table. The long midwinters enabled a number to make ends meet with earnings from schoolteaching.

The students lived under stiff surveillance both in and out of the classroom. This vigilance doubtless reflected belief in original sin and had further justification because of the immaturity of the undergraduates and their freedom from home restraints. The usual age at admission varied from fifteen to seventeen, with some even younger. Of the last colonial generation, for example, Thomas Hutchinson and John Hancock respectively registered at Harvard when twelve and thirteen; John Trumbull and Timothy Dwight at Yale when each was thirteen; and Gouverneur Morris and John Jay at King's when thirteen and fourteen. The boys had to rise early, attend daily prayers as well as Sunday services, defer unquestioningly to tutors and upperclassmen, and avoid fighting, profanity, lying, hard liquor, gambling, or nocturnal outbreaks. William and Mary, because of its large contingent of planters' scions, went further in 1752 by banning race horses and game-cocks. Everywhere the outbreak of pent-up high spirits during commencement raised almost unmanageable problems. Disciplin-ary measures ranged from public censure and fining of offenders to suspension and expulsion.

Moral standards imposed by edict inevitably invited defiance, sometimes even on the part of preachers' sons who when later in the pulpit would themselves castigate falls from grace. As time went on, violations increasingly took the form of collective dis-obedience. The student rebellion at Harvard in 1766, however, which coincided with and perhaps aped the public opposition to the Stamp Act, was directed not against faculty supervision but against the bad butter served in the commons. As in all under-graduate uprisings, the insurgents, upon being threatened with dismissal, quickly gave in with a "Promise of future good Conduct."

Despite sporadic breaches, the surprising thing is that, in the absence of organized sports and entertainment as safety valves for undergraduate exuberance, riots were so few. Group activity typically found an outlet in literary and oratorical societies, al-though even these developed late. The Linonian, formed in 1755, and the Brothers in Unity, in 1768, throve at Yale. Jefferson belonged at William and Mary to the Flat Hat Club and James Madison at New Jersey College to the American Whig Society. These groups provided a welcome relief from the prescribed course of study. The Phi Beta Kappa Society, instituted at William and Mary late in 1776, differed from the others only in its plan of establishing branches elsewhere, thus anticipating the practice of Greek-letter fraternities in the nineteenth century. It was not until 1831 that it assumed its present character of an honorary scholar-ship society.

Occasionally, youths went abroad for their higher education, although not all remained long enough to earn degrees. The principal outflow came in the last quarter-century with the increase of the colonies in population and wealth. More than half the entire number set out from Virginia and South Carolina. In the Old Dominion the gentry sometimes by-passed William and Mary to give their sons the broadening experience of a European sojourn, while South Carolina lacked a college of its own. Over a hundred young Americans in the colonial period enrolled at Oxford and Cambridge with a scattering as well at Glasgow and Aberdeen in Scotland, Trinity in Dublin, and also at Leyden and half-a-dozen other Continental universities. A still greater number —more than three hundred—seeking a professional rather than a liberal-arts education attended London's Inns of Court for a grounding in law and Edinburgh for medical training.

Some apprehensive colonials, however, feared that the European exposure at so impressionable an age would wean the youths away from their native land. As the Reverend James Maury of Virginia, himself a William and Mary product, put it in 1762, "The Genius of our People, their Way of Life, their Circumstances in Point of Fortune, the Customs & Manners & Humours of the Country, difference us in so many important Respects from Europeans."

Actually, such anxieties had little basis. Almost the reverse proved true, for when the Anglo-American quarrel erupted virtually all those who had studied abroad supported the patriot party. Eight of the group, not counting President Witherspoon of New Jersey College, became signers of the Declaration of Independence. The older civilization had seemed too effete, dissolute, and corrupt to inspire trust. Furthermore, as in the case of those who remained at home, what Americans studying abroad learned from the classics reinforced their natural libertarianism. In Plutarch's *Lives,* the orations of Demosthenes and Cicero, and the events of ancient history they perceived a mirror of their own time.

Undergraduates speaking out against British policy could count on a sympathetic public. "The young gentlemen" at Harvard, a contemporary attested, sometimes got "wrought up to such a pitch" as to nonplus their tutors who "are fearful of giving too great a check to a disposition, which may, hereafter, fill the country with patriots." There and elsewhere students held forth in declamations, forensic disputes, and commencement theses on such incendiary topics as "Oppression and Tyranny," "All Men are Free by the Law of Nature," and "The People Are the Sole Judges of Their Rights and Liberties." New Jersey College lads backed up the Boston Tea Party by burning their steward's supply, and Yale boys went so far in 1775 as to expose in the press a student who had cast aspersions on the cause.

By 1776, colonial colleges had three thousand living alumni. Along with their fellows who had gone abroad, they occupied a special status in their communities. Not all, to be sure, chose to take a stand, and some even sided with the British but, if one may judge from the Harvard graduates, Tories and their sympathizers among the college-bred numbered fewer than one in six. Of the fifty-six signers of the Declaration of Independence nineteen had attended American institutions. Only two of the college presidents —Myles Cooper of King's and John Camm of William and Mary, both Anglican clergymen of English birth—stuck by the mother country. Cooper fled in 1775 to Britain out of fear for his life at the hands of the populace, and Camm suffered dismissal by the college authorities a few years later. From the beginning to the end the thrust of higher education was to further the patriot cause.

Politics distracted only slightly, however, from the substantive development of the curriculum. For all the commitment to the medieval system of courses, the American colleges were far from static. Thus, although natural philosophy, as science was termed, received relatively slight attention in the academic curriculum, it reflected to a surprising degree the epochal advances after the work abroad of such masters as Copernicus and Newton. Notwithstanding an atmosphere steeped in Scriptural lore, no one in colonial times, however religious, considered that the new ideas and discoveries undermined the primacy of God. Rather, such findings merely revealed how the marvelous mechanics of His creation worked. Science, wrote Cotton Mather in *The Christian Philosopher* in 1721—his credulity as to Salem witchcraft then far behind him—"is no *Enemy*, but a mighty and wondrous *Incentive* to *Religion*." Nor was the belief in special providences to be abandoned, since obviously the Great Legislator when occasion demanded could suspend His own laws. The conflict between science and theology, although it was later to become acute, did not actually occur in America until the nineteenth century, when disputes over the age of the earth and the descent of man threatened, in the eyes of the pious, to subvert the pillars of faith.

The Copernican system was taught at Harvard at least as early as 1659, only ten years after being introduced at Oxford, and Newtonian physics received a similar welcome at a little later date. The other colleges showed comparable tolerance toward the new learning. Among the most appreciated gifts to the institutions were scientific instruments ("philosophical apparatus"): celestial and terrestrial globes, telescopes, quadrants, microscopes, and the like. The teachers, for their part, labored to disseminate the fresh insights and methods rather than to advance any of their own, although they sometimes sent meteorological and other data and materials to Europe for the use of researchers there. Lest this idea of their function be ascribed to the handicaps of a frontier environment or to an inadequate conception of their role, it should be remembered that in Britain as well the new work in science was being done largely outside academic walls.

The shining colonial exception was John Winthrop, the fourth of his name in the famous New England family, who served as Professor of Mathematics and Natural Philosophy at Harvard from 1739 until his death in 1779. In the age before scientific specialization, he explored many kinds of physical phenomena and always with valuable results. He delivered lectures on electricity with classroom demonstrations; made in 1739 the first authoritative study in America of sunspots; investigated in 1740 the transit of Mercury across the face of the sun and similarly in 1759 the reappearance of Halley's comet, visible for the first time since 1682; and induced the Massachusetts legislature in 1761 to join the college in fitting out the first American astronomical expedition, which under his direction recorded in Newfoundland, despite the "venemous stings" of "infinite swarms of insects," the transit of Venus across the sun.

A severe earthquake in 1755 provided Winthrop with a dramatic setting for the thesis that, like wind and gravity, the shocks were due to natural causes—not "the tokens of an incensed Deity," as even some of the learned believed. This attack on the doctrine of special providences brought down on his head a stern rebuke from the Reverend Thomas Prince of Boston's South Church; but in a vigorous newspaper exchange he put that eminent cleric to rout. In similar fashion he championed Franklin's lightning rods in face of the widespread view that they were impious attempts to thwart the divine will. "It is as much our duty," he retorted, "to secure ourselves against the effects of lightning as against those of rain, snow, and wind, by the means God has put into our hands." In all, Winthrop contributed eleven papers to the *Philosophical Transactions* of the Royal Society of London. In addition he found time when the troubles broke out with England to take active part in the patriot movement.

By and large, however, original additions to natural philosophy came mostly from gifted amateurs. Of the twenty-two men elected to the Royal Society from America before 1776, nineteen had no academic connections. Untrained in science, these men operated on principles of common sense. Their work tended to be descriptive and classificatory rather than analytical and interpretative. Nonetheless, their findings increased knowledge of the material world by supplying European natural philosophers with valuable data from a little-known quarter of the globe. Among their supporters abroad were such notables as Newton, Halley, and the physicist Robert Boyle. In botanical investigations transatlantic relations proved especially close. Besides John Fothergill, Peter Collinson, and others in the mother country, the correspondents included the supreme authorities—Linnaeus in Sweden and Gronovius in Holland. In this area, moreover, interchanges sometimes produced financial aid through the buying of colonial seeds and plants. American researchers thus had the sense of participating in an international enterprise.

Since so much remained to be discovered and so few barriers had been erected between fields of inquiry, the characteristic colonial scientist wandered from one field to another as interest dictated. Franklin, who explored a dozen fields, was at once the greatest and the most versatile; but his versatility reflected the state of the art. The environment of the New World, of course, directed particular attention both to what was distinctive in America and what was useful for Americans. Thus the mapping of the country and the ocean adjacent, the enumeration of new plants and animals, and the exploration of factors affecting conditions of living commanded first interest. Pure science—the pursuit of knowledge for its own sake—was a secondary incentive. Even Franklin, who ceaselessly concerned himself with theory, hoped through his discoveries to improve man's well-being. "What signifies Philosophy," he asked, "that does not apply to some Use?"

The earliest contributions were geographical: depictions of the routes of explorers on maps, some made before the colonies were founded. But, informative as these efforts were, the real development of American cartography came through the more exact knowledge gained in the occupation of the country and the need for a definitive marking of provincial boundaries by surveyors. By the mid-eighteenth century maps of the known parts of the continent had become reasonably accurate and complete. The crowning achievements, both in 1755, were Lewis Evans's *General Map of the Middle British Colonies* and John Mitchell's *Map of the British and French Dominions in North America*. Evans, a Philadelphia surveyor, had derived his material mainly from personal observation; Mitchell, a Virginia physician of divers gifts then living in England, assembled his largely from official documents. The Mitchell map served as a guide to the peace negotiators at the close of the Revolutionary War and continued in wide use for many years thereafter.

In determining colonial boundaries the most famous achievement, through an accident of history, was that of the Englishmen Charles Mason and Jeremiah Dixon in the mid-1760's, when they laid out some three hundred miles of the border between Pennsylvania and Maryland, which had long been in dispute. Their memory lived on because in the troubled era before the Civil War the Mason and Dixon Line by an imaginary extension westward became the popular term for the respective limits of free and slave soil. It was forgotten that when the survey was made Pennsylvania no less than Maryland sanctioned human bondage.

From the outset exotic plants excited the settlers' interest and prompted investigations into their possible value for man. By the eighteenth century a host of persons—more than in any other scientific field—dabbled in botany, and the Pennsylvania Quaker John Bartram, the most dedicated of them, made it an almost exclusive pursuit.

From classical days onward physicians in Europe had inquired into the curative properties of plants, and this quest was pursued in America. Dr. John Lining of Charleston, for instance, proclaimed the virtues of Indian pinkroot; Dr. John Tennent in Virginia cried up seneca (rattlesnake root); while Bartram, though lacking a medical degree, recommended numerous herbs, roots, and barks. Such claims, often but not always ill-founded, did much to popularize botany. The colonial activity led to the collection and description of hitherto unknown flora, introduced new species into Europe, and aided Linnaeus in constructing his famous system of classification. In recognition of the work of the Charlestonian Dr. Alexander Garden the gardenia was named for him. The Philadelphia fur merchant and provincial official James Logan established through a series of controlled experiments the function of pollen in fertilizing maize—the first conclusive demonstration in history of the sexual reproduction of plants.

In breadth of accomplishment, however, Bartram, a youthful protégé of Logan, outshone all his fellows. A farmer with little formal schooling, from 1738 onward he collected specimens from the Gulf of Mexico to the Great Lakes and New England, and cultivated them in a botanical garden a few miles outside Philadelphia. He also studied plant hybridization and by crossbreeding produced new beauty in flowers. His tireless exertions caused Linnaeus to call him "the greatest natural botanist in the world" and brought him appointment in 1765 as botanist to George III for the recently acquired Floridas. His son William, whom he trained, was to emulate him in the next generation. The elder's garden, with the stone dwelling he built with his own hands and some of the trees he planted, is maintained today as a municipal park.

Animals and birds attracted far less scientific attention. This was partly because in the colonists' eyes the native beasts, except when they could be killed for food or pelts, offered no prospect of human benefit, only dire perils to the advance of settlement. Cotton Mather and others, however, interested by the differences from Old World animals, did attempt accounts of American deer, pigeons, rattlesnakes, and the like; and in response to the urging of Linnaeus Dr. Garden took time off to collect fish, insects, and reptiles in the Carolinas, transmitting observations along with specimens. Otherwise zoology in British America was almost entirely neglected.

Geology fared little better, for here too the human advantages seemed remote. Why strive for possible wealth concealed in the earth when so much was readily available on the surface? Farming, fur-trading, commerce, and the fisheries held more enticing rewards. Jared Eliot, the Connecticut agricultural reformer, was one of the few to diverge from the pattern when in 1762 he devised a feasible means of producing malleable iron from a variety of beach sand. The principal interest centered on earthquakes, those seemingly senseless disturbances of the natural order which recurrently endangered life and property. These, however, seldom called forth more than plain narrative accounts. Content with description, the writers, unlike Professor Winthrop, did not probe into the underlying causes.

Even if the workers in geology and the other branches had been more inclined to theorizing, they, like their brethren abroad, would have been handicapped by the biblical version of the Creation. On the basis of *Genesis* the Anglican prelate James Usher in the mid-seventeenth century had authoritatively determined that the world and all forms of life on it came into existence in 4004 B.C. The Reverend Thomas Prince, for example, cited the figure as a matter of course in his *Chronological History of New-England* in 1736. So short a time span obviously precluded insights that might have ascribed the earth's organic and inorganic life to processes operating through eons.

Interest in astronomy began with ancient folk beliefs about the influence of heavenly bodies on human affairs. Although celestial superstitions receded among the better educated toward the close of the seventeenth century, even as late as the 1750's many respected Rhode Islanders—and doubtless their like elsewhere— consulted astrologers or pondered the signs of the zodiac before making important business deals or sending ships to sea. Steadily, however, the need for greater precision in the plotting of ocean voyages and the conduct of land surveys with the skies serving as a guide encouraged the more rational approach. In addition, the discoveries of Newton had given the study new intellectual appeal. Now, as a result, one's own telescope could glimpse the symmetry and functioning of the universe and perhaps even find confirming evidence for Newtonian theorems. This latter service the Boston merchant Thomas Boylston notably rendered when his observations of the great comet of 1680 yielded data that Newton used in his *Principia Mathematica* several years later.

The Pennsylvanian David Rittenhouse, starting as a farm boy, became in turn a clockmaker and surveyor and finally an internationally known astronomer. In 1767 he constructed an orrery, or planetarium, which, though not the first in America—President Clap of Yale having preceded him with a cruder one in 1744— displayed with extraordinary exactness the motions of the heavenly bodies, including solar and lunar eclipses, "for a period of 5000 years either forward or backward." New Jersey College promptly purchased the mechanism, the College of Philadelphia acquired a replica, and the Pennsylvania legislature awarded Rittenhouse £300 for the achievement. With his superior astronomical attainments he also conducted important boundary surveys for over half the colonial governments, employing at times instruments of his own devising.

Naturally Rittenhouse engaged actively in the most ambitious astronomical enterprise of the time: the recording on an interprovincial basis of the transit of Venus across the sun in 1769. The phenomenon had not been observable in the thirteen colonies eight years before when Professor Winthrop voyaged to Nova Scotia to witness it, and it was not to occur again for more than a century. The prime scientific motive was to ascertain through a comparison of findings the distance of the earth from the sun, with secondary benefits anticipated for navigation and trade.

In America watchers kept vigil at twelve or more places from Massachusetts to Virginia. In Pennsylvania, the main center of activity, the legislature appropriated funds for the project, and Rittenhouse built an observatory on his premises for which he made his own refracting telescope, the first known to have been constructed in the colonies. Winthrop collected data in Massachusetts, while up and down the coast ordinary folk, keyed up by the newspapers, scanned the sky with smoked glasses. The best observations, when correlated with those made abroad, helped establish the sun's position at approximately 93,000,000 miles from the earth, not far off the present determination.

In the closely related field of physics Franklin stood pre-eminent, although his ceaselessly questing mind led him in accord to pursue side inquiries into optics, meteorology, oceanography, geology, biology, and the like. His studies of the properties of heat and ventilation bore practical fruit, as noted earlier, in the invention of the fireplace stove. His profoundest achievements, however, rested on his electrical researches.

Observing the resemblance of lightning to electricity, he conducted his famous kite experiment in 1752 to confirm the identity; and this along with kindred findings made him the internationally acknowledged master in the emerging field of physics.

Among his contributions Franklin devised the first workable theory to account for all known electrical phenomena as well as for those of the future. His concepts of "positive" and "negative," "plus" and "minus," and the like are still fundamental. Through the invention of the lightning rod, moreover, as has already been seen, he tried to harness "the Electrick Fire from Clouds," thus evidencing again his wish to make theoretical knowledge useful whenever possible. These epochal investigations all took place in the few years from 1746 to 1752. Had not the continuous demands of public service thereafter diverted his energies, his stature in the world of science might have been greater yet. Even so, his fame as an experimentalist stood him in good stead in his diplomatic career. When he went to the French court during the Revolutionary War, he was received not as an obscure agent of a desperate cause but as a scientist—a man admired and esteemed by the best minds of Europe.

Although no one else approached Franklin as a physicist, it was thorough command of physical principles that enabled Rittenhouse to attain his great precision in the making of instruments and that helped the Philadelphia glazier Thomas Godfrey in 1730 to invent a more reliable quadrant. Similarly, the New Englander Edward Bromfield in the 1740's devised an improved microscope that revealed "wonderous Views of the inside Frames and Works of Nature." His death shortly afterward prevented him from seeking to apply the sun's rays with greatly intensified lenses to the heating of houses, a limited accomplishment as yet even in the twentieth century.

In the realm of pure theory the New York royal official Cadwallader Colden, less discreet than Franklin in his electrical inquiries, tried in an ambitious treatise, *The Principles of Action in Matter* (1751), to correct and surpass Newton's overarching synthesis. But, by general agreement of competent critics both at home and abroad, Colden's understanding of Newton was faulty and his reasoning poorly supported, although the work afforded some striking insights. Colden's reputation as a scientist continued to rest on his factual findings, after the manner of the times, in such disparate fields as botany, astronomy, and geology.

The most obviously useful branch of science, if such it could be called, was medicine, or "Physick." Disease posed a constant peril, greater even than that from savage beasts or hostile Indians. The rigors of the long sea voyage followed by the wilderness exigencies of deficient housing, unaccustomed bodily exertion, and recurring food shortages threatened the survival of the original settlements, while "fevers" and "agues"—malaria, dysentery, and typhoid—due to impure water or pestilential insects persistently stalked the backwoods clearings. Overindulgence in hard liquor, often induced by belief in its medicinal value, doubtless increased the settlers' susceptibility to disease. As though all this were not enough, the slave trade introduced yellow fever and hookworm from Africa, and with the rise of towns the filth on the streets bred noxious flies and polluted the drinking water.

So great was the demand for doctors that for many years clergymen had to fill the gap. As the most learned and revered members of the community they by common consent assumed the function of curing bodies as well as souls. This *"Angelic Conjunction,"* as Cotton Mather termed it, comported with a widespread view that fleshly ills sprang from divine displeasure or satanic malice, whence it logically followed that a holy man would know best how to deal with whichever might be the cause. Trained physicians at first were few, but in time growing numbers of laymen embarked upon the career by indenturing themselves to established practitioners for three to seven years or by serving under them informally for a period. Such apprenticeship might afford access to medical works and the experience of observing the treatment of patients, although often it taught them little more than to pound drugs, tend the doctor's horse, and perform other menial tasks. For many, therefore, the real education came when they struck out for themselves and learned by doing.

The special branch known as surgery, or "Chirurgery," enlisted relatively few regular followers. Hardly any progress had been made in the procedures since the thirteenth century. The worker had no anesthetics to administer—although he sometimes stupefied his patients with liquor—nor did he establish aseptic conditions for recovery. Understandably, then, the colonial surgeon engaged mostly in emergency operations like bone setting, amputations, and tending gunshot wounds. Seldom if ever did he pry into the more sensitive interior of the body.

Dentistry was even more primitive, though, and if travel accounts are reliable, Americans stood in greater need of dental care than Europeans. The observers speculated that this was due to gorging on hot foods or, more wildly, they laid it to the extreme changes of temperature. They could not blame it, as one might in some part today, on a neglect of toothbrushes, since these were then unknown. A folk prescription for stopping "the pains of the Teeth" was to carry about the tooth of a dead man, and other alleged remedies were no less traditional; but after the early years the custom grew, especially in the towns, of having the family doctor or a self-styled "Surgeon-Dentist" extract the cause of the trouble. The resulting demand for false teeth created a thriving business for ingenious artisans, the one best known to history, though for other reasons, being Paul Revere, the Boston silversmith and engraver.

Midwifery, an inevitable resort in a society that prized large families, devolved, as the word indicates, almost exclusively on women. The prejudice against men in this capacity reflected the feeling, brought over from Europe, that male performance of so intimate a task would be improper if not immoral. Since virtually all the practitioners learned their calling by trial and error, some of the high infant mortality may doubtless be laid at their door. On the other hand, contemporary accounts repeatedly attest to the value of their services. Mrs. Thomas Whitmore of Marlboro, Vermont, for example, presided at two thousand births prior to her death in 1763 at the age of eighty-seven, and the "greatly lamented" Mrs. Elizabeth Hunt of South Carolina, dying in 1766 at seventy-three, officiated at "near 4000." Of persons of historical note, Anne Hutchinson in seventeenth-century Boston acted as midwife before moving on to religious controversy.

Women also sometimes ventured into the male precincts of the profession. Two Virginia "doctresses," probably no better trained than the ubiquitous midwives, stand out on the official record. Mary Johnson in the 1740's and Constant Woodson in the 1760's asserted that they had achieved cures for cancer, thereby earning such repute that the legislature granted them in turn £100 for divulging their method. Testimonials from patients ardently supported the claims, so that there is no reason to believe that all parties concerned were not acting in the utmost good faith. Such credulity at this stage of the history of medicine was normal.

The colonists in fact knew little more about the causes of diseases than did the ancient Greeks. The basic treatment for virtually all disorders was to sweat, purge, or bleed the patient and in acute cases to do all these things at once. The aim was to expel the malady, whatever the effect on lowering bodily resistance. Time-honored folk remedies oftentimes supplemented this system, and the colonial physician also borrowed practices from the Indians and the Negroes. Most people, however, chose to dose themselves, and as a manual for the purpose Dr. John Tennent in Virginia compiled *Every Man His Own Doctor,* which professed to set forth "Plain and Easy Means for Persons to Cure Themselves" with concoctions "Chiefly of the Growth and Production of This Country." Published at Williamsburg in 1734, it also found wide favor outside the Old Dominion. Franklin in his role of printer brought out four editions of the work to meet the demand in the Middle colonies, including a translation for the German inhabitants.

From the red and the black races the white man learned the therapeutic properties of many herbs, roots, and barks. A seventeenth-century Virginia clergyman John Clayton collected three hundred varieties of plants used by the tribes of the region to combat disease, and settlers elsewhere obtained similar knowledge. The most fundamental contribution, however, came from outside the colonies. This was cinchona bark, a remedy for the ever-threatening malaria which the Spanish conquerors of Peru had acquired from the natives and which early in the eighteenth century reached the colonists by way of England.

The Negroes, for their part, not only brought with them familiarity with herbal and other African methods of healing, but in the new land appear to have developed more of their own. In any event no white prejudice rendered the practices unacceptable. On the contrary, the Virginia government, for instance, in 1729 granted a bondsman his freedom and £60 for divulging his "many extraordinary cures" for "venereal distempers." Later, however, fears arose that slaves through ignorance or malice sometimes concocted lethal potions, so that the lawmakers in 1748 forbade on pain of death any further such activity in Virginia except under strict supervision. Still, as late as 1750, the South Carolina legislature awarded a black his liberty and an annual £100 for revealing his secret of counteracting poisoning and rattlesnake bites. Unhappily, however, the dominant race ignored for many distressing years the knowledge the Negroes possessed of smallpox inoculation in Africa.

The folk remedies, mainly of venerable European origin, generally contained ingredients of miscellaneous and revolting character. Toads, dried and beaten into a powder or boiled to a jelly, formed the favorite component. Among others were pulverized snails, bees, and sow bugs, spider webs, cow dung, even the scrapings of human skulls. These substances and their like, when mixed with honey, liquor or animal grease, were made into brews and pastes, then perhaps seasoned with spices and herbs. For the utmost potency some of the concoctions were to be applied in a special phase of the moon.

However bizarre to us today, the "elixirs" and "electuaries" could hardly have maintained their hold on generation after generation without at least the appearance of curative or ameliorative results. Many of the sick, having only imaginary ills, no doubt derived psychological benefit from using these "medicines." Others recovered regardless of the medication when the disease ran its course. But, beyond such deceptive effects, modern research has revealed that toads, the most common of the ingredients, possess an external secretion of the powerful heart stimulant, adrenalin, as well as a chemical responsible for vitamin D. There may have been equivalent virtues in other instances.

With the advertising rendered possible in the eighteenth century by newspapers, patent medicines, mostly from England, cut into the use of the home variety. The convenience of ready-to-be-taken nostrums plus the sweeping claims made for them and the fascination of the boasted secret formulas offered an attraction that has not wholly spent its force even today. Typical of the lot was the General Cordial of Dr. Godfrey, who, without revealing its ingredients, engaged to heal "the Cholick, and all Manners of Pains in the Bowels, Fluxes, Fevers, Small-Pox, Measles, Rheumatism, Coughs, Colds, and Restlessness in Men, Women, and Children," as well as "several Ailments incident to Child-bearing Women," and so on. The cure-alls could be obtained not only from apothecaries but also from printers, booksellers, and others and were even prescribed by many physicians. No one, at least in the towns, needed to go without. The good effects, if there were any, doubtless came from the same factors that operated in the case of certain of the folk remedies.

In coping with epidemic diseases the colonists were on firmer ground. From the very start they recognized the need for prevention and control, and although little knowledge existed even in Europe of the bacteriological causes, provincial authorities followed the common-sense Old World practice of imposing quarantine regulations on incoming ships during outbreaks and of confining persons already affected in pesthouses or in their homes. Town officials also displayed activity of a sort, hoping to improve the health of the inhabitants as well as the ease of transit by ridding the streets of sewage and other suspected deleterious matter.

These precautions, however, never proved sufficient, although the wide dispersion of population rendered the onslaughts less deadly than in dense European communities. The most feared pestilence was smallpox, which was more or less endemic. It was followed by yellow fever, communicated as we know now by a particular variety of mosquito native to Africa but usually entering the colonies on ships from the West Indies. Other scourges, generally less destructive, were malaria (borne by a local mosquito), dysentery, influenza and kindred respiratory ailments, scarlet fever, and diphtheria. Only a few of these disorders, though, were clearly identified at the time.

Smallpox inspired the supreme terror because, besides being very often fatal, it left permanent scars on the survivors—among them George Washington, who contracted the disease at the age of nineteen. In Massachusetts, where the people had experienced six tragic outbreaks since 1635, Cotton Mather resolved to meet the visitation of 1721 head on—a decision that led to the first important experiment in preventive medicine in American history. The means he employed was inoculation—that is, the conferring of immunity on the healthy by injecting smallpox pus in modified form into their blood. Having learned of the efficacy of the method in Africa from his "Negro-man" who himself had benefited from it, then reading in the Royal Society *Transactions* of the Turks' use of it, Mather not only prevailed upon his friend Dr. Zabdiel Boylston to inoculate the physician's six-year-old son and some 250 other persons in Boston and the vicinity, but in addition he subjected his own son Samuel to "transplantation," as the treatment was called. To many of the pious, this application of a pagan usage defied God's will, while even most of the medical fraternity remonstrated on what they held to be scientific grounds. A bomb flung into Mather's home betrayed the intensity of the feeling; by good luck it failed to explode. The results of the treatment in this and later epidemics, however, proved so convincing that it gradually won general acceptance in Massachusetts.

Elsewhere, too, the procedure met with resistance. One objection with real basis, also urged in the Bay Colony, was that if an inoculated person went about too soon, he would spread the infection. Another was that an inept doctor sometimes caused deaths. At Charleston, South Carolina, where a newspaper and pamphlet battle was precipitated by an outbreak in 1738, the legislature prohibited the practice in and near the town during the continuance of the scourge. Similarly Governor George Clinton in 1747 forbade by proclamation anyone in or around New York City to inoculate "on pain of being prosecuted to the utmost rigour of the law." As late as 1768 an inoculation in Norfolk, Virginia, resulted in the adoption of a province-wide regulatory statute. A common reason for such displays of hostility, however, was not the treatment itself but the absence of proper safeguards. As these were supplied, the opposition everywhere subsided. The American soldiers in the Revolutionary War were inoculated as a matter of course. In the longer run the controversy helped prepare the public mind for the acceptance a generation later of the then newly discovered and more efficacious method of vaccination—inoculation with cowpox vaccine—which is still the modern way.

The eighteenth century brought other advances in medical usage. Homemade remedies relinquished some of their hold, especially in the towns, although, as has been seen, prepared concoctions forged ahead. Likewise clergymen-practitioners steadily lost out to regular doctors. Although the great majority of future doctors continued to get their professional training from established physicians, a growing number now studied abroad, generally at the University of Edinburgh, which was reported to offer the best medical education in the British Empire. Here and there, too, the newer generation took up obstetrics, seeking to place that hitherto female vocation on a scientific basis. Dr. James Lloyd in Boston, entering the field in the 1750's, has been called America's pioneer "man-midwife," but others preceded him in Philadelphia, Charleston, and elsewhere.

There were parallel improvements in medical institutions. In 1752 the first general hospital in the colonies was opened in Philadelphia, with Franklin one of its principal backers, and it was followed in 1773 at Williamsburg by an establishment exclusively for the mentally deficient. This provision for their isolation and separate care marked a genuine advance—customarily such folk were simply jailed—but unfortunately the methods employed involved whipping and chaining the unruly as well as bleeding them copiously, in accordance with the approved system in Europe. Real understanding of the nature and treatment of insanity lay far in the future.

Still other steps sought to protect the community against the pretensions of impostors or "empiricks." New York in 1760 passed the first law requiring practitioners to be examined and licensed; and in the next few years physicians' associations sprang up to promote better standards in Connecticut, New Jersey, and Philadelphia. To the same end the College of Philadelphia in 1765 began offering instruction in medicine, with King's College following two years later. These signs of the times, though scattered and tardy in appearing, evidenced a hopeful trend toward greater professionalization.

A number of colonial doctors in the eighteenth century, moreover, published empirical observations to help their colleagues in the treatment of patients; to some degree these influenced European practice as well. Besides the writings already mentioned on herbal cures and smallpox inoculation, important clinical descriptions of scarlet fever and yellow fever were published by, respectively, Dr. William Douglass of Boston in 1736, and Dr. John Lining at Charleston in 1753. Studying a broader problem, Dr. Lionel Chalmers brought out in 1776 his *Account of the Weather and Diseases of South-Carolina,* an examination of the relations of climate to sickness. And, to include just one other name, Dr. Benjamin Rush of Philadelphia, destined to become a leader of the profession in the next generation, set forth in the early 1770's cogent views on such matters as personal hygiene, the merits of certain mineral waters, and the utility of Indian remedies. The colonists, to be sure, made no fundamental contributions to medical science, but, handicapped as they were by an ocean's distance from Europe's research centers and by their heavy daily duties, they displayed powers of inference and generalization which suggest that they might well have held their own with the Old World under equally favorable conditions.

In an over-all view the population, despite the inroads of disease, suffered relatively less than the masses in Europe. It was mainly the physically fit who settled the country, and the great majority of the colonists pursued healthful outdoor occupations. Besides, their better food and housing as compared with Europe conduced to robustness and increased their resistance to illness. Even the slaves, the one depressed class, were usually kept in good

condition, if only for economic reasons. The average life expectation, as calculated in 1789 for areas in Massachusetts and New
Hampshire, was thirty-five years, and it was doubtless the same
before the break with England. Although this span seems dis-
tressingly small today, its brevity owed much to the ill effects of
the high infant mortality. Once this dangerous period of infancy
was passed, youngsters had an excellent chance of surviving to a
ripe old age. Jefferson, Franklin, and John Adams, for example,
despite exacting public responsibilities, lived on respectively to
eighty-three, eighty-four, and ninety-one.

Although the workers in the various areas of science were
scattered up and down the coast, Philadelphia stood forth as the
pre-eminent center as the colonial period drew toward a close. This
was not only because of the stimulating presence there for many
years of Benjamin Franklin, but also because persons of scientific
bent could exchange ideas with fellow spirits in this largest of
America's cities. Furthermore, Philadelphia's great consequence
as a trading community kept the people in touch through travel,
correspondence, and the printed word with contemporary currents
of thought abroad. Not surprisingly, therefore, such significant
figures congregated there—in addition to Franklin—as Thomas
Evans, John Bartram, James Logan, David Rittenhouse, and
Thomas Godfrey, as well as Benjamin Rush, John Morgan, and
other acute minds on the medical faculty of Philadelphia College.

Inevitably, the pervasive interest in science, or "philosophy,"
led to a more formal association, the founding in 1769 of the
American Philosophical Society dedicated to "promoting useful
Knowledge" and admitting qualified persons elsewhere. It was a
direct copy of the Royal Society, which numbered Franklin and
Dr. John Morgan among its Fellows. Two smaller, earlier groups
joined forces to set up the organization, with Franklin serving as
president until his death in 1790, although prolonged absences
from the country restricted him during most of the time to a
nominal role. The original membership of 251 included 55 from
sister provinces and 26 from Europe, Canada, and the British
West Indies. Its scope was thus international as well as intercolonial.

The planning and partial financing of the local observations of

the transit of Venus in 1769 was the Society's first signal undertaking, and two years later it issued the initial volume of its
Transactions. Colonial science had at long last achieved a strong
sense of community and looked confidently to the future. To the
ebullient Tom Paine, lately arrived from England, it seemed, as he
wrote in the *Pennsylvania Magazine* in 1775, that "no nation"
had ever "in so short a time" accomplished so much in "the
labyrinth of art and science; and that not in the *acquisition* of
knowledge only, but in the happy advantages flowing *from* it."

CHAPTER XII

Artistic Groping

STRUGGLING TO BUILD a homeland in the wilderness, the colonists had little time for the arts. As in other affairs of life, utility remained the prime concern. In the words of a New England writer in 1719, "The Plow-Man that raiseth Grain, is more serviceable to Mankind, than the Painter who draws only to please the Eye. . . . The Carpenter who builds a good House to defend us from the Wind and Weather, is more serviceable than the curious Carver, who employs his Art to please the Fancy." This, he asserted, "condemns not Painting or Carving, but only shows, that what's more substantially serviceable to Mankind, is much preferable to what is less necessary." Besides, the settlers, coming by and large from the less cultivated classes of the Old World, had inherited no conscious interest in beauty for its own sake.

Unconsciously, however, they displayed a simplicity of taste that delights the eye of later generations. This appeared most strikingly perhaps in their intimate daily surroundings. Whether of British, Dutch, German, or other descent, the settlers fashioned for their homes objects that were attractive as well as functional. Just as they had brought folk medicine to the colonies, so, too, they brought folk art—an inbred feeling for simple lines and proportions going back to the craftsmanship of the Middle Ages. In due course some of the more talented artificers discovered they had salable articles and so converted their proficiency into a source of livelihood. By the eighteenth century no sizable community lacked such men.

The furniture in common use was above all else sturdy. Constructed of maple, oak, or other convenient timber, the pieces often served several purposes in the compact living quarters. A small table, for example, could by extension become a large one, while the back of a chair when tilted down became a table. Wood, pewter, and iron provided the usual materials for both dishes and kitchen utensils; the floors, formed of broad boards, were either sanded or partly covered with homemade rugs; and whitewash generally coated the walls. An unaffected simplicity and candor of design marked all the equipment.

With the growth of a wealthy class, both vanity and a desire for more opulent living wrought changes. Gentlefolk demanded elegant furnishings, preferably of English workmanship. They rejoiced in Windsor and Chippendale chairs and tables and took pride in their Venetian blinds, wallpaper in scenic patterns, silverware, china and glassware, oil paintings, four-poster and canopied beds, and other appurtenances befitting their station. Mahogany, imported from the West Indies or Central America, vied with local woods in their furniture. Basic good taste almost invariably underlay the sumptuousness.

To help meet the desire for these finer furnishings, native craftsmen strove to copy the best work done abroad and often-times equaled it. Paul Revere in Boston, for instance, was a silversmith who fashioned bowls, pitchers, candlesticks, and other pieces so exquisitely that they are esteemed as museum pieces today; and Henry William Stiegel in Pennsylvania, of German birth, turned out goblets, bottles, flasks, and other glassware of rare delicacy and charm. His products were sold by agents in towns from Philadelphia and Baltimore to Boston and are greatly prized by modern collectors.

Beauty for its own sake, however, was most deliberately pursued in the lovely colonial gardens, although the desire to grow medicinal herbs, berries, and such for household use was a supporting factor. Decorative plants of native origin grew beside those from the Old World. A contemporary has recorded, for instance, that the rich Charlestonian Henry Laurens in the mid-eighteenth century set out "everything useful or ornamental that Carolina produces or his extensive mercantile connections enabled him to procure." Amid the harshness of untamed nature, people rich and poor evidently sought solace and serenity in the fragrance of gardens. No group was indifferent, whether of Puritan, Quaker, or other religious background or of non-British lineage. Nearly all the varieties of flowers common today were in evidence: roses, lilacs, peonies, phlox, pansies, daffodils, asters, sweet peas, foxgloves, and pinks, to mention a few. Humble folk cultivated their small plots, while the affluent maintained spacious, formal grounds intersected with winding hedge-lined walks which, for greater effect, were often terraced.

As in the case of house interiors, domestic architecture also acquired a growing degree of decorative splendor among the rich. Dugouts and other rude lean-tos met the temporary needs of the first English comers; but for permanence they generally built houses of the sort they remembered from the old country. The log cabin, brought from their homelands by the Swedes to New Sweden on Delaware Bay in the seventeenth century and by the Germans to Pennsylvania early in the eighteenth, provided an exceptionally durable style of shelter. Built of horizontally laid logs interlocking at the corners and chinked with clay, moss, or wood chips, the log cabin rapidly commended itself to the Scotch-Irish and other colonists. It could be constructed of timber without the use of nails, which were both expensive and scarce; and the only tool required was an ax. Primarily a frontier house, the log cabin also became a common habitation of poorer folk in the coastal communities and of slaves in the South. After the colonial period, of course, it was to attend the march of the pioneers through the forested trans-Appalachian region.

More ambitious architectural styles began to appear in major towns as well as on country estates as the eighteenth century approached. These styles mirrored the transformation of taste in England that had followed the devastating London fire of 1666. In rebuilding the city the great Sir Christopher Wren was the dominant figure; and a host of architectural manuals, prepared to speed the undertaking, in due course found their way across the Atlantic. There, in the absence of professional architects, the colonial carpenters ransacked the handbooks for ideas they might apply themselves.

The first result was a rather slavish imitation of the classic Renaissance forms that had swept England; but, as the builders

grew in skill, they were wise enough and accomplished enough
to adapt it to local needs and circumstances. The outcome was
Colonial Georgian, in full fashion by the second quarter of the
eighteenth century. Reduced to its elements, the Georgian house
was, as in England, a rectangular structure of two or three stories
with a balanced arrangement of windows and dormers and a
chastely decorated entryway. Inside it displayed an exquisite
composition of paneling, cornices, mantelpieces, and staircases.
Its satisfying proportions breathed an atmosphere of stateliness,
fitness, and charm.

The modifications of English Georgian were due largely to the
distinctive building materials and climatic conditions of the colonies. The New England gentry, for example, commonly substi-
tuted timber for stone, making the end walls of brick when they
contained chimneys, as a safeguard against fire, while from New
York southward full brick construction was the rule, thanks to the
abundant clay deposits. The Southern planters, in addition, liked
pillared front porches for comfort during the hot summers, and
they situated their kitchens and slave quarters away from the main
house, oftentimes connecting them with it by means of colon-
nades. Whatever the local variations, the effect everywhere was
less austere, the lines pleasanter and more restful, than the transatlantic original.

Public architecture was best represented in the omnipresent
places of worship. In early New England the Puritan determination to avoid the ostentation of the hated Church of England
produced the simple square, white meetinghouse, which on occasion could serve also as a town hall and courthouse. Even in the
South, where Anglicanism held sway and churches were restricted
to devotional exercises, they at first were nearly as plain, possessing at most a cube-shaped tower over the entrance and leaded-
glass windows. Religion in the first century of settlement was not
deemed to require a distinctive outer appearance.

But, as in the case of private houses, the architectural revolution in England and the mounting wealth in the colonies wrought
a change. The trend in the eighteenth century was for churches to
signify their holy mission by external appearance. The Quakers
alone among major faiths persisted in unadorned meetinghouses

befitting their creed. The characteristic feature of the new mode was the slender, perfectly proportioned spire. Foremost among church designers was the English-born Newport merchant and shipowner, Peter Harrison, active in the mid-eighteenth century. An accomplished amateur, who also designed several secular edifices, he never accepted a fee for his services. Boston and Cambridge, as well as Newport, benefited from his work, which was invariably marked by individuality and monumental qualities. He stands out as the ablest architect in the entire colonial period.

Painting meanwhile ran a somewhat similar course before it too attained the status of a fine art. Even as late as 1767 John Singleton Copley wrote, "The people generally regard it no more than any other usefull trade, . . . not as one of the most noble Arts in the World." Copley's view of its lofty character was amply sustained by the quality of his own work, but the attitude he bewailed grew naturally out of the circumstances of colonial life.

Painting for practical ends had, as Copley indicated, prospered from early times; and the results, if crude to the modern eye, met the needs of the day. Thus the making of signs gave men in business a potent means of attracting customers. A silversmith might display the likeness of a teakettle with a candlestick, a watchmaker the picture of a clock dial, and so it went with their fellow tradesmen. Innkeepers, more picturesquely, exhibited symbols less representative of their vocation, though undoubtedly equally appealing to their patrons. Typical was a bull's head or a prancing horse, a ship in full sail or a bunch of grapes. A Philadelphia tavern waggishly justified its name of "The Quiet Woman" with the painting of a female without a head. These practices, all borrowed from the Old World, incidentally lent a welcome relief of color to the otherwise somber streets.

Almost from the outset, too, there was a demand by families for "face-pictures." In an age before the invention of photography these supplied the sole means of recording personal resemblances. Thus they also accomplished at bottom a utilitarian purpose. Only the well-to-do, however, could afford to have their portraits painted, and even they had at first no choice but to sit to self-taught amateurs whose brushwork was typically stiff and lifeless.

But the artistic quality improved as the ranks of the rich increased and the practitioners gained in experience. Occasionally, too, upper-class worthies patronized European portraitists while on sojourns abroad or when the painters visited America. Even lesser folk, if they desired, could gratify their vanity at small cost by having their own faces added to standardized bodies by itinerant limners.

By the second quarter of the eighteenth century some of the artists had achieved an intercolonial reputation. Outstanding were the Swedish-born Gustavus Hesselius of Philadelphia, the Scottish-born John Smibert in Boston, and the Newporter Robert Feke. Even so, they were eclipsed by two who followed them: Benjamin West and John Singleton Copley, who won international as well as intercolonial fame. Both were natives of America, and both, to their country's loss, later found residence in England artistically more congenial.

West, born near Philadelphia in 1738, the son of an innkeeper from England, displayed youthful talent in pictures of birds and flowers and at the age of fifteen struck off a likeness of a lady in Lancaster. Constantly improving his technique by practice with some guidance from established practitioners, he secured passage in 1760 on a trading vessel to Italy, the first native colonist to view with a painter's eyes the masterpieces of the art center of the West. Stopping in London on his way back three years later with examples of his work, he was so cordially received that he remained till his death in 1820.

One of West's early English compositions inaugurated an epoch in British art. In his "Death of Wolfe" (1771), inspired by the tragic event of the siege of Quebec in the recent French and Indian War, he disregarded long-established convention by putting the heroic figures not in robes, helmet, and breastplates, but in the clothes they actually wore. Appointed shortly afterward historical painter to the King, he divided his time thenceforth between executing royal commissions and depicting suavely the fashionable and prominent of the day, vying for sitters with such eminent portraitists as Thomas Gainsborough and Sir Joshua Reynolds. Even so, West never forgot his American roots and made no secret of his sympathy with the patriots in their struggle for freedom. His greatest service to the land of his birth, however, lay in the unfailing encouragement he gave young American artists studying abroad. For half a century his studio was a training school for some of the gifted painters of the generation following Independence.

Copley, born the same year as West, was the son of Irish immigrant parents who ran a tobacco shop in Boston. He, too, learned by perseverance from childhood, turning out at the age of fourteen his first recorded likeness, that of a half-brother. Growing steadily in proficiency, he portrayed in the next score of years a whole gallery of richly clad worthies in Boston, New York, and Philadelphia. Nor did he disdain persons of humbler station. His portrait of Paul Revere, for instance, shows the silversmith in his work clothes admiring a teapot of his own making. Whether delineating high or low, Copley strove for rigorous and exact truth.

Urged by repeated letters from West, and spurred on probably by the fact that his wife's family were Tories and he himself had been threatened by mob violence, Copley went to Europe in 1774. After a preliminary pilgrimage to Italy, he settled down in England, where he died in 1815. Like West, he painted historical episodes in London as well as the celebrities of the time; but his severe, penetrating work—even though his painting in exile was more uneven than in his American period—has lasted far better than West's softer and more romantic pictures.

The colonies were not entirely the aesthetic wasteland perceived by the two expatriates. West, indeed, had succumbed to the lure of London without giving America a real try; and Copley by 1768 was earning three hundred guineas a year in Boston—an income he estimated to be worth treble the sum in England. If these painters left no one of equal stature behind them, the larger towns all had artists with sufficient skill and patronage to make a living. On the other hand, none of their canvases—not even those of Copley or West—conveyed the full sweep of colonial life. Since portraiture supplied the surest income, the practitioners rarely treated religious themes—Hesselius being a striking exception—and notwithstanding the wonders of primeval nature they also neglected landscapes. No doubt the savage forest and rugged terrain excited in colonial breasts emotions other than artistic.

Paintings, moreover, whatever their kind or merit, reached at best a limited audience, since they were confined to the homes of the well-off. Nowhere were there art museums to shape the average man's taste. Common folk throughout most of the colonial period saw only the rude black-and-white illustrations of almanacs and short-lived magazines. Newspapers, because of inadequate mechanical facilities, carried none at all until 1754 save for occasional stock cuts. Then Franklin, a pioneer in all he touched, published in his *Pennsylvania Gazette* on the eve of the Albany Congress the likeness of a snake split into sections representing the colonies and captioned: "JOIN or DIE."

Twice again, after the rise of the difficulties with Britain, editors resorted to the device—at the time of the Stamp Act in 1765 and of the Coercive Acts in 1774—but otherwise they based the colonial case on words. The patriots found it more feasible to make their visual appeals through cartoons circulated as broadsides and often hand-colored for greater emphasis. A memorable instance was Paul Revere's gory engraving of the Boston Massacre. With such transitory attempts at art the mass of people had to content themselves.

Sculpture showed no development comparable to architecture and painting, perhaps because latent talent failed to obtain the same support from the wealthy. The accomplishments, such as they were, took the form mainly of gravestones chiseled by self-trained craftsmen. These varied from death's-heads, hourglasses, scythes, and other grim reminders of mortality to happier symbols like floral designs and winged cherubs. Workmen also carved figureheads for ships and made weathervanes out of wood or iron for steeples. A venturesome few late in the colonial period went farther afield. For instance, a Boston artificer in plaster advertised in 1768 busts of the King and Queen along with images of cats, dogs, and parrots—no *lèse-majesté* intended—while Patience Wright, a widow of Bordentown, New Jersey, did her modeling in colored wax. For added effect she dressed her life-size figures in real clothing. Going to England in 1772, Mrs. Wright received so many commissions that she stayed abroad the remaining decade or so of her life. It was not until the nineteenth century was well under way that Americans demonstrated any genuine capacity in sculpture.

Music fared hardly better as a creative endeavor, although otherwise the interest in it was widespread and deep. As a matter of course the colonists cherished the melodies brought with them from the Old World, both for religious purposes and as a deep-seated folk custom. Churches, to be sure, differed in their attitudes. To the Anglicans, Lutherans, Dutch Reformed, Baptists, and Methodists, as well as to the Catholics and most of the German Pietistic sects, music redounded to the glory of God. But the Congregationalists and Presbyterians worried lest it woo the senses of worshipers to the detriment of true piety. The Quakers, entertaining no doubt on the point, rigorously banned all music, whether vocal or instrumental.

The moral problems posed by music to the Congregationalists were, first, whether psalms should be spoken by a deacon line by line before being sung by the congregation; then, after this system was abandoned, whether the members should proceed alone or with the help of a choir; and, finally, whether instrumental music should accompany the singing. With much searching of souls and at an uneven pace, music infiltrated the service, although as late as 1790 no meetinghouses in Boston had organs. The increasing tolerance led William Billings, a twenty-four-year-old Boston tanner, to bring out in 1770 a collection of his own hymns, which, he asserted, had "more than twenty times the power of the old slow tunes." These with other pieces written later in the century—over three hundred in all—won wide favor both in and out of New England, although they have not stood the test of time. Billings is also credited with having introduced the pitch-pipe and the violoncello to improve church music.

The Moravians, centered in Bethlehem, Pennsylvania, went furthest in wedding music and godliness, employing congregational singing and choirs as well as assortments of musical instruments. Franklin was charmed on attending a service in 1746 to find that "flutes, oboes, French horns, and trumpets, accompanied the organ." The membership also maintained a community orchestra that, alive to the best European music, played the works of such composers as Handel, Haydn, and Johann Christian Bach. Moreover, in their zeal to convert the aborigines, the Moravians published in 1763 a collection of hymns in the language of the Delawares. Had the Moravians not dwelt in rural solitude, their example might have brought about an ampler use of music by the Anglo-American denominations.

Even more deeply embedded in the heritage from overseas were the folk songs. They recited the joys and tribulations of this life instead of the next one, and most had been handed down from generation to generation. Those of more recent vintage came from London on inexpensive handbills. Lighthearted or plaintive, as suited the occasion, the words were sung in the home, at neighborhood gatherings, and, most noisily, by roisterers at the taverns to the scraping of fiddles. Sometimes, to lend local color, the lines were appropriately altered, and as partisan feeling heightened over provincial issues, a political purpose now and then crept in, sometimes to the wrath of the authorities. Thus in 1734 a New York grand jury friendly to the governor ordered the burning of two "Seditious Songs" by the public executioner, and in 1751 the Massachusetts legislature demanded the arrest forthwith of the distributors of a ballad whose sentiments, the lawmakers asserted, "tend very much to weaken if not subvert the happy Constitution of this Government."

Therefore, it was natural for the colonists, once trouble broke out with England, to use the same method against the Ministry and Parliament. Each crisis called forth a fresh crop of songs. "Hearts of Oak," "Derry Down," "Smile Britannia," and "The British Grenadiers" were the favorite airs, with patriots of the standing of Joseph Warren, Thomas Paine, and John Dickinson among the versifiers. Dickinson's offering, "The Liberty Song" (1768), proved especially effective, since he brought to it the enormous prestige of having written the influential *Farmer's Letters*. Set to the strains of "Hearts of Oak," his spirited words were circulated on broadsides and to a still wider public in newspapers and almanacs. John Adams considered the musical efforts an excellent way of "cultivating the sensations of freedom," while Joel Barlow, later the "Connecticut Wit," asserted impudently, "One good song is worth a dozen addresses or proclamations."

Religious and folk music held sway almost exclusively until the eighteenth century was well under way and enough people in the towns began to crave the kind of music relished by cultured Europeans. Public concerts had their beginning in the 1730's at Boston, New York, and Charleston, with performers from abroad; and the same decade saw the introduction of light opera in the latter two places. Then, after a time, interested citizens in these and other sizable communities joined together to sponsor musical events regularly on a subscription basis and availed themselves increasingly of native talent. The outstanding instance was the St. Cecilia Society of Charleston, formed in 1762, which outlived all its contemporaries, not disbanding finally until 1912.

Such organizations drew on an expanding pool of colonial musicians as well as an ever larger number of amateurs playing for their own enjoyment. With the upper class in both town and country, indeed, musical skills became a mark of gentility. The instruments embraced virtually all of those known today—the flute, flageolet, oboe, clarinet, mandolin, harpsichord, pianoforte, and others—and members of both sexes could learn to play from instructors advertising in the press. Among the Revolutionary leaders Jefferson whiled away time on the violin and violoncello, and Franklin diverted himself with the violin, harp, guitar, and harmonica (the name then for musical glasses). Dissatisfied, however, with the harmonica's imperfections, Franklin in 1761 characteristically devised one that was both truer in pitch and simpler to play. His version so commended itself to Europe that Mozart and Beethoven composed pieces for it.

However, despite the widespread interest in the best secular music abroad, only one American—and he very late in the colonial period—showed much interest in composing. In 1759 Francis Hopkinson, a twenty-two-year-old Philadelphian and recent graduate of the College, struck off "My Days Have Been So Wondrous Free" and three companion songs; but these, remaining in manuscript, were known only to his friends. Later pieces were published during and after the Revolution and won contemporary praise. None of his efforts proved of lasting worth, however, and his place in the history of American music lies in his priority as a composer, anticipating the hymnologist Billings by more than a decade. A lawyer tireless in public affairs, Hopkinson wrote songs simply as a pastime. To posterity he is better known as a signer of the Declaration of Independence.

Thus the colonists, while achieving some musical sophistication as consumers, made no lasting additions of their own to the world's fund of music. Nor did they even contribute much to America's own store. The one tune that has never lost its appeal, "Yankee Doodle," was of a popular, catchy character and, in any case, was almost certainly of English folk origin. The air seems first to have come into prominence during the French and Indian War when a British officer is said to have set words to it deriding the motley appearance of the New England forces. In like spirit the redcoats at the opening of the Revolutionary War started off to Lexington in step to the melody. But the pert, staccato rhythm so tickled the rebels that in short order they appropriated it for themselves by substituting their own jocular verses—a prize seized from the enemy. When Cornwallis surrendered at Yorktown, the American musicians played "Yankee Doodle" and the British band wailed "The World Turned Upside Down." It was in this unpremeditated fashion, then, that the new republic acquired its first and sprightliest national song.

In sum, the colonists in their attitude toward the arts, whether music or other fields, never altogether ignored esthetic values, despite their remoteness from the centers of European culture and the burden of taming a new continent; and they progressed in appreciation as time went on. "After the first Cares for the Necessaries of Life are over," Franklin wrote in 1763, "we shall come to think of the Embellishments. Already some of our young Geniuses begin to lisp Attempts at Painting, Poetry, and Musick." But the insistent demands of daily living continued to divert interest from "the Embellishments" to the close of the colonial era, as well as for some time thereafter. As John Adams lamented in 1776, "I wish I had Leisure, and Tranquility of Mind to amuse myself with these Elegant, and ingenious Arts of Painting, Sculpture, Statuary, Architecture, and Musick. But I have not."

The greatest progress was associated as a matter of course with the cities, where the majority of those with wealth and taste resided and where the closest ties existed with Europe. And, as was logical with a transplanted people, the accomplishments were essentially imitative, aiming to reproduce as well as possible the amenities of the older civilization. In none of the fine arts did the colonists achieve an authentically American style. This had to await greater cultural maturity and a more vivid sense of national purpose.

CHAPTER XIII

The
Lighter Side of Life

In TAKING UP a new life across the Atlantic, the settlers had no thought of abandoning the diversions with which their ancestors had traditionally relieved the tedium of life. Neither the harshness of existence on the new continent, nor the scattered population, nor clerical disapproval discouraged the majority from the pursuit of pleasure.

City and country, of course, conducted this pursuit in different ways. Farm dwellers in their isolation not only found it harder to locate companions in play but also, thanks to the unending demands of their work, felt it necessary to combine fun with purpose. No other set of colonists took so seriously Poor Richard's admonition: "Leisure, is Time for doing something useful." In the countryside men therefore tempered the daily grind with such double-purpose relaxations as hunting, fishing, and trapping. When a neighbor needed help, families rallied from miles around to assist in a house or barn raising, a corn husking, a sheep shearing, or a chopping bee. The resulting social respite, accompanied by food, drink, and rough merrymaking, soothed weary muscles.

The crowning social events were the rural fairs. These, continuing for several days, took place once or twice a year outside New England and at irregular times there. Hundreds of men, women, and children attended from far and near. The men bought or traded livestock and secured needed merchandise; their wives displayed preserves, pickles, and other creations of their kitchens; and everyone, including the youngsters, watched or participated in a variety of competitive sports, with prizes awarded the winners. These events typically included horse races, wrestling bouts, foot races (for each sex), and, on the comic side, greased-pig chases and grinning and whistling matches, while the Southern fairs often added beauty contests. No other occasions did so much to relieve the isolation of farm existence.

With the open countryside everywhere at hand, townsfolk naturally shared in some of the rustic diversions. No less a personage than Boston's Cotton Mather, for instance, found time for fishing; and on one jaunt, his friend Judge Sewall records in his diary, the learned angler tumbled into a pond, "the boat being ticklish." Other favored recreations were hunting, sleighing, skating, and swimming. But city dwellers also developed pleasures which only compact communities made possible and which, in any event, their rural brethren had neither the time nor the means to enjoy. Central to most of them were the urban taverns.

These hostelries not only offered lodging for man and beast but also provided places where the men of the locality could forgather for convivial drinking, to read the latest newpapers, exchange ideas, and otherwise disport themselves. Everybody could find something to his taste. The grounds outside the inns provided facilities for target shooting, bowling, and quoits as well as, in the South, rings or pits for animal baiting and cockfighting. Indoors one could indulge in chess, backgammon, billiards, and, above all, cards—a game provocative of widespread gambling. An austere citizen like John Adams scorned cards, wherever or however played, as "great antidotes to Reflection," but the popular addiction may be judged from the fact that they were sold in stores from Portsmouth to Charleston and as far inland as settlements in the Shenandoah Valley. Six thousand packs were imported into supposedly strait-laced Boston alone in 1772.

The taverns further provided accommodations for dancing, which was popular with both high and low. Although clerics in early Massachusetts had denounced *"Gynecandrical Dancing"* (that is, jointly by the sexes) as a satanic invention, few people heeded this warning, since the Bible itself cited the practice without disapproval. By the eighteenth century dancing classes flourished in Boston as in all other sizable towns. A fiddle or banjo provided the music at simpler gatherings; perhaps a flute, violoncello, and spinet at the fashionable ones. Similarly, the dances varied from spirited jigs and reels to the dignified minuets and gavottes so popular with the gentry.

At the taverns, too, the men's clubs usually held their meetings. These groups existed even in small towns. Some were purely social in character and some were reading circles, but the great majority coupled good fellowship with a civic, moral, or charitable purpose. The Junto, fathered in Philadelphia by Franklin in 1727 and described for posterity in his autobiography, well illustrates the aim of community welfare. Designed as a means for self-improvement for mechanics and small tradesmen, the Junto succeeded so well that it stimulated the formation of five or six counterparts within the city.

Among colonial organizations the Masonic order occupied a special place. It enjoyed the prestige of extending across provincial borders and offered the enticements of ritual and secrecy to a people having little of either in their lives. Introduced at Philadelphia in 1730 following the revitalization of the parent body in England in 1717, the Masons numbered more than forty lodges from Portsmouth to Savannah before 1776. Their ranks included well-known figures in their respective communities such as James Otis, Paul Revere, Franklin, and Washington. Nonetheless, the oath of secrecy at times excited popular hostility. The New York members on one occasion were "complimented with Snow Balls and Dirt" when parading the streets. In Philadelphia, resentment over the death of an apprentice in a bogus initiation caused the lodge, though blameless in the affair, to suspend its activities from 1738 to 1749. This practice of joining together for larger purposes prepared the colonists for collective political action when the breach developed with Britain. Then the merchants' and mechanics' committees, the committees of correspondence, and other groups provided the structure of the movement for Independence.

The taverns also served as headquarters for the sale of lottery tickets, a legal form of gambling that appealed to the sporting instincts of all classes. George Washington, for one, purchased chances time and again. Some lotteries were public in origin, providing the authorities painlessly with money for building roads and bridges and for reducing government debt, as well as for churches and colleges. Others were conducted by private individuals for personal gain. A New York carpenter in 1762 spent ten shillings in a lottery for erecting a lighthouse and won the grand award of £5,000—an achievement that no doubt kept hopes alive in many other breasts. Lesser prizes in lotteries included clothing, jewelry, furniture, houses, and land.

As time went on, the lotteries became so crooked that in the half-century before 1776 every province but Maryland and North Carolina banned all but government ventures. The British government, going further, in 1769 forbade public as well as private varieties except with express Crown approval. This action accorded with London's new policy of tighter imperial control, although for reasons largely rooted in their charters the prohibition did not apply to Rhode Island, Connecticut, Maryland, and Delaware.

The twofold set of restrictions brought about a reduction in the number of duly authorized projects and an increase of those run surreptitiously. So long as the rules were honestly administered, few Americans saw anything wrong in the transactions. Life had accustomed them to taking chances. Even among the religious, the Quakers were the only sect who throughout and unfailingly pronounced the undertakings immoral. It was not until fifty years or more after Independence that a radical reversal of the popular attitude at last brought effective steps to outlaw every form of lottery.

The upper classes increasingly imitated the diversions of the English aristocracy, and most of all in the plantation South. There the dances of the gentry typically took the form of sumptuous balls or "assemblies," and horse races consisted of the matching of blooded steeds for lavish prizes. There, too, sports like cockfighting and fox hunting flourished, the latter conducted by parties of gaily attired horsemen with baying hounds. Washington and Jefferson relished such pastimes, disporting themselves at balls, maintaining fine horses and hunting dogs, and donning the latest styles in riding apparel. During January and February 1769, Washington rode to the hounds fifteen times.

A fashionable diversion, reaching its peak in the closing colonial years, was the seasonal migration to mineral springs. These resorts, lying within easy reach in both the North and the South, enabled the elite to cultivate each other's company while seeking to heal the gout or kindred complaints or to stay the inroads of more serious ills. The major retreats, like Bristol and Yellow Springs in Pennsylvania, drew patrons from afar and thus incidentally served to promote attachments across provincial boundaries. In the growing troubles with Britain this commingling proved an impalpable factor in consolidating a common American sentiment.

Of annual holidays Christmas was the most widely celebrated, although Puritan New Englanders shunned it as savoring of Popery and the Quakers rejected it as detracting from true spirituality. For the rest the occasion called for church attendance but, even more, for merriment, feasting, and the exchange of gifts. Two modern features, however, were absent. Only the Dutch in New York had a role for St. Nicholas, their Santa Claus, whose legend they had brought from their homeland. The Knickerbocker Santa, though, was not a jolly sprite but stern and dignified of mien. He flew through the sky with reindeer and sleigh and descended chimneys with gifts or switches for children according to their deserts. The other symbol of the observance—the Christmas tree—remained unknown to Americans until German immigrants introduced it in the mid-nineteenth century.

Other commemorations tended to be regional or local in scope. Thanksgiving, a practice that originated in Virginia and was popularized by the Pilgrims of Plymouth, was solemnized for many years whenever occasion arose to attest gratitude for a teeming crop, a military success, or some other good fortune. Gradually, however, it assumed the guise of a regular autumn event at harvest time. All work then ceased, and families went to church, after which they would gorge at their tables on roast turkey and pumpkin pie. Although Thanksgiving did not become a universal American custom until long after the Revolution, the culinary traditions of colonial times continue to mark the day.

In addition, people in the larger centers held observances of a more special type. Royal birthdays prompted fireworks and the din of cannons, topped off by civic banquets with oratory and the imbibing of countless toasts. Ethnic groups honored their patron saints in somewhat comparable manner. It was also usual for young men and boys on the fifth of November—the so-called Gunpowder Plot or Guy Fawkes Day—to parade the streets in fantastic garb, bearing effigies of the Pope and his presumed ally, the devil, and creating general confusion. The curious, moreover, could on almost any day escape boredom by watching the flogging of evildoers and their exhibition in the stocks and the pillory. The hanging of extreme offenders proved the climactic show. When, for example, two pirates met their fate at Newport in 1760, a crowd of five or six thousand looked on. Instances are on record of women in their excitement even leaping on death carts with condemned men.

As the eighteenth century advanced, itinerant showmen from abroad visited the principal cities offering brand-new uses for leisure. The enlarging populations now assured them adequate patronage. Audiences gazed entranced at slack-wire performers, equestrians, tumblers, and jugglers, also conjurors, marionettes, midgets, and waxworks. One self-styled "Master of sleight of hand" notified *Pennsylvania Chronicle* readers in 1769 that he would throw in as a bonus an infallible cure for nagging wives. There were likewise exhibits of exotic animals: lions, tigers, leopards, camels, and a polar bear in Boston in 1733 ("a sight far preferable to the Lion in the Judgment of all Persons who have seen both"), and a domestic cat in Philadelphia in 1737 "having one head, eight legs, two tails and from the breast down two bodies." These attractions foreshadowed the nineteenth-century circus.

Even the theater had gained a firm foothold, though in face of considerable opposition. Stern religionists condemned stage plays as conducive to impiety and loose morals—"highways to hell"— while many who were worldly-minded pronounced them an unconscionable waste of time and money. Cried a multisigned Philadelphia protest of 1767, the performances "divert the minds of the people and more especially of the unwary youths from the necessary application of the several employments by which they may be qualified to become useful members of society."

The Friends, with allies among the Pennsylvania Presbyterians, Lutherans, and Baptists, waged unceasing war against the stage, but their efforts had only temporary effect and in the final decades suffered total rout. Besides this determined resistance from outside their ranks they encountered Britain's repeated vetoes of prohibitory legislation. In New England, however, puritanical bias plus the Yankee passion for thrift succeeded in averting the threat of playhouses. But elsewhere in the colonies no substantial barriers existed, and the theater needed only a sufficient degree of local enterprise to flower.

The earliest performances were given in taverns, warehouses, and courtrooms by local amateurs, supplemented perhaps with strolling players. As audiences became more critical, they demanded ampler staging and more finished acting. Between 1716 and 1736 buildings suitable for plays were erected in Williamsburg, New York, and Charleston; Philadelphia and Annapolis followed in 1759 and 1771, with New England of course continuing to stand aloof. Of these places Williamsburg and Annapolis were sleepy hamlets most of the year until in their role as provincial capitals they drew to them during legislative sessions members eager to indulge with their wives and friends in playgoing on the side.

For a better quality of performance, Americans had to wait until after the mid-century for the arrival of a company of professional performers from England. Led by Mr. and Mrs. Lewis Hallam, and outfitted, as the *Virginia Gazette* reported, with "scenes, Cloaths, and Decorations entirely new, extremely rich, and finished in the highest Taste," they made their New World debut at Williamsburg in 1752. So warm was the reception of their first effort, *The Merchant of Venice,* as well as of the pieces which followed, that they proceeded during the next twenty-three years—until stopped by the outbreak of war—to play repeatedly in cities from New York to Charleston, touring even communities where the stage accommodations were still primitive. The American Company, as it came to be called, shortly lost Hallam by death, so that his talented wife, who presently married a fellow actor, thereafter continued under her new name of Mrs. David Douglass to head the outfit, with her son Lewis Hallam, Jr., as a leading man.

In the larger towns the troupe usually remained several months, presenting as many as thirty or more plays. The London public in a single season probably saw no greater number. Along with Shakespeare and other standard works the offerings included contemporary favorites like Garrick's *Miss in Her Teens,* Addison's *Cato,* Otway's *The Orphan* and Gay's *The Beggar's Opera.* For good measure a farce was generally added to the main attraction as an afterpiece. The American Company's production in New York in 1769 of Dibdin's version of Bickerstaffe's *The Paddock* within eight months of its London premiere affords a striking illustration of how closely colonial theatergoers kept abreast of the current drama in the old country. The troupe's acting received lavish praise as well as occasional criticism in the press, and obviously its true worth cannot rightly be judged at this distance in time. But the unfailing patronage accorded the players for nearly a quarter of a century attests convincingly to the popular acclaim.

Thus, after a slow and laborious start, the theater became the principal commercial amusement. George Washington, a devotee of the drama from youth to old age, witnessed eleven performances of the American Company in Williamsburg and eight at Annapolis during the theatrical season 1771–2. In Philadelphia, to be sure, the company, faced with religious opposition, felt it prudent to announce it had taken care to "expunge" from Congreve's *The Mourning Bride* "every passage that might be offensive to either decency or good manners." Doubtless similar concessions were made in other instances and places before or after the fact.

In the long run, indeed, even perverse New England somewhat succumbed by condoning plays when blandly billed as public readings or moral discourses. Thanks to this subterfuge, Bostonians in the 1760's and 1770's were able to listen without legal retaliation to *The Orphan, The Beggar's Opera,* Rowe's *Tamerlane,* and the like. And by the same casuistry Newporters in 1762 attended *Othello,* described as "a series of MORAL DIALOGUES in *Five Parts*

Depicting the evil effects of jealousy and other bad passions and
Proving that happiness can only spring from the pursuit of Virtue."

Despite the zest for playgoing, however, no colonists prior to
the decade preceding the Revolution tried their own hands at
writing for the theater; and, even then, only one succeeded in
having his brain-child produced professionally. This drama, *The
Prince of Parthia,* a tragedy in blank verse on an Oriental theme,
was acted by the American Company in Philadelphia in 1767. It
was the posthumous work of Thomas Godfrey, Jr., a Philadelphia
migrant to Wilmington, North Carolina. But apparently it did not
survive the single performance, and its sole claim to memory
today lies in its having been the first full-length play by a native
author to be actually staged in America.

Another effort of the same year got as far as rehearsal. This
was *The Disappointment; or, The Force of Credulity,* a rollicking
comedy by Thomas Forrest, a Philadelphian using the pseudonym
"Andrew Barton," of whom little else is now known. The Forrest
piece freely lampooned local citizens—their identity only thinly
disguised—as determined to recover the supposed buried treasure
of Blackbeard the pirate. At the last moment threats against the
management by some of those ridiculed prevented it from being
shown. The text, however, doubtless to the glee of many, had
already seen print at the safe distance of New York.

Forrest's play, though of little intrinsic merit, possessed at
least the virtue of treating an American theme—a course that was
consistently emulated by the handful of colonial authors who
followed. They, however, wrote for fireside perusal instead of for
the stage, their works appearing in newspapers and pamphlets.
Robert Munford, a Virginia planter, thus set down in 1770
(though without publishing) *The Candidates: or, The Humours
of a Virginia Election,* a bit of drollery for his friends prompted by
his service in the House of Burgesses. As tension with the mother
country tightened the writers aimed their shafts at British "tyranny," and the humor, when present, was savagely satirical. In
these circumstances Mrs. Mercy Warren in Massachusetts, sister
of James Otis, wrote *The Adulateur* (1773), which pilloried
Governor Hutchinson and his associates, as well as *The Group*
(1775), portraying the dire effects of Parliament's recent emascu-

lation of the provincial charter. And early in 1776 Munford, now in deadly serious vein, penned *The Patriots,* which contrasted the genuine with the spurious variety in the Old Dominion. These dramatic discourses—and there were others—possessed little artistic worth, but that was not their aim: they were tracts for the times.

To Dr. Benjamin Rush in Philadelphia it was distressing that through the passage of years urban pastimes had come more and more to involve mere passive participation. "Man was formed to be active," he argued in a pamphlet of 1772 urging a return to healthy recreations like walking, running, swimming, skating, pitching quoits, and bowling. And, thanks to his sojourn as a medical student at the University of Edinburgh, he further recommended the introduction of golf, "an exercise which is much used by the Gentlemen in Scotland" and "is played with little leather balls stuffed with feathers." Unknown to Rush, however, the game of *kolf* had long since been brought over from Holland by the settlers of New Netherland, though without yet spreading to the English colonies. The wildness with which the balls were driven had indeed caused some of their towns to exclude it from their more densely settled parts.

Rush voiced undue alarm. What he inferred from indications in America's largest city he magnified into an impending danger to colonial urban dwellers everywhere. In reality, of course, the debilitating effects of spectator entertainments lay in the far distant future. Nevertheless, his fears presently received seeming confirmation from a distinguished intercolonial gathering. The First Continental Congress in 1774 bound its members by "sacred ties" to discourage "all Horse Racing, and all Kinds of Gaming, Cock Fighting, Exhibitions of Shews, Plays, and other expensive Diversions and Entertainments." The motive, however, was in no sense anxiety over the ill consequences to health but an intent to make it easier for the public to bear the hardships of the economic nonintercourse which had been adopted by the body to extort concessions from Britain. In any case, the outbreak of hostilities not long afterward discouraged every type of leisure-time activity.

The colonists in building a new society had thus never lost sight of the saving element of fun. Whether in country or town they had managed to leaven hard work with play. Where rural distractions, whatever their form, almost always had also a utilitarian purpose, urban living instilled a taste for pleasure for its own sake and an increasing bent toward commercial entertainments. The action of the Continental Congress in face of the crisis with Britain provided impressive evidence of the vital place recreation had come to occupy in colonial life.

CHAPTER XIV

The Emerging Pattern of Americanism

By 1776 nine generations of colonists had dwelt in North America since the landings at Jamestown and Plymouth. This was almost half the history of white settlement in the subcontinent; the years since 1776 have seen only ten more generations pass across the stage. And the first nine generations, despite the width of the ocean and the adjustments required by their new life, had never in these years lost their sense of being Englishmen. Indeed, time, distance, and the wilderness, instead of estranging them from the motherland, had dimmed the memory of the tribulations that had driven them across the Atlantic and, if anything, had increased their feeling of identity. As for the other European nationalities migrating to the New World, they had to a remarkable degree absorbed the habits and outlook, as well as the language, of the dominant English strain.

In every way possible the colonists had worked to reproduce the essentials of English civilization in the wild land beyond the sea. They read English literary works, cherished English political values, followed English commercial practices, paralleled English religious beliefs, adopted English educational methods, imitated English architecture, sang English songs, copied English dress, played English games. Even as the long years passed and as the colonies began to evolve institutions and purposes of their own, England remained their pervasive ideal.

This fidelity gained strength from the fact that rivalries among the colonies hindered the development of a common American loyalty that might otherwise have lessened the filial attachment. Founded for different reasons and at different times—more than a century separated the beginnings of Virginia and Georgia—each colony pursued its own course with scant regard for the well-being of others. In many cases the relationship to London was more direct and continuing than that to colonial neighbors.

Theological and national antagonisms were the first source of discord. As these faded, boundary disputes engendered constant friction, forcing the home government in nearly every instance to intervene to settle the differences. In trade, the colonies did not hesitate to levy discriminatory customs duties against one another. The absence of a uniform currency further impeded relations, since varying standards of value complicated business transactions up and down the coast. Even when need arose for joint action against the French or the Indians, it was hard to enlist cooperation from provinces not immediately endangered. To Andrew Burnaby, an English visitor in 1759–60, it seemed that "fire and water are not more heterogeneous than the different colonies in North-America. Nothing can exceed the jealousy and emulation, which they possess in regard to each other." He thought that civil war would rage "from one end of the continent to the other" should the colonies ever break away from Britain.

Until nearly the end, indeed, no event appeared more improbable than collective secession. The Boston merchant Thomas Banister expressed a universal view when he declared in 1715, "Different schemes, notions, customs, and manners will forever divide them from one another and unite them to the crown." No less emphatically, Governor William Shirley of Massachusetts four decades later stressed "how different the present Constitutions of their respective Governments are from each other; how much the Interests of some of them clash, & how opposite their Tempers are." And five years afterward, in 1760, Franklin stated out of his unrivaled knowledge of conditions that "they all love much more" the land "with which they have so many connexions and ties of blood, interest, and affection . . . than they love one another." He, however, presciently added that "tyranny and oppression" could change the situation.

Even when Britain in the period following 1763 imposed taxes and other irksome restraints on the Americans, their expressions of loyalty and devotion continued unchanged; and there can be little doubt of their sincerity. Almost to the very point of proclaiming Independence they still sought redress of grievances within the framework of the Empire. No patriot pamphleteer, however impassioned, then called for anything more. "Torn from the body to which we are united by religion, liberty, laws, affections, relations, language, and commerce," declared John Dickinson in the famous *Farmer's Letters* (1768), "we must bleed at every vein," and John Adams went so far as to say in *Novanglus* (1774) that "there is not a man in the province among the whigs, nor ever was," who wanted a separate existence.

Patriot assemblages reinforced such assurances. The Stamp Act Congress in 1765 asserted that the colonies "most ardently" desired the "perpetual continuance" of their ancient tie with London. The Massachusetts House of Representatives three years later not only flatly disavowed "the most distant thought of an Independency" but said that "the colonies would refuse it if offered to them, and would even deem it the greatest misfortune to be obliged to accept it." In its turn, the First Continental Congress, in 1774, stressed that "we shall always carefully and zealously endeavour to support and maintain" the connection. And when six months afterward the patriots resorted to arms, the Second Continental Congress, in July 1775, justifying the action, affirmed, "Honour, justice, and humanity, forbid us tamely to surrender that freedom which we received from our gallant ancestors, and which our innocent posterity have a right to receive from us," and still earnestly disclaimed any intent "to dissolve that union which has so long and so happily subsisted."

This deep-rooted devotion to the mother country did not rest on sentiment and habit alone. It reflected the tangible benefits of the relationship. These, as has been seen, affected every important aspect of the colonists' life. In matters of government they had through the years been permitted a latitude comparable if not superior to that of their brethren at home. Hence maxims like "no taxation without representation" and "government by consent" arose out of their actual experience in provincial affairs long before they became issues with distant London.

No traditional barriers, as in the Old World, had stood in the way of everyone's making full use of his talents. Although attempts were made in various provinces to impose the feudal system of quitrents, they met with such resistance from the settlers as to prove of little or no effect. The humblest person, therefore, could rise to a position of dignity and even of wealth on the basis of native ability. As James Russell Lowell put it, perhaps with his own forebears in mind, "Here, on the edge of the forest, where civilized man was brought face to face again with nature and taught mainly to rely on himself, mere manhood became a fact of prime importance." Nor did this prove any less true of indentured servants who after their temporary bondage struck out for themselves. Only the African slaves, not regarded as true members of society, faced an insuperable impediment.

Materially the colonists had prospered beyond compare under Britain's rule. The tiny settlements at the water's edge had expanded into an inhabited zone fifteen hundred miles along the seaboard and reaching inland to the Appalachians or farther, the whole comprising an area exceeding that of most Old World countries. While performing this herculean task, moreover, the people had diligently exploited extensive natural riches on both land and sea. Their surplus agriculture and fisheries had come to feed much of Europe. Their commerce had grown to more than a third the size of Britain's, and their shipyards built nearly an equal amount of her merchant marine. All this and more had been due in some degree to London's active help, inasmuch as the home government—for its own purposes, to be sure—stimulated the progress at various points with bounties, protective tariffs, and the security afforded trade routes by the imperial navy.

The settlers had likewise found religious asylum. Despite the initial persecution suffered by a few individuals and sects at the hands of fellow colonists, they, as well as the inhabitants in general, early acquired the liberty to worship as they pleased or not at all, even where the Church of England was officially established. In addition, the clergy, notably in New England, acted as political mentors, freely preaching doctrines of civil disobedience toward tyrants long before the difficulties arose with London. The colonists, moreover, as a result of the expansion of educational facilities, had become probably the most literate people on the globe. They had on their own made creditable contributions in letters and the arts and notably in science, where some had won international recognition.

All these opportunities and advantages had come to them under the British flag, enhancing their pride in being Englishmen. But the peace settlement of 1763, ending the Seven Years' War with France and Spain, wrought a change in the attitude of the mother country toward the colonies and a corresponding one in theirs toward her. In little more than a dozen years the colonists underwent an intellectual revolution that made political rebellion inevitable. At the end, they could see no alternative but to sever the connection they had so long and dearly prized.

The emergence of a transatlantic civilization, similar to the homeland's, yet necessarily somewhat different, had always held dangers if the relaxed conditions of the relationship should ever radically alter. Suddenly the time had come. Britain's territorial gains from the Seven Years' War tripled the size of her overseas possessions. On the North American mainland she received from France Canada and the region west of the thirteen colonies to the Mississippi, as well as Florida from Spain. In London's eyes the vastly enlarged responsibilities required a drastic reorganization of Empire to ensure that her domains, old and new, yield unreservedly to central direction and be rendered militarily secure. In part, too, London may have been responding to a dimly perceived need for greater central control within the North American colonies in order to deal with common problems of defense, trade, and expansion—a need that the Americans themselves would only fitfully recognize until the experiences of war and independence gave them new perspectives.

The imperial program in its application to the thirteen colonies had as its main features taxation by Parliament without their consent, vigorously enforced restrictions on their commerce, restraints on expanding into the former French territory beyond the Appalachians, and the stationing of armed forces in America to fend off possible Indian attacks. All this meant a greater sub-servience to London than the colonists had ever before known or envisaged or were willing to accord. It went against the grain of their whole way of life. And now that Canada was in Britain's hands and they no longer needed the home government for armed aid, they were freer to offer an unremitting resistance.

Unfortunately for the success of the new British policy, the means adopted were wavering and bungling. This was a time, as David Ramsay wrote in his *History of the American Revolution* shortly after the war, which called for men at the head of affairs who had "a great knowledge of mankind, and an extensive com-prehension of things," but "the helm of Great-Britain was not in such hands." Moreover, the authors of the legislation not only had to sail an uncharted sea, but also encountered at every turn per-sistent obstruction from adversaries in Parliament. This domestic factional strife, aggravated by differences on other scores, over-turned successive ministries, and contributed to the ambiguous, and oftentimes contradictory, policies toward the colonies.

Yet it seems unlikely that even the highest statesmanship could have won over the Americans. Even the colonists' champions in Westminster, Pitt and Burke, questioned only the wisdom of par-ticular measures, not Parliament's unlimited right to pass them. The colonists, however, totally rejected the doctrine of parlia-mentary supremacy as heartlessly nullifying a time-honored rela-tionship that had worked to the advantage of both parties. Hence, as the program of imperial control unfolded, they warily resisted every move to apply the principle lest acquiescence in one in-stance end in a complete surrender. In Dickinson's words in *The Farmer's Letters*, "A free people therefore can never be . . . too firm in opposing the beginnings of alteration either in form or reality, respecting institutions formed for their security," since "each new encroachment will be strengthened by a former." And the Virginia patriot Richard Henry Lee saw all history showing that "nations which have lapsed from liberty . . . have been brought to this unhappy condition, by gradual paces."

The ministerial measures provided substance for such fears. From the start they struck at both the material welfare of the inhabitants and their exclusive right to tax themselves. To make matters worse, the initial blows fell during the economic depression that lasted until the end of the sixties. The crucial enactments —the Sugar Act of 1764, the Stamp Act of 1765, the Townshend Acts of 1767, and the East India Company Act of 1773—provoked legislative remonstrances, newspaper, pamphlet, and clerical protests, nonimportation pacts, and mob violence; and in the case of every law but the last, resistance produced partial or total repeal. Passionate language like "tyranny" and "oppression" increasingly supplemented reasoned arguments as the controversy roared on. Patriots ceaselessly exhorted the people never, never, to trade their birthright for "slavery."

At the very beginning of the difficulties, opposition was virtually unanimous. Those who did not think the legislation unconstitutional nevertheless condemned it as misguided, inequitable, and financially disastrous. The merchant class in particular took a bold stand. But as subsequent enactments revealed the fixity of Parliament's purpose, the more conservative either deserted the agitators or sought with little avail to moderate their methods. As a result, the direction fell increasingly to radical hands. Tried beyond endurance by the Boston Tea Party, the most daring of the riots, the Ministry in 1774 devised the Intolerable Acts to punish Massachusetts and sent four regiments there under General Gage to enforce the terms. The patriot party, seeing no alternative, now took up arms themselves, and the historic clash at Lexington and Concord followed on April 19, 1775.

Compliance with the Intolerable Acts would have put the province in a state of complete subjection. The legislation in its major features not only closed Boston to ocean trade until the tea should be paid for and the people accept the law, but it also annulled basic democratic provisions of the Massachusetts charter. The sister colonies rightly perceived in these terms a grim warning to them as well. An accompanying Quebec Act, though adopted on quite different grounds, incidentally magnified the sense of injury, principally by extending the boundaries of Canada southward from the Great Lakes to the Ohio River. This action canceled the sea-to-sea claims of Connecticut, Massachusetts, and Virginia to a region important to traders, prospective settlers, and land speculators, now presumably destined for a form of government the colonists disliked. In drawing the sword, however, the patriots still expected to achieve their ends within the British Empire. More than a year was to pass before they reluctantly came to the conclusion that they must strike out on their own.

Although the Americans were characteristically men of action rather than reflection, they advanced a wealth of theoretical arguments in behalf of their cause. Leading the war of words were members of the bar, seconded by clergymen and prominent Southern planters. They based their case, varying the emphasis as events required, on guarantees in the colonial charters, on "the rights of Englishmen" as derived from the Magna Carta, the common law, and the Bill of Rights of 1689, and, with ever increasing stress, on "the immutable laws of nature." These precedents and principles, in the colonists' view, defined the British constitution, a priceless heritage which, if infringed by Parliament, rendered its actions invalid. If on practical grounds they accepted Parliament as the logical body to supervise all ocean traffic except for the purpose of raising revenue, they did not for a minute concede that Britain's altered global standing after the Peace of 1763 in any way affected their own position in the Empire.

The First Continental Congress gave these contentions quasi-official expression, contending that the colonies alone had jurisdiction "in all cases of taxation and internal polity" and that therefore, with the one exception of *bona-fide* trade regulations, they were linked to the homeland only by the same sovereign. Consistent with this stand, if not with the historical record, the Second Congress in the Declaration of Independence about two years later entirely ignored Parliament's part in the "long train of abuses and usurpations" that occasioned the action and ascribed them exclusively to the King. Most significant of all, the delegates, scrapping the arguments they had invoked when they still considered themselves Englishmen, now rested their decision on universal principles—"the laws of nature and of nature's God."

Contributing to the American disaffection were subtler factors. One was resentment at the British practice of saving choice provincial appointments for fellow islanders. The colonists, accustomed to governing themselves, inevitably took offense at being denied a hand in the application of imperial policies touching their own well-being. They also felt a personal affront at the slight to colonial merit. Of the governors in these final critical years there were only three, for example—in New Hampshire, Massachusetts, and New Jersey—who were natives of America.

To add to the sense of injury, the colonists witnessed an influx of persons in connection with the parliamentary program, whom Josiah Quincy, Jr., angrily characterized in the *Boston Gazette*, October 3, 1768, as "pensioners, stipendiaries, and salary-men." In South Carolina, William Henry Drayton complained specifically of the needy strangers from the old country on the Executive Council, their only interest in the province, he alleged, being to draw their salaries of £200 or £300 a year. The Declaration of Independence itself recited as a grievance the "swarms of officers" sent over "to harass our people, and eat out our substance."

Bitterness resulted further from the unblushing nepotism practiced at times by the governors. In New Hampshire, for instance, Governor John Wentworth's relatives by blood or marriage provided not only a judge and the clerk of the Superior Court but also all members save one of the Executive Council. In Massachusetts, Governor Hutchinson and his Lieutenant Governor Andrew Oliver were brothers-in-law, and each had a brother on the Superior Court as well as children married to members of that body. In New York, Lieutenant Governor Cadwallader Colden's three sons and five of his grandchildren filled official berths. Countless colonists must have reacted as John Adams did to the Hutchinson-Oliver sway. "Is not this amazing ascendancy of one Family, Foundation sufficient on which to erect a Tyranny?" he raged in his diary. "Is it not enough to excite Jealousies among the People?" (The ascendancy of the Adams family still lay in the future.)

Still another source of indignation came as a side effect of Britain's application of the doctrine of parliamentary supremacy. Reducing the power of the legislative assemblies reduced in like degree the political and personal status of individual members. This, as the observant Adam Smith wrote in *The Wealth of Nations* early in 1776, gave them a special stake in "preserving or defending their respective importance," for "ambitious and high-spirited men" could not endure the idea of being "so far degraded" as to become mere "executive officers" of remote London. In addition, a dozen years of participation in committees, conventions, and other extralegal bodies had given former nobodies a relish for power. "From shopkeepers, tradesmen, and attornies,"—and he might have added artisans and the like—they have "become statesmen and legislators," with each achieving "a station superior not only to what he had ever filled before, but to what he had ever expected to fill." Just as the members of the Continental Congress, he went on, "feel in themselves a degree of importance which, perhaps, the greatest subjects in Europe scarce feel," so "five hundred different people, perhaps, who in different ways act immediately under the continental congress; and five hundred thousand, perhaps, who act under those five hundred, all feel in the same manner a proportionable rise in their own importance." Thus Britain had heedlessly brought to political life a segment of the community that would not willingly return to obscurity.

Adding to all other causes of anti-British feeling was disillusion on moral grounds. These years revealed deep corruption in English public and private life: overt buying and selling of seats in Parliament, scandals in high society, disregard for the suffering of the masses. Traditionally, the colonists had accorded the motherland reverence and affection; now, as more and more of them came to know her at first hand or by reputation, they reacted with distaste when not abhorrence.

William Samuel Johnson of Stratford, Connecticut, for instance, writing from England in 1767, voiced dismay at the contrast between "the Wealth, Magnificence & splendour of the Nobility Gentry & rich Commoners" and "the extreme Misery & distress's of the Poor," and at another time observed that Americans used to "sober, regular, fair, & righteous Elections can hardly form any Idea, without being on the spot, of those made here, where . . . the whole depends upon Intrigue, Party, Interest, and Money." Benjamin Rush after a year or so in Edinburgh as a medical student told a correspondent in 1768 that every Philadelphian "should be sent abroad for a few years if it was only to teach him to prize his native land above all places in the world." And the Charleston merchant-planter Henry Laurens, repelled by

"the wretched state of female virtue," recounted in 1772 a string
of unsavory episodes involving the King's brothers, who, he said,
"debauched men's wives and daughters throughout the island."

Such expressions of disenchantment came with singular authority from Benjamin Franklin, whose many years' residence in
Britain yielded exceptional opportunities for knowledge. From an
attitude of great admiration he came, upon fuller acquaintance, to
score a system that kept "Multitudes below the Savage State that a
few may be rais'd above it," and avowed, "Had I never been in the
American Colonies, but was to form my Judgment of Civil Society
by what I have lately seen, I should never advise a Nation of
Savages to admit of Civilization." Three years later, in 1775,
particularizing his indictment of "this old rotten State," he wrote,
"Here Numberless and needless Places, enormous Salaries, Pen-
sions, Perquisites, Bribes, groundless Quarrels, foolish Expeditions, false Accounts or no Accounts, Contracts and Jobbs, de-
vour all Revenue, and produce continual Necessity in the Midst of
natural Plenty."

Newspapers kept Americans at home well acquainted with the
decadence of the motherland. For example, John Adams as
"Novanglus" told the readers of the *Boston Gazette,* February 13,
1775, the "melancholy truths" that the people were "depraved,
the parliament venal, and the ministry corrupt." "An American"
in the New London *Connecticut Gazette* on October 20 of that
year termed the old country "an hundred years behind us" in
"Humanity, Temperance, Chastity, Justice, a Veneration for the
Rights of Mankind, and every Moral Virtue." "Salus Populi" in
the *Pennsylvania Journal,* January 24, 1776, added that "From
the King on the throne to the meanest freeman in the nation, all is
corrupt." "Candidus" in the *Pennsylvania Gazette,* March 6,
blamed the taxing of America on the fact that "Luxury (and the
search of ways and means to support it) is arrived at such a pitch
in Britain." "Americans!" exhorted the New York *Constitutional
Gazette,* March 20, "Remember the corrupt, putrefied state of
that nation, and the virtuous, sound, healthy state of your own
young constitution."

This conviction of British decay fed the sense of moral
superiority already strong in the colonists. On every side Bishop

Berkeley's prophecy of half a century before seemed on the verge of fulfillment: the course of empire was indeed taking its way westward. "The American Whig" declared in the *New-York Gazette and Post-Boy,* April 11, 1768, that "in proportion to the abatement of national glory in Europe would be the brightness of its resurrection in America." Similarly, Philip Freneau and H. H. Brackenridge devoted their commencement poem at New Jersey College in 1771 to "The Rising Glory of America"; and the Salem *Essex Gazette,* March 1, 1774, quoted for Massachusetts readers the Duke of Orrery's thought that "the ball of empire might well roll westward and stop in America; a world unknown when Rome was in its meridian splendor." "American Solon" in the *Boston Gazette,* January 27, 1772, forecast that another twenty years would give the colonies as many inhabitants as England; and "Sydney," pointing a similar moral, demanded in the *Massachusetts Spy,* November 11, 1773, "Shall the island BRITAIN enslave this great continent of AMERICA which . . . is capable of supporting hundreds of millions of people? Be astonished all mankind, at her superlative folly!"

This belief in a dazzling future was in part, of course, a projection of the colonists' amazing progress in the past. As the Philadelphian Jacob Duché wrote an English correspondent in 1772, "All the powers of nature seem to be on the stretch, as if they were in pursuit of something higher still." Such forecasts, however—unless subconsciously—did not at this juncture envision a breakup of the Empire. They sought rather to convince Britain that if she should restore her former relationship with the colonies they would in time contribute even more materially to her substance and might. But a very different conclusion could be drawn from this prospect, and Thomas Paine did draw it in *Common Sense* early in 1776. It was, he said, "something absurd" for "a Continent to be perpetually governed by an island"; this reversed "the common order of nature." A recent arrival from England, Paine was peculiarly sensitive to the disparities in size.

And, still short of seeking Independence, the patriots drew further inspiration from animadversions in other times and places on oppression. Their wide reading provided them with copious material. John Adams, for instance, appealed in his "Novanglus" essays to "the principles of Aristotle and Plato, of Livy and Cicero, and of Sidney, Harrington, and Locke." They levied also on the works of Plutarch, Tacitus, Burlamaqui, and the like, as well as on those of Englishmen such as Coke, Bracton, Addison, and Gordon and Trenchard, the joint authors of *Cato's Letters.* To lend symbolic authority to their writings they even signed them on occasion with the names of such commanding figures.

The colonists similarly identified their resistance with contemporaneous movements of defiance in other lands. Whig gatherings drank toasts to "The distressed Poles," "Dr. Lucas and the patriots of Ireland," "Added vigour to the spark of liberty kindling in Spain," "The brave Dantzickers who declare they will be free in the face of the greatest monarch in Europe," and "Paschal Paoli and his brave Corsicans." John Hancock called one of his vessels *Paoli,* and admiring New Yorkers in 1770 organized the Knights of the Order of Corsica.

This association of their cause with the aspiration of oppressed peoples everywhere—"The Sons of Liberty throughout the World," in the words of one of the toasts—gave an altruistic flavor to the patriots' opposition. They deeply felt that on them had fallen a historic duty extending far beyond their own shores. "Anglo-Americanus" in the *New-York Journal,* July 7, 1774, called America "the only remaining seat of liberty" on the globe, now that despotism had triumphed in Poland, Corsica, and Sweden and declared that Britain faced the same fate "unless propp'd by the virtue and spirit of the colonies." As "A Freeman" put it in the Cambridge *New-England Chronicle,* November 23, 1775, ". . . if tyranny should prevail in this great country, we may expect LIBERTY will expire through the world." Benjamin Rush, looking back to this time, observed, "I was constantly animated by a belief that I was acting for the benefit of the whole world, and of future ages." Paine's statement in *Common Sense* that "The cause of America is in a great measure the cause of all mankind" voiced a fundamental conviction.

Something more, however, was needed to turn an armed effort to attain reform within the Empire into a war for independence from the Empire. Such incidents piled up on one another in the weeks and months following the initial skirmish at Lexington. As the Continental Congress organized an intercolonial army and the fighting spread, the King in August 1775 proclaimed a state of rebellion; Parliament in December prohibited American trade with all the world; and British warships in October burned Falmouth (now Portland), Maine, and in January 1776, Norfolk, Virginia. But no single event did so much to incense the colonists and to convince them of the mother country's utter malignity as word that Britain had hired German mercenaries.

In taverns, at public gatherings, in the pulpit, in legislatures, in pamphlets and newspapers, the debate now grew ever angrier. Vocal Tories by this time were few, and in the highly charged atmosphere they risked their possessions and even their lives by arguing for submission to British rule. Myles Cooper, for instance, the Anglican churchman and president of King's College, had twice found it necessary in the seventies to take refuge from mob violence on a royal frigate in New York harbor and in mid-1775 fled America permanently. The threat of the Hessians drove the discussion to the last stage. The issue by the spring of 1776 was whether any point remained in seeking redress of grievances within the imperial connection or whether the argument should be ended by striking out for Independence.

Those who still clung to the hope of reconciliation advanced a variety of reasons. They maintained that, unconstitutional and hurtful though some of the measures had been, these were "rather complained of, as establishing precedents for future violations, than as severely felt." Moreover, the precedents would now surely never be used, for "Great-Britain by this dispute will be taught that her true interest lies in a friendly connexion with us and a few years hence a similar attempt will be rendered impracticable by our increase in numbers and strength." Why, then, they argued, fly to ills that we know not of? Total separation would create fearful problems. With the stabilizing influence of London removed, there would almost certainly follow social anarchy, the impairment of property rights, and constant conflict among the newly formed commonwealths with the strong exploiting the weak. In any event, how could the Americans hope to wrest freedom from the mightiest nation on earth? A victory achieved with French or Spanish aid might well put the people at the mercy of despotisms worse than anything imaginable under Britain. Independence, in short, would be "a leap in the dark." Advocates of "the dark and untrodden way" were either "adventurers who have nothing to lose" or "men exalted by the present confusions into *lucrative* offices, which they can hold no longer than the continuance of the public calamities."

The champions of Independence sternly rejected these contentions as faint-hearted and as a betrayal of the patriot cause. If Britain's actions had not been "severely felt," it was only because the colonists had again and again forced repeal of the measures. Now, however, she had undeniably disclosed her malign purpose by unleashing war to enforce her will. The hostilities, a writer estimated in Dixon and Hunter's *Virginia Gazette*, May 6, 1776, had already caused innumerable American deaths, besides costing £7,850,000 in military outlays, damages to towns, the cutting off of trade, and the like. The motherland had plainly forfeited all claim to further allegiance.

Nor, it was maintained, could anyone rightly doubt America's ability to win liberation. By turning to foreign hirelings for help, Britain had revealed her military weakness. Moreover, she must send her forces across three thousand miles of ocean to wage war on a strange terrain with her soldiers obliged to live off the country. The Americans, on the other hand, fighting defensively on familiar ground, possessed inexhaustible manpower as well as excellent marksmanship. Furthermore, France or Spain or both would gladly enter the fray merely for vengeance against their traditional enemy and nothing more. Far from being "a leap in the dark," the attainment of Independence would bring the thirteen commonwealths together in a general government to promote their general welfare and give them greater weight as a newcomer in the family of nations.

Paine's *Common Sense* holds a special place in the controversy because it set forth the grounds for a final break in passionate prose that overwhelmed many who still hesitated. Every word was a sword. After restating the stock reasons for separation, Paine unmercifully assailed the institution of the monarchy—the one link with the Empire which, apart from Parliament's minimal control of trade, the patriots continued to acknowledge. Reviewing kingship from pre-Scriptural times onward, he pronounced the institution "the most prosperous invention the devil ever set on foot for the promotion of idolatry" and declared, "Of more worth is one honest man to society, and in the sight of God, than all the crowned ruffians that ever lived." Now George III, true to form, had acted the "royal brute" by spilling American blood. No other recourse remained but to disown the "sullen-tempered Pharoah." Paine performed his cardinal service in rending the sentimental veil that had immemorially clad the sovereign with divinity.

Circumstances reinforced arguments: common sense as well as *Common Sense* hastened the movement toward independence. For the widening hostilities and the flight of royal officials left an administrative vacuum that the patriots had no choice but to fill with their own legislative, executive, and judicial organs. Thus the Second Continental Congress, assembling in May 1775, while continuing earnestly to disclaim any thought of Independence, proceeded step by step under the pressure of events to acquire comprehensive governmental functions. It not only organized an army but also assumed control of Indian relations, established a postal system, issued currency, authorized privateering, opened American trade to the world in defiance of the parliamentary ban, and in May 1776 directed the colonies that had not yet acted to set up popularly elected regimes. The colonial womb was slowly producing a state. Even so, the bulk of the delegates considered these measures merely as necessary means to demonstrate the purpose of resistance and wring the desired concessions from London.

Meanwhile, voices from the country in increasing volume urged the Congress to "cut the Gordian knot." Reflecting the tide of opinion, the New York *Constitutional Gazette,* May 18, 1776, commented, "Many honest persons two years ago, would have trembled at the thought of such a thing, who are now fully convinced of the expediency, the safety and necessity of this measure, as our only security." The Independence advocates in Congress felt the time was at hand. War left no alternative; unless the goal were clearly avowed as Independence, it would be hard to mobilize the colonies for a long struggle and impossible to hope for French and Spanish assistance. On June 7 Richard Henry Lee of

Virginia, with John Adams as his seconder, introduced the motion. Opponents, however, led by John Dickinson, succeeded in postponing the vote to allow for more deliberation. One argument against hasty action was the still lingering hope that Britain might back down. Another was that a permanent national government should first be formed.

Finally, on July 2, with the delegates balloting by colonies under the unit rule and so concealing personal dissents, the resolution went through without a recorded negative; and on the fourth the Declaration of Independence proclaimed to "a candid world" the maxims of human rights and the "repeated injuries and usurpations" that had compelled so drastic a decision. Dickinson purposely absented himself that day, but, patriotically accepting the result, he joined the armed forces to uphold it.

As in all revolutions, an energetic minority had brought matters to this pass. Even as late as the First Continental Congress the members, according to John Adams, were "one third tories, another whigs, and the rest mongrels" or, as he said elsewhere, "half Way Men, Neutral Beings." The Second Congress's resolve for separation, made with such travail, obliged the people scattered through the towns and countryside also to take a stand. St. John de Crèvecœur has feelingly described their predicament. Each had to decide, "Shall I discard all my ancient principles, shall I renounce that name, that nation which I held once so respectable? . . . On the other hand, shall I arm myself against that country where I first drew breath, against the play-mates of my youth, my bosom friends, my acquaintance?—the idea makes me shudder!" Crèvecœur himself, a French-born New York farmer with an American wife, after much anguish chose Britain, having been antagonized by zealots who in his judgment were "perpetually bawling about liberty without knowing what it was."

A multitude of factors—social, political, economic, ethnic, geographic, religious, intellectual, sentimental—influenced men's attitudes. There were, besides, persons "among the lower ranks" by whom, as the Philadelphia patriot Alexander Graydon noted, "the true merits of the contest, were little understood or regarded" and who reacted, if at all, out of ignorance. Tories and Whigs, not to mention neutrals, were therefore to be found at every level of society. For example, of the more than three hundred loyalists banished by Massachusetts in 1778 nearly a third were merchants, professional men, and "gentlemen," a roughly equivalent number farmers, and the rest artisans, small shopkeepers, and day laborers. Clearly the economic motive was not the only or necessarily the governing consideration when men made their choices. Indeed, one's notion of material advantage might turn one either way. Some merchants, for instance, believed they would prosper more by remaining under England, while others saw greater promise in the free trade and unchecked industrial growth of an independent country. Likewise ordinary folk might disagree whether their standard of living might be better under a different rule.

In after years John Adams judged that about one out of three people in the country opposed separation. Whatever the exact figure, the Tories lacked effective leadership and organization and, when they spoke out, they risked reprisals at the hands of their neighbors or patriot committees. Some, like William Byrd III and Lord Fairfax in Virginia and the noted Maryland lawyer Daniel Dulany, kept to their homes to avoid trouble. In the Carolinas and Georgia the Crown supporters may have numbered a majority. They were weakest in New England and Virginia. As for the intervening region, Adams said that "New York and Pennsylvania were so nearly divided, if their propensity was not against us, that if New England on one side and Virginia on the other had not kept them in awe, they would have joined the British."

The neutrals, who made up perhaps another third, embraced a wide variety. There were those who, while favoring Independence, did not hold it worth fighting for. Others were too preoccupied with their own concerns to take a position, or, like John Ross of Philadelphia, "loved ease and Madeira, better than liberty and strife." Ross quipped that "let who would be king, he well knew he would be subject." Still others, such as the respected New York attorney Peter Van Schaack, stood aloof for conscientious reasons. He had wholeheartedly supported the patriot cause until early 1776, when, reading deeply in Locke, Grotius, and other libertarian thinkers, he could not convince himself that Britain's acts betokened "a preconcerted plan to enslave us." He ascribed the measures instead to "human frailty" and hence not justifying Independence. Although he did not become a Tory, life was made so difficult for him because of his earlier stand that in 1778 he sought refuge in England, there to remain until a few years after the peace.

The only sizable organized group to take this middle ground was the Society of Friends. Its pacifist principles, of course, discountenanced armed resistance to constituted authority. Yet, even so, individual members out of personal conviction joined one side or the other. Nathanael Greene, one of the ablest Revolutionary generals, was a conspicuous example. But his fellow Rhode Island Quaker Job Scott expressed the dominant attitude. "I had no desire," he wrote in his memoirs, "to promote the opposition to Great Britain; neither had I any desire on the other hand to promote the measures or successes of Great Britain."

The confirmed revolutionists, though numbering probably no more than either the Tories or the neutrals, included the most enterprising and aggressive souls, those unrestrained by prior loyalty, by religious commitment, or by faintheartedness from hazarding their future on an uncertain outcome. Having matched wits and will with Britain for over a decade, they had acquired the unity of action, the self-confidence, and the fortitude needed to reject her rule in entirety. "Old men were seldom warm whigs," wrote David Ramsay in his firsthand account of these days. "Attached to ancient forms and habits, they could not readily accommodate themselves to new systems." Yet there were striking exceptions, as in the case of three signers of the Declaration of Independence—John Witherspoon, Samuel Adams, and Benjamin Franklin—who ranged in age from fifty-two to seventy. More representative were three of their fellows—Benjamin Rush, Thomas Jefferson, and James Wilson—who were thirty, thirty-three, and thirty-four respectively. Ramsay himself, laboring for the cause in South Carolina, was then twenty-seven.

Inevitably the agonizing choice split families asunder. In the most famous instance, Benjamin Franklin's son William was a Crown adherent whom the New Jersey Provincial Congress in June 1776 ousted from the office of royal governor as "an enemy to the liberties of this country." In New York, Gouverneur

Morris, a member of the patriot Council of Safety and later of the Continental Congress, had a Tory mother, and one of his half-brothers became a British general. In Virginia, Edmund Randolph, an original aide-de-camp of General Washington, was the son of Attorney General John Randolph, who in the fall of 1775 fled to England for refuge. In South Carolina, Thomas Heyward, a signer of the Declaration, had a loyalist father, and three nephews of the Carolina royal governor sided against England. In Georgia the three sons of Joseph Habersham, a veteran Crown official, likewise joined the revolutionists.

Such examples show how poignantly the war penetrated and divided American households. When Independence was finally won, William Franklin wrote his father, then in his seventy-eighth year, seeking a reconciliation. Nothing had ever hurt him so much, came the elder's reply, as to have his only son oppose him when "my good Fame, Fortune, and Life were all at Stake." Nonetheless, he forgave him on the ground that men could honestly differ in opinion and welcomed a resumption of "that affectionate Intercourse that formerly existed between us."

The contest with Britain begot in the course of a dozen years the most remarkable generation of public men in the history of the United States or perhaps of any other nation, and this in a country containing no more than two million white inhabitants. An explanation of the phenomenon lies beyond the wit of the historian. It is not satisfactory to suppose, for example, that, as has sometimes been said, dire peril automatically evokes superlative leadership. One need only recall that this magic did not work when North and South confronted each other nearly a hundred years later over the question of preserving the Union bequeathed by the Revolutionary generation. Lincoln alone of all the men then at the head of affairs proved equal to the crisis. Had his two predecessors in the White House—Pierce and Buchanan—shown enough statesmanship, the tragic war between the sections might never have occurred; and had his two successors—Johnson and Grant —possessed sufficient caliber, the blunders of Reconstruction might likewise have been averted.

As for the Revolutionary period, no doubt the wide diffusion of education, the challenging economic opportunities, the social mobility and fluidity of classes, the training in self-government, and the saturation in classical principles of government and liberty all created a favorable milieu. It may be assumed that they opened vistas for persons in every walk of life, enabled all to cultivate their political aptitudes to the utmost, and vastly enlarged the base from which men of public stature might rise. For with the church declining in prestige, and with business, science, and art yet to emerge as compelling fields for individual endeavor, statecraft remained almost the only outlet for men of energy and purpose. It was statecraft practiced, moreover, under the burden not only of local but of world responsibility. "Providence," declared John Adams in the *Boston Gazette* in 1765, had expressly intended America "for the illumination of the ignorant, and the emancipation of the slavish part of mankind." And the commitment the patriots felt to the oppressed of the world was no less than that to their own children and children's children. Adams articulated it again in a letter to his wife after signing the Declaration of Independence: "Through all the gloom I can see the rays of ravishing light and glory. *Posterity* will triumph in that day's transaction."

All these things both concentrated and heightened the public genius of the Revolutionary generation. Yet the mystery remains. Puritan divines of the preceding century would have explained the flowering as the result of a "special providence." Our scientific age would doubtless attribute it to a lucky concatenation of genes. Whatever the elements responsible, the leaders who came on the stage in the 1760's were extraordinary by any standard. They were fearless, high-principled, deeply versed in ancient and modern political thought, yet withal astute and pragmatic, convinced of man's power to improve his condition through the use of intelligence, and unafraid of experiment. They were men of vision without being visionaries. John Adams, who was ordinarily chary of praise, said of his colleagues in the First Continental Congress, "The Art and Address, of Ambassadors from a dozen belligerent Powers of Europe, nay of a Conclave of Cardinals at the Election of a Pope, or of the Princes in Germany at the Choice of an Emperor, would not exceed the Specimens We have seen." And from the other side of the Atlantic William Pitt, the Earl of

Chatham, went further: "I have read Thucydides," he told the House of Lords, "and have studied and admired the master states of the world," and found that "no Nation or body of men can stand in preference to the General Congress at Philadelphia."

This generation, moreover, unlike its counterparts in most successful revolutions, knew how to create as well as to destroy. While the war was still raging, many of the members participated in the formation of the first state governments, proceeding, in Adams's words, "by the use of reason and the senses," not after "any interviews with the gods." They operated, he said, in the way that "Godfrey invented his quadrant, and Rittenhouse his planetarium." Although the initial attempt at a central political structure—the Articles of Confederation—did not long survive the hostilities, its deficiencies brought into being the Federal Constitution, the oldest written frame of national government in the world today. And, as further evidence of the quality of the generation, its members supplied all the Presidents during the first thirty-six years after the adoption of the Constitution.

Any roll of honor of these giants would include Franklin, Jefferson, Washington, John and Samuel Adams, Hamilton, and Madison and, not far behind them, James Monroe, George Mason, James Wilson, John Jay, George Wythe, Robert Morris, Richard Henry Lee, Edmund Pendleton, Joseph Reed, Christopher Gadsden, James Iredell, Gouverneur Morris, Roger Sherman, Henry Laurens, Stephen Hopkins, and Elbridge Gerry, to name no others. All played a vital role in both the revolutionary and restorative aspects of building the new nation.

Was the opposition to Britain's imperialistic program a radical movement? The patriots themselves did not so consider it, since until nearly the end they strove simply to safeguard old and cherished liberties within the Empire. Whether by peaceful means or (during the fifteen months after Lexington) by armed resistance, the avowed purpose was to maintain the established order against acts they deemed unconstitutional and unwarranted. In their view they were the conservators, the London authorities the innovators.

Even in declaring Independence they betrayed a similar conservative bent, for, instead of asserting a doctrine peculiar to a new people, they based their case on the teachings of the revered John Locke of the preceding century. In framing state constitutions they likewise invoked principles of the past. Aside from removing every trace of the imperial connection, they kept the tripartite system of government with little change except insofar as they strengthened the legislative branch at the expense of the executive. Rhode Island and Connecticut in fact, save for severing the transatlantic tie, retained their colonial charters intact. Pennsylvania and Georgia alone diverged from the pattern by instituting single-house legislatures, which, however, they presently abandoned.

Neither at the state nor at the national level did the generation seek to write on a clean slate. No firebrands demanded the replacement of the social and economic order with some sort of utopian dream. There was not even any significant outcry against the continuance of the upper-class leadership that had characterized British dominance.

To the outside world, however, the actions of the Americans trumpeted sheer radicalism. While still subject to England, they had enjoyed rights and privileges utterly repugnant to the Continental European powers. Now, although they were revolutionaries by chance rather than by choice, they had instigated the first great anticolonial uprising in history. They had, moreover, not only rejected Parliament but spurned the very institution of the monarchy, pledging their lives, fortunes, and sacred honor to a governmental system that should rest on popular authority and ensure the equality of "all men."

True, the abstractions of natural rights had long been current in Old World thought, but no people had hitherto tried to give them concrete application. "In no age before, and in no other country," exulted David Ramsay in his account of the times, "did man ever possess an election of the kind of government, under which he would choose to live." In John Adams's words, a more important question perhaps "never was or will be decided among Men." Official recognition of the transcendent event was accorded by the Great Seal of the United States. Adopted in 1782, it displays a pyramid symbolic of timelessness with the roman numerals for 1776 and, below it, the inscription "NOVUS ORDO SECULORUM" (a new order of the ages), a drawing of which appears on the back of the dollar bill as a reminder to our own generation.

Little wonder that the governing classes on the Continent reacted with consternation. Nonetheless, the two most powerful countries, hoping to wreak revenge on their old adversary, took sides against England. Only a few months after the Americans battled a British army into surrender at Saratoga in October 1777, France made an alliance with them and sent military and naval help. Spain, however, did not go so far, fearing the effects of a successful colonial rebellion within her own vast empire in the Western Hemisphere. As an ally of France, therefore, but not of the United States, she entered the conflict to recover territory earlier lost to Britain.

On the other hand, the example of the revolutionists enraptured liberty-loving Europeans, affording hope that they might achieve their own "NOVUS ORDO SECLORUM." Franklin, in Paris for the Continental Congress, found it was "a Common Observation" that "our Cause is *the Cause of all Mankind,* and that we are fighting for their Liberty in defending our own." "In a little while," rhapsodized one Frenchman, "there will be nothing to which man cannot attain." Reading the Declaration of Independence led Lafayette to join Washington's army. From a temporary refuge in Holland, Mirabeau exhorted the German mercenaries to imitate the Americans by breaking their chains and using their weapons for freedom. A German enthusiast stated that "a secret bond . . . links the cause of the Colonies with the welfare and uplifting of the human race." A writer in *Die Zukunft,* observing that not only North America but also South America would be free, asked whether the Old World would then be content to remain in darkness. A Swiss journalist charged well-wishers of Britain with sinning against humanity. In Italy the great prophet of the *risorgimento,* the poet Alfieri, published a cycle of odes, *L'America libera.*

History in fact had reached a signal turning point for all humankind as well as for the Americans. Even before the outbreak of war John Adams and other patriot spokesmen had in challenging the mother country denounced tyranny as unbearable in whatever land it was practiced. Upon America's final victory in the struggle there emerged, in Edmund Burke's words, "a new state, of a new species, in a new part of the globe," whose advent would, he foresaw, render "as great a change in all the relations, and balances and gravitations of power, as the appearance of a new planet would in the system of the solar world." Shortly thereafter came the French Revolution; popular upheavals erupted in other European countries; and across the Atlantic the Latin peoples threw off their dependency on Spain and Portugal. While these events were still unfolding, John Adams, pondering in his old age the "effects and consequences" of the spirit of 1776, wondered prophetically, "And when and where are they to cease?"

Qualitative differences remained between the American Revolution, which began in hope and concluded in democracy, and later modern revolutions, which began in bitterness and concluded in authoritarianism. The Americans were happy revolutionists, fighting as much to protect as to achieve a free and equalitarian society. Their purpose was national independence rather than social upheaval and reconstruction. In rejecting Britain, they were confining themselves to a specific proposition—that, in the words of the Declaration of Independence, "all *political* connection . . . is and ought to be totally dissolved" [my emphasis]. No one in the new nation, high or low, expressed a desire to repudiate the social, intellectual, cultural, and moral heritage. A common history, language, literature, a common set of legal principles and social institutions—these invisible threads continued to bind the first colonial country to win its independence to the country against which it had rebelled.

The American War for Independence was therefore limited in its aims and limited in its outcome. It freed the American state but not yet the American mind. Nationalism and democracy, in their more ardent expression, followed rather than accompanied the Revolution. It was not until the early nineteenth century that a truly distinctive American civilization began to emerge. Still, when it came, it found its inspiration and its sustenance in the ideals of the Revolution; for, if the Revolution itself was limited, its principles were universal. To this day the nation and the world are committed to the unending quest to unfold the ultimate meaning of those quiet phrases, written nearly two centuries ago by a young man in a small room in an unknown city on the far margin of Western civilization: "We hold these Truths to be self-evident, that all Men are created equal, that they are endowed by their Creator with certain unalienable Rights, that among these are Life, Liberty, and the Pursuit of Happiness."

Selected Bibliography

Adams, James Truslow: *Provincial Society, 1690–1763*. New York, 1927.

Adams, John: *Diary and Autobiography*, ed. L. H. Butterfield. 4 vols. Cambridge, 1961.

Adams, John and Abigail: *Familiar Letters . . . during the Revolution*, ed. Charles Francis Adams. New York, 1876.

Alden, John R.: *The South in the Revolution, 1763–1789*. Vol. III of *A History of the South*. Baton Rouge, La., 1957.

Andrews, Charles M.: *Colonial Folkways: A Chronicle of American Life in the Reign of the Georges*. New Haven, 1919.

————: *The Colonial Period of American History*. 4 vols. New Haven, 1934–8.

Bailyn, Bernard: *The New England Merchants in the Seventeenth Century*. Cambridge, Mass., 1955.

————, ed.: *Pamphlets of the American Revolution, 1750–1776*. Cambridge, Mass., 1965.

Baldwin, Alice Mary: *The New England Clergy and the American Revolution*. Durham, N.C., 1928.

Barbé-Marbois, François, Marquis de: *Our Revolutionary Forefathers: The Letters of François, Marquis de Barbé-Marbois . . . 1779–1785*, trans. and ed. Eugene Parker Chase. New York, 1929.

Baxter, W. T.: *The House of Hancock; Business in Boston, 1724–1775*. Cambridge, Mass., 1945.

Boorstin, Daniel J.: *The Americans: The Colonial Experience*. New York, 1958.

————: *The Lost World of Thomas Jefferson*. New York, 1948.

Bridenbaugh, Carl: *Cities in the Wilderness: The First Century of Urban Life in America, 1625–1742*. 2nd edn. New York, 1955.

————: *Cities in Revolt: Urban Life in America, 1743–1776.* New York, 1955.

————: *The Colonial Craftsman.* New York, 1950.

————: *Mitre and Sceptre: Transatlantic Faiths, Ideas, Personalities, and Politics, 1689–1775.* New York, 1962.

————: *Myths and Realities, Societies of the Colonial South.* Baton Rouge, La., 1952.

————, and Jessica Bridenbaugh: *Rebels and Gentlemen: Philadelphia in the Age of Franklin.* New York, 1942.

Brissot de Warville, Jacques Pierre: *New Travels in the United States of America, 1788,* ed. D. Echeverria. Cambridge, Mass., 1964.

Burchard, John Ely, and Albert Bush-Brown: *The Architecture of America: A Social and Cultural History.* Boston, 1961.

Burnaby, Andrew: *Burnaby's Travels through North America.* With intro. and notes by Rufus Rockwell Wilson. New York, 1904; repr., 1960.

Byrd, William: *The Prose Works of William Byrd of Westover: Narrative of a Colonial Virginian,* ed. Louis B. Wright. Cambridge, Mass., 1966.

Calhoun, Arthur W.: *A Social History of the American Family from Colonial Times to the Present.* New York, 1945.

Channing, Edward: *A History of the United States.* 6 vols. and index. New York, 1905–32. Vol. II, *A Century of Colonial History, 1660–1760* (1927).

Chastellux, François Jean, Marquis de: *Travels in North America, in the Years 1780, 1781, and 1782.* 2 vols. Rev. trans. with intro. and notes by Howard C. Rice, Jr. Chapel Hill, N.C., 1963.

Cohen, Hennig: *The South Carolina Gazette, 1732–1775.* Charleston, S.C., 1953.

Cresswell, Nicholas: *The Journal of Nicholas Cresswell, 1774–1777.* New York, 1924.

Crèvecœur, Michel-Guillaume St. Jean de: *Letter from an American Farmer.* New York, 1961.

Dorfman, Joseph: *The Economic Mind in American Civilization.* 3 vols. New York, 1946–9.

Duffy, John: *Epidemics in Colonial America.* Baton Rouge, La., 1953.

Earle, Alice M.: *Stage-coach and Tavern Days.* New York, 1935.

Fairlie, John A.: *Local Government in Counties, Towns, and Villages.* New York, 1906.

Fitzpatrick, John C.: *George Washington Himself.* Indianapolis, Ind., 1933.

Forbes, Esther: *Paul Revere and the World He Lived in.* Boston, 1942.

Franklin, Benjamin: *Writings,* ed. A. H. Smyth. 10 vols. New York, 1905–7.

Gage, Thomas: *The Correspondence of General Thomas Gage,* ed. Clarence Edwin Carter. 2 vols. New Haven, 1931–3.

Gipson, L. H.: *The British Empire before the American Revolution.* Vols. 1–10. Caldwell, Idaho, and New York, 1936–61.

Goodman, N. G.: *Benjamin Rush, Physician and Citizen, 1746–1813.* Philadelphia, 1934.

Gowans, Alan: *Images of American Living: Four Centuries of Architecture and Furniture as Cultural Expression.* Philadelphia, 1964.

Green, Constance McL.: *The Rise of Urban America.* New York, 1965.

Greene, Evarts B.: *The Revolutionary Generation, 1763–1790.* New York, 1943.

Hamilton, Alexander [physician]: *Gentleman's Progress; Itinerarium, 1744,* ed. Carl Bridenbaugh. Chapel Hill, N.C., 1948.

Hardwick, Katharine D.: *Boston Private Charities from 1657 to 1800.* Boston, 1964.

Hindle, Brooke: *The Pursuit of Science in Revolutionary America, 1735–1789.* Chapel Hill, N.C., 1956.

Howard, George Elliott, *A History of Matrimonial Institutions.* 3 vols. Chicago, 1904; New York, 1964.

James, Sydney V.: *A People among Peoples; Quaker Benevolence in Eighteenth-Century America.* Cambridge, Mass., 1963.

Kittredge, George Lyman: *The Old Farmer and His Almanack; Being Some Observations on Life and Manners in New England a Hundred Years Ago.* Boston, 1904.

Klees, Frederic: *The Pennsylvania Dutch.* New York, 1950.

Kraus, Michael: *Intercolonial Aspects of American Culture on the Eve of the American Revolution.* New York, 1928.

Lowens, Irving: *Music and Musicians in Early America.* New York, 1964.

Main, Jackson T.: *The Social Structure of Revolutionary America.* Princeton, N.J., 1965.

Malone, Dumas: *Jefferson and His Time.* 2 vols. Boston, 1948–51.

Mittelberger, Gottlieb: *Journey to Pennsylvania,* ed. and trans. Oscar Handlin and John Clive. Cambridge, Mass., 1960.

Morison, Samuel Eliot: *Builders of the Bay Colony.* Boston, 1930.

————: *Harvard College in the Seventeenth Century.* 2 vols. Cambridge, Mass., 1936.

————: *The Intellectual Life of Colonial New England.* 2nd edn. New York, 1956.

Morris, Richard B.: *Studies in the History of American Law, with Special Reference to the Seventeenth and Eighteenth Centuries.* New York, 1930.

Palmer, Robert R.: *The Age of the Democratic Revolution.* 2 vols. Princeton, N.J., 1959 64.

Perry, Ralph Barton: *Puritanism and Democracy.* New York, 1944.

Pumphrey, Ralph E., and Muriel W. Pumphrey, eds.: *The Heritage of American Social Work: Readings in its Philosophical and Institutional Development.* New York, 1961.

Ramsay, David: *The History of the American Revolution.* 2 vols. Philadelphia, 1789.

Rossiter, Clinton: *Seedtime of the Republic: The Origin of the American Tradition of Political Liberty.* New York, 1953.

Sachse, W. L.: *The Colonial American in Britain.* Madison, Wis., 1956.

Savelle, Max: *The Foundations of American Civilization.* New York, 1942.

————: *Seeds of Liberty: The Genesis of the American Mind.* New York, 1948.

Schafer, Joseph: *The Social History of American Agriculture.* New York, 1936.

Schlesinger, Arthur M.: *The Colonial Merchants and the American Revolution. 1763–1776.* New York, 1918.

————: *Learning How to Behave: A Historical Study of American Etiquette Books.* New York, 1946.

————: *Paths to the Present.* New York, 1949.

————: *Prelude to Independence: The Newspaper War on Britain, 1764–1776.* New York, 1958.

Sewall, Samuel: *Diary,* ed. Mark Van Doren. New York, 1963.

Smith, Abbot Emerson: *Colonists in Bondage.* Chapel Hill, N.C., 1947.

Spruill, Julia C.: *Women's Life and Work in the Southern Colonies.* Chapel Hill, N.C., 1938.

Sydnor, Charles S.: *Gentlemen Freeholders: Political Practices in Washington's Virginia.* Chapel Hill, N.C., 1952.

Tolles, F. B.: *James Logan and the Culture of Provincial America.* Boston, 1957.

————: *Meeting House and Counting House, Quaker Merchants of Colonial Philadelphia.* Chapel Hill, N.C., 1948.

United States, Bureau of the Census: *Historical Statistics of the United States, Colonial Times to 1957.* Washington, D.C., 1960.

Van Doren, Carl C.: *Benjamin Franklin.* New York, 1938.

Van Tassel, David D.: *Recording America's Past: An Interpretation of the Development of Historical Studies in America, 1607–1884.* Chicago, 1960.

Ver Steeg, Clarence L.: *The Formative Years, 1607–1763.* New York, 1964.

Wertenbaker, Thomas Jefferson: *The First Americans, 1607–1690.* New York, 1927.

————: *The Founding of American Civilization: The Middle Colonies.* New York, 1938.

————: *The Golden Age of Colonial Culture.* 2nd edn. New York, 1949.

————: *The Old South: The Founding of American Civilization.* New York, 1942.

————: *The Puritan Oligarchy: The Founding of American Civilization.* New York, 1947.

Williamson, Chilton: *American Suffrage from Property to Democracy, 1760–1860.* Princeton, N.J., 1960.

Woolman, John: *The Journal of John Woolman, and A Plea for the Poor,* ed. J. G. Whittier, intro. by F. B. Tolles. New York, 1961.

Wright, Louis B.: *The Cultural Life of the American Colonies, 1607–1763.* New York, 1957.

Index

Arthur M. Schlesinger was born in Xenia, Ohio, on February 27, 1888. After studying at Ohio State University (B.A., 1910) and Columbia University (Ph.D., 1917), he joined the history department at Ohio State in 1912. Leaving Ohio State in 1919, he became head of the history department at the University of Iowa, moving on in 1924 to Harvard, where he was Francis Lee Higginson Professor from 1939 until his retirement in 1954. He served as visiting professor in European universities, was president of the American Historical Association, and was awarded numerous academic and other honors. His published books include *The Colonial Merchants and the American Revolution* (1918), *New Viewpoints in American History* (1922), *The Rise of the City* (1933), *Paths to the Present* (1949), *The American as Reformer* (1950), and *Prelude to Independence: The Newspaper War on Britain, 1764–1776* (1958). He was co-editor of *A History of American Life* (13 volumes, 1927–44). Professor Schlesinger died in 1965 and is survived by his wife, Elizabeth Bancroft Schlesinger, who shared his historical interests, and two sons, Thomas B. and Arthur M. Schlesinger, Jr., also a well-known historian.

A NOTE ON THE TYPE

The text of this book was set on the Linotype in a face called TIMES ROMAN, designed by Stanley Morison for The Times (London), and first introduced by that newspaper in 1932.

Among typographers and designers of the twentieth century, Stanley Morison has been a strong forming influence, as typographical advisor to the English Monotype Corporation, as a director of two distinguished English publishing houses, and as a writer of sensibility, erudition, and keen practical sense.

Composed by American Book–Stratford Press, Inc., New York, printed and bound by The Haddon Craftsmen, Scranton, Pa.